Praise for *The Inner Edge:*
Effective Spirituality in Your Life and Work

"A clearly thought out, workable guideline for Spirituality in Business dealing with profound issues both on the individual level and at work. Every thoughtful businessperson could benefit from this timely book."

—DEEPAK CHOPRA
Author, *How to Know God*

"People debate the idea of spirituality in business. They long for what the phrase implies, even though on the surface they may be afraid of it. And for a long time the concept has just bounced around as some vague management tool. But now this book changes all that. It shows us how spirituality is the only way to succeed in business in these times. And it shows us how bringing out your spirit in your life can inspire you to a new kind of success. *The Inner Edge* is a gift to businesspeople who need to find their way in this chaotic, but beautiful world."

—MICHAEL RAY
Professor of Creativity and Innovation (Emeritus)
Stanford Business School
Author, *Creativity in Business*

"One of the consequences of the September 11th attacks is that many U.S. employees are thinking differently about the work they do, their relation to it, and also to the organizations for which they work. This book provides a straightforward yet rich methodology for individuals to reconsider their activities and relationship to work in a powerful way."

—BOB GARDELLA
Author, *The Harvard Business School Guide to Finding Your Next Job*

"If you're ready to discover who you really are and go to the depths of your spirituality, this book is for you!"

—MARK VICTOR HANSEN
Co-creator, #1 New York Times bestseller series
Chicken Soup for the Soul®

"Most organizations are in dire need of transformation, and it takes personal transformation in order to achieve deep and lasting organizational change. *The Inner Edge* provides a simple yet powerful program that draws on spiritual wisdom and practices to help you transform your work and your organization. You'll be amazed at the results you create!"

—JUDITH A. NEAL, PH.D.
Executive Director
Association for Spirit at Work

"This is a direct, practical, honest, and powerful book. I found new and profound insights into my own spiritual experience. I highly recommend *The Inner Edge*."

—MARTIN RUTTE
Co-author, *Chicken Soup for the Soul at Work*

"The authors of *The Inner Edge* offer a rich assortment of techniques and processes for readers to enrich their experience of work, find greater fulfillment, and enjoy more balance in their lives."

—JOHN RENESCH
Business Futurist
Author, *Getting to the Better Future*

". . . provides the first practical approach to releasing the power of spirituality not just to 'do good,' but to enhance the 'bottom line,' both for the individual and the organization. Those that master the simple straightforward tools, designed to efficiently tap into one's logical and intuitive self, will enjoy a definite competitive edge. A must read!"

—JOHN A. THOMPSON
Founder, IMCOR, The Interim Management
Company
Author, *The Portable Executive, Building Your Own Job Security*

"Based on a solid understanding of the changed business environment, *The Inner Edge* offers a distinctive and workable approach to organizational and individual productivity and renewal. Its perspectives and techniques—particularly Quantum Decision Making—can be applied by individuals and by business managers at every level."

— JIM HENDERSON
Retired Chairman and CEO
Cummins Inc.

". . . provides a common sense approach to achieving a balanced and productive life. I found scores of insightful observations that explain feelings and experiences I have had and have observed in others."

— J. LAWRENCE WILSON
Retired Chairman and CEO
Rohm and Haas Company

"*The Inner Edge* is above all else a practical guide. When followed, it reaches and touches much more deeply than the many other guides to business 'success.' It taps into one's inner spiritual core. The result is personal integrity, which leads to success in business and in life."

— WARREN R. RADTKE
Executive Coach
Boston, Massachusetts

"Takes the mystery out of 'spirituality in business.' A great resource for those who want to learn how to take their whole selves to work."

— RICHARD BARRETT
Fellow of the World Business Academy
Managing Partner of Richard Barrett Associates

THE INNER EDGE

Effective Spirituality

in Your Life and Work

RICHARD A. WEDEMEYER | RONALD W. JUE, PH.D.

McGraw-Hill

Chicago New York San Francisco Lisbon London Madrid Mexico City
Milan New Delhi San Juan Seoul Singapore Sydney Toronto

Library of Congress Cataloging-in-Publication Data

Wedemeyer, Richard, A., 1936–
    The inner edge : effective spirituality in your life and work / Richard A. Wedemeyer, Ronald W. Jue.
        p.   cm.
    Includes index and bibliographical references.
    ISBN 0-8092-9541-5 (alk. paper)
        1. Spiritual life.   2. Business people—Religious life.   I. Jue, Ronald W. II. Title.

    BL625.9.B87W43   2002
    291.4—dc21   2002022400

McGraw-Hill

A Division of The **McGraw·Hill** Companies

1 2 3 4 5 6 7 8 9 0   DOC/DOC   1 0 9 8 7 6 5 4 3 2

ISBN 0-8092-9541-5

McGraw-Hill books are available at special quantity discounts to use as premiums and sales promotions, or for use in corporate training programs. For more information, please write to the Director of Special Sales, Professional Publishing, McGraw-Hill, Two Penn Plaza, New York, NY 10121-2298. Or contact your local bookstore.

This book is printed on acid-free paper.

The Inner Edge is dedicated to the vision of the Dalai Lama for individuals to become enlightened leaders with purposeful hearts. We also dedicate it to all those who hunger to understand and fulfill their purpose for being on this planet, and who feel a deep desire to leave their part of the world a bit better than they found it.

CONTENTS

FOREWORD BY HIS HOLINESS THE DALAI LAMA XI

ACKNOWLEDGMENTS XIII

INTRODUCTION XV

I

Your Inner Edge

1. The Inner Edge   3

2. Spirituality in Life and Business   9

3. An Overview of Pragmatic Spirituality   17

II

Pragmatic Spirituality at the Personal Level

4. Unfinished Business: Its Nature and Resolution   29

5. Your Self-Resolves: Self-Accountability, Self-Maintenance, and Self-Discipline   47

6. Identity: The First Dimension of Pragmatic Spirituality   57

7. Integration: The Second Dimension   73

8. Inspiration: The Third Dimension   85

9. Achieving Your Inner Edge: The Fully Functioning Adult   99

III

Pragmatic Spirituality in Your Workplace

10. Applying Pragmatic Spirituality in Your Job   119
11. QDM: Quantum Decision Making   135
12. Adaptability, Rapport, and Politics   149
13. Loyalty and Responsibility Redefined   161
14. Accountability   171
15. Pragmatic Spirituality and Your Career Management Cycle   181

IV

The Potential for Pragmatic Spirituality in the Organization

16. From the Traditional to the Evolving Organization   197
17. QDM: The Bottom-Line Power of Intuition in the Organization   207
18. The Potential for Pragmatic Spirituality in the Organization   219
19. Introducing Pragmatic Spirituality in the Organization   235
20. Spirituality in Business—Can It Work?   251
21. The Inner Edge and the Outer Limits   263

APPENDIX A: YOUR PRAGMATIC SPIRITUALITY VISUALIZATIONS 269
APPENDIX B: THE RADICALLY CHANGING WORKPLACE 277
APPENDIX C: SELF-ASSESSMENT EXERCISES FROM *IN TRANSITION* 281
APPENDIX D: ON THE JOB 285
APPENDIX E: THE MOTIVATIONAL PROFILE 289
APPENDIX F: *THE INNER EDGE* CD AND SEMINARS 291
RECOMMENDED READING 293
QUOTE SOURCES 301
INDEX 303

FOREWORD

THE WORKINGS OF BUSINESS, COMMERCE, and economics are fields about which I have very little knowledge. However, they have long been a focus of human activity and continue to exercise great influence over our lives today. Business management and commercial transactions concern human beings, so their success is not merely a question of whether they generate a profit like the efficient running of a machine consisting of inanimate parts. Because they involve human beings, a proper sense of human values is important.

In the world in which we live, a great deal depends on money and power, and there is not much concern about the real value of love. But, if human society loses the value of justice, compassion, and honesty, we will face greater difficulties in the future. Some people may think that these sorts of ethical attitudes are not much needed in the areas of business or economic activity. I strongly disagree. The quality of all our actions depends on our motivation. In business, if you have a good motivation and seek to contribute to a better human society, you will be a good and honest businessman. Business itself is not bad; it is a necessary instrument to make goods and services available. However, if people lacking a good motivation—who only have selfish and short-term ends, and whose concern for profit is dominated by greed—undertake business, then of course it becomes bad.

From my Buddhist viewpoint all things originate in the mind. Actions and events depend heavily on motivation. A real sense of appreciation of humanity, compassion, and love are the key points. When we develop a good heart then whatever activities we engage in will have beneficial results since the motivation is the most important. With proper motivation our activities can help humanity; without it they have the opposite effect. This is why the compassionate thought is so very important for humankind. Although it is difficult to bring about the inner change that gives rise to it, it is absolutely worthwhile to try.

I first met Ronald Jue in 1989 during an interaction I had with businessmen in Newport Beach, California. Since then, Ron has pursued his interest in reconciling spirituality and business. One of the results of this deep interest is the book, *The Inner Edge*, written by Richard Wedemeyer and Ronald Jue, who have combined their experience of business practice with the cultivation of inner values. Their idea of practical spirituality incorporates what I think of as fundamental human values. I believe their explanation of how it can be developed and how it can be a source of success will be of compelling interest to anyone interested in creating a satisfying approach to business with a more human face.

March 10, 2002

THE DALAI LAMA

ACKNOWLEDGMENTS

Our primary acknowledgment goes to David Christel of Santa Fe, New Mexico—a man of many talents who helped us finalize the manuscript for *The Inner Edge*. His editorial skills, empathy, computer expertise, and ability to stay on top of myriad details proved invaluable—particularly in the middle of the project, when a routine elective surgery for Dick escalated to a near-catastrophe. Without David's competence, wisdom, and hard work, *The Inner Edge* would never have been completed. We are most grateful for everything David did for us and *The Inner Edge*, and we commend his talents to anyone desiring to achieve clear and cogent written communication.

We also recognize Nancy Trichter, our literary agent, and our editors at Contemporary Books/McGraw-Hill, Danielle Egan-Miller and Kathy Dennis, who understood our vision and slogged with us through the long, tedious process of producing a book.

Dick's Acknowledgments

I am most grateful to all the factors that combined in bringing me back from my recent brush with death to experience life with a renewed sense of appreciation and joy: my wife, Jane; the medical professionals who ministered to me; friends and acquaintances, for their prayers and support; and the divine power who determines each of our destinies. I also acknowledge the contributions of all the people who have influenced this book and those who have been generous with their insights and encouragement, among whom are Bonnie Brown, Alex Platt, Jessie Turberg, Sherry Cupac, Gabe Campbell, and my children, Laura Hanson and Trevor Wedemeyer. And most of all, I acknowledge the unfailing and dedicated support of my wife and life companion, Jane, who not only tolerated the book's seemingly endless intrusions on our relationship but was always ready with valuable insights, words of encouragement, and a timely smile and hug. Thank you, my love!

Ron's Acknowledgments

I would like to acknowledge the individuals and mentors who had a tremendous influence on my spiritual growth: Jiddu Krishnamurti, Ajan Nep, and His Holiness the Dalai Lama, who taught me the importance of presence and the revelation of spirit in everyday life. I am grateful for the inspiration and vision from my professional colleagues, Peter Müri, François Cusano, and Nicole Roux, who developed the seminars and institute for this work in Switzerland and France. I am indebted to the healing work of Ernst Pecci, Narajan Singh, and Angeles Arrien, whose seminars taught me a great deal about the intuitive dimensions of the mind and the need to look from a place of the heart to find meaning. A special thanks to Richard A. Williams, Ronald Hoefer, Bob Beers, and the businesspeople from my seminars, who helped me to see the importance of finding spirituality in the workplace. Thanks to Richard Wedemeyer and David Christel, who saw the potential of our collaboration. And a heartfelt thanks to my beautiful wife, Naomi, and two daughters, Lian and Karin, whose spirit and presence have given me great dimensionality and purpose to my life.

Finally, Dick and Ron acknowledge one another for the separate talents each brought to this project, their good fortune in coming together, and their common beliefs that energized this book.

INTRODUCTION

*The Muppets dream, aspire, attempt and fail—and they do so
unbitterly, humorously, endearingly. We (whose lives and
aspirations are not so dissimilar) can both stand the comparison
and take heart from their example.*

—ALAN COREN, Editor, *Punch* magazine

LIFE ISN'T EASY, yet each of us can take heart in knowing that we're all in this
together—fumbling, stumbling, and bumbling about, much like the Muppets.
But as we aspire to a greater quality of life and to bring deeper meaning to our
endeavors, we can follow the example of those "not live, but oh-so-alive" characters: their lightheartedness, their resiliency, their playfulness. If there is anything we can come away with from their "world," it is their sense of hope—and
that is the spirit in which this book is written.

There are many books out in the marketplace about business and about spirituality, some extolling their virtues and others deriding them. But there seem to
be no books that combine the two into a fluid and functional whole. Our purpose in writing this book is to do just that. Our perspective is derived from our
experiences in the fields of business, psychology, spirituality, and the humanities.
We both have a strong desire to share what we've discovered through years of
leading seminars and working with people questing to make sense of a world of
multilayered complexities and trying to maintain a sense of balance and integrity
while honoring their values and beliefs—at home, in the workplace, and glob-
ally. The result is *The Inner Edge*: a straightforward, organized approach to finding deeper levels of balance, congruity, and fulfillment in all aspects of your life.

The concepts and techniques we offer in this book have been life changing
for both of us, and for others. Our hope is that you will explore the broader perspectives found within these pages, and through its exercises discover more

expansive levels of self that will enable you to go forth into this frenetic world as a clear and steady light unperturbed by the fears, responsibilities, and liabilities of daily living.

The Inner Edge is grounded on a concept we call—for reasons explained in more detail later—*Pragmatic Spirituality*. This is *not* connected with any religious belief or practice, but is related to the universal sense of spirituality as *seeking*: seeking to satisfy a hunger or to find meaning or to discover one's fullest potential. The objective of Pragmatic Spirituality (PS) is to achieve enhanced authenticity and appropriateness in everything you do while accessing resources and capabilities beyond the limits of your rational mind, no matter what your belief system or religion may (or may not) be. In developing the concept of Pragmatic Spirituality, we have drawn upon Eastern practices, psychology, right/left brain theory, and other means through which people have accessed the potential within themselves. We have also drawn from our own personal and professional experiences over the years.

Our process invites you to use your intuition as a resource by means of visualizations, imaging, and meditative techniques. Ron's success with the *Quantum Decision-Making (QDM)* process in organizational contexts—a harbinger for the benefits of intuitive potential for many other aspects of an organization—offers concrete examples of the process. We feel this provides a valid conceptual basis for the bottom-line organizational potential of Pragmatic Spirituality, and that the principles and practices of Pragmatic Spirituality can be effective in all aspects of life.

We are very much aware of the limitations imposed in presenting our concepts and techniques in a book format. In a one-on-one situation, the PS process can be matched to the circumstances, needs, and pace of each individual's perspective, beliefs, values, and level of awareness. A book format, on the other hand, imposes a "one message for all" approach, so each reader will find certain portions more relevant and useful than others.

The book is divided into four sections:

- Section I places Pragmatic Spirituality in an approachable context.
- Section II discusses the concepts and techniques of Pragmatic Spirituality at the personal level.
- Section III examines Pragmatic Spirituality as it applies to the rigors of the workplace.

- Section IV explores the potential for Pragmatic Spirituality in the organization to truly achieve the benefits of "spirituality in business."

Be advised that this is not a quick-fix or easy-answer book. The Pragmatic Spirituality process requires a commitment to candid self-assessment and the devotion of necessary time on a daily basis. It also involves patience and trust throughout the process. If you are willing to make that commitment, Pragmatic Spirituality is a means of finding renewal and fulfillment in your life, along with greater effectiveness in all your endeavors.

We are realistic enough to know that *The Inner Edge* is unlikely to change the world, but we do believe there are businesspeople out there who want to change *their* world (and possibly take a small step toward changing *the* world). To these adventurers, we offer Pragmatic Spirituality and this book as a guide. We also dedicate this book to all spiritual seekers—including those who may have experienced dissatisfaction with their lives but never considered that dissatisfaction in "spiritual" terms. We are eager to share what we have learned and experienced, not as a teacher with a student, but as one pilgrim with another journeying on the same road. And we offer it to you in the spirit of that wonderful saying, "We teach what we need to learn."

Note on Ammonites

The chambered nautilus featured on the book's cover is directly related to fossilized ammonites of the Triassic era. The ancient Egyptians worshipped the god Ammon (he who is everywhere but remains unseen) as the undifferentiated form of the divine, and considered the ammonite's evolving spiral chambers as a metaphor for the divine unfolding in the material world.

Likewise, we embrace the nautilus as a metaphor for the evolution of human consciousness and for the potential awaiting to be discovered in every individual.

YOUR INNER EDGE

I

1

THE INNER EDGE

You have to leave the city of your comfort and go into the wilderness of your intuition. What you'll discover will be wonderful. What you'll discover will be yourself.

—ALAN ALDA

SUCCESS IN TODAY'S FAST-MOVING, complex business world depends on many factors. Some of these are largely within your control, such as working hard, working smart, and using your resources, experience, and credentials. Other success factors are pretty much beyond your control, such as luck, timing, chemistry, the economy, and public sentiment.

However, there is a *third* set of success factors that is increasingly relevant to today's fast-changing, chaotic business conditions: the subtle but very powerful *inner* factors that profoundly influence every aspect of your life, both business and personal.

The inner factors we are referring to include instinct, intuition, inner balance, motivation, confidence, appropriateness, passion for work, and creativity, among others. It is quite possible that your logical thought process is unaware of these powerful but subtle influences. Although you have little if any direct control over these inner factors, it is possible to learn how to better align them to achieve your goals—to create your *Inner Edge*.

More widely recognized by Eastern cultures, inner factors have long been viewed with suspicion by the objective world of left-brain/rational thought. Recent years, though, have seen a growing interest in and awareness of these inner factors, possibly brought about by discoveries of logical paradoxes and contradictions in a number of leading-edge scientific fields, including quantum physics and chaos theory. Such growing and well-documented evidence that the

traditional Western rational thought process has its limits is in turn sparking interest in the untapped intuitive potential and resources of the mind.

The Benefits of an Enhanced Inner Edge

Most of us have grown up learning to distrust or even disavow the validity of our
intuitive resources, yet commonly used business vernacular evidences a respect
for gut feelings, acting on hunches, and "sleeping on it" before making a decision. Preoccupied with objective data obtained through our five senses, we have
forgotten or are otherwise unaware of the myriad inner factors that indelibly
influence us—for better or for worse. *The Inner Edge* equips you to access these
inner factors with a new level of consciousness, and provides you in your work
and all facets of your life with specific techniques to reawaken and enhance your
own Inner Edge in two ways:

1. By identifying and transcending behavioral patterns (of which you are
   largely unaware) that limit your potential by causing you to self-sabotage
   your best interests
2. By finding and drawing on new resources *beyond* your customary rational
   thought processes, thus opening up new energies and abilities in perception, decision making, and relationships

The overall outcome is a fuller expression of the essence of who you are. It's
not about power and authority over others or situations, but about capitalizing
on your strengths and gifts and letting go of behaviors and attitudes that no
longer serve you—aspects of yourself that actually hinder your ability to evolve
as an individual, as an employee or employer, and as a contributing member of
your family, organization, and community. As we'll discuss in Chapter 2, it's all
about "coming home" to *yourself*.

The Inner Edge *Deals with* Spiritual *Issues*

Understandably, developing your Inner Edge requires going inside to deal with
the many factors that make you unique. It involves asking the questions "Who
am I? How should I best allocate my time and talents?" and "What is my destiny?" These are, at their heart, *spiritual* issues—not spiritual as related to any

type of religious belief or practice, but in the sense of your intrinsic self. (We'll examine this distinction in the next chapter.)

We believe that there is a growing hunger to address these inner, spiritual issues—that beneath the bustle and affluence of today's life, many people experience an inner sense of hollowness and lack of grounding. The hunger to fill this void has been demonstrated in the last several decades by a flourishing interest in topics related to "spirituality" and "soul"—on an individual level and in group practices. Even more striking has been the growing fascination with "spirituality in business"—which not too long ago would have been regarded as an oxymoron, diametrically opposed terms struggling for supremacy and resolution.

How Compatible Can Spirituality and Business Be?

Many people would find it hard to believe that business and spirituality could coexist in the same context. Yet we believe that as the human species evolves, business and spirituality are being drawn together inexorably toward a confluence. What will be the outcome?

From our perspective, this drawing together of business and spirituality is transforming old understandings and behavioral patterns into a greater and more expansive blueprint for human endeavor—an intrinsic and consistent striving for *identity* and *meaning*. At the initial stage of this confluence, two extremes exist.

- One camp—the old-school perspective—embraces the way business has traditionally been conducted and regards religion and spirituality as having little compatibility with the realities of business.
- The other camp stretches its perspective so far in the opposite direction as to be unreasonable with their expectations, demands, and naïveté about bringing spirituality into business and what business should do to be "socially responsible."

We are heartened by the prospects of an amalgamation of business and spirituality, but we have been disappointed in what has been offered thus far to people seeking to create this merger.

- Too often, spiritual practices, which offer fulfillment when used by oneself or in a safe environment (such as a retreat center), don't hold up to the rigors of day-to-day life in the real world or over a period of time, especially in the workplace.
- And so far, offerings about spirituality in business either suffer from the same lack of practicality or are simply old concepts and techniques with new labels.

This causes frustration, creating a self-fulfilling scenario: the more spirituality is regarded as esoteric, the less applicability or impact it will be perceived to have for dealing with the nitty-gritty concerns of life, thus short-circuiting spirituality's potential contribution. Just as an individual's logical and routine existence can be changed and enhanced, we feel that spirituality has the potential for leveraging and expanding into various parts of society to achieve a new level of authenticity and appropriateness. This requires an *effective* form of spirituality.

The Search for an Effective Spiritual Technique

Many types of spiritual practices, done alone or in safe group environments, have helped countless people address their sense of inner hunger and hollowness. However, all too often these spiritual techniques are not robust enough to deal with complex real-world situations. In some cases, this is because the techniques are intrinsically flawed—offering a superficial quick-fix or feel-good approach that fails to solve essential problems.

Other spiritual techniques may be satisfying and effective within protected or controlled situations, but they fail to take into account realities that are commonly encountered when interacting with others in real-world circumstances. For example: people are not always well intentioned; interactions and spiritual growth are often blocked by unresolved psychological issues; individuals are not always honest about their agendas; and people respond differently in larger groups or more public circumstances than they might in small groups or one-on-one situations.

Most demanding and difficult to deal with constructively is the on-the-job environment, where competition and bottom-line issues can seem diametrically opposed to spiritual concepts and goals.

A Pragmatic *Spirituality*

In this book we offer an effective form of spiritual practice that allows you to address your intrinsic issues and to bridge your inner potentials with your outer realities. We call it *Pragmatic Spirituality* (*pragmatic* comes from the Greek word *pragmatikos*, meaning "business"). The goal of Pragmatic Spirituality is for you to draw upon your inner stability and resources to be able to function more authentically and appropriately in the most difficult circumstances.

Pragmatic Spirituality addresses the desire to understand and enhance one's individual intrinsic identity, as well as to bring together the realities and potential of business (logical and quantitative) with the resources and expanded sphere of spirituality (intuitive and qualitative). Logic and inner intuitive resources can be two quite complementary views or systems. This new paradigm is, in reality, a refocusing toward a broader perspective that takes into account the inherent respect due each of us as individuals on all levels, our creativity and capacities, our dreams and aspirations, and the need for each individual to not just "survive," but to *thrive*—without compromising our values and beliefs in the process of doing our work. The result is a pragmatic approach for integrating business and spirituality and creating an Inner Edge.

Like business and spirituality, the combination of "inner" and "edge" may suggest polar opposites, yet when brought together they produce a new image: that of accessing information and creative inspiration from a more *authentic* source—one that is congruent with universal principles of respect, responsibility, honesty, and a deep connection with the world around us. *The Inner Edge* is not about throwing all you know out the window, but about integrating what you do know from an external context with a much larger picture derived from

---

WE CHOSE *THE INNER EDGE* for our title because it evokes several images:
- *Inner* suggests working from within oneself to elicit inspiration and greater clarity in all aspects of one's life.
- *Edge* implies being on the cutting edge—in the forefront, the vanguard.
- In business, the term *competitive edge* is used to describe the ability to stay ahead of the competition.

an interior landscape of "unconstrained comprehension" in order to ensure a more fulfilling and richer quality of life in all your endeavors.

In Chapter 3, we'll take the first step toward developing *your* Inner Edge with an overview of Pragmatic Spirituality, its core elements, and how it can be applied on a day-to-day basis in every aspect of your life. But before that, we feel that it is important to discuss some aspects of *spirituality* to ensure a firm base of clear communications.

2

SPIRITUALITY IN LIFE
AND BUSINESS

*It has been said that Spirituality is the "courage to look within
and trust." What is seen and what is trusted appears to be a deep
sense of belonging, of wholeness, of connectedness, and of the
openness to the infinite.*

—Definition of *spirituality* adopted by the California
State Psychological Association Task Force on
Spirituality and Psychology

ALL WORDS ARE SYMBOLS representing something. The usefulness of a particular word for effective communication depends on how similar are the images
evoked by that word for each of the parties involved. Simply put, words are fal-
lible agents of communication.

The word *spirituality* can be problematic for effective communication in two
ways. First, it is a symbol for something that is not only intangible but also inef-
fable (inexpressible, indescribable, transcendent). Second, since spirituality tends
to be associated with words representing *religious* concepts, for many people it
evokes strong emotions—positive or negative, or both.

In spite of the loaded nature of the word *spirituality*, it does have one very
important thing going for it: it is the common denominator among the very
diverse universe of people who are seeking meaning and identity in life and work.
It is in this sense that we use *spirituality* in this book, including the capacity for
achieving one's full potential.

We like the definition of spirituality at the beginning of this chapter, as it
embraces the idea of coming home to oneself—*discovering one's essence*—while

at the same time expressing the expansive possibilities of personal growth derived from the self-discovery process of looking within and trusting the information provided. It emphasizes the "inner" focus, as compared to more outward-directed activities such as religion.

Spirituality and Religion

It is essential to recognize the distinction between spirituality and religion, although the difference is not always clear-cut. Both may deeply affect intrinsic human nature, with differing manifestations—from outward and visible forms of religious practice to inner results known only to the individual. Religion represents organized vehicles or practices that translate a specific set of spiritual beliefs or doctrines, often involving adherence to dogma and a hierarchical organizational structure.

The word *spirituality* is less focused on forms, practices, or personages, but embodies the idea of *spirit* or *soul*—the essential part of a person that transcends physical limitations. Spirituality tends to focus more on the discovery of personal truth as opposed to taught truth.

We respect existing religious traditions, acknowledging the insights and influence of belief systems throughout history. From our own personal experiences, we recognize the benefits that can come from participation in an organized religious community.

The spiritual techniques offered in this book focus on a practical form of spirituality that transcends differences in such definitions. These techniques can be practiced on their own or in combination with any form of organized religion or belief system. This practical form of spirituality, which we call *Pragmatic Spirituality*, focuses on the *authenticity* of one's identity and the *appropriateness* of one's actions and interactions, as well as openness to guidance *from resources and wisdom beyond the limits of one's rational mind.*

AUTHENTICITY: Congruency between the truth of what is experienced and what is expressed; genuineness and sincerity.

Growing Interest in Spirituality in All Aspects of Life

Recent years have seen an expanding interest in spirituality at several levels: on a personal basis, for group environments, and most recently in the context of business. Many types of spiritual practices are effective for "turning down the volume" of concerns and distractions in order to find the inner places of quiet and inspiration. All too often, as we discussed in Chapter 1, such practices that are effective when done alone or in like-minded company don't stand up to the stress of real-life situations.

A realistic spiritual approach must be able to work in *all areas* of an individual's life, as well as with life's "updrafts" and "downdrafts." Life needs to be addressed in its entirety in order to create a spiritual context for growth.

Greater Effectiveness Through Spirituality

Although most people have only sensed it at a very subtle level, there is ample evidence that one's effectiveness in very practical aspects of life can be enhanced significantly by one's inner or spiritual factors.

One of Ron's clients, a young surfer, described how surfing gave him a highly spiritual experience. When he had the right balance on the waves, he felt connected with the air, wind, and waves—he knew he was in the groove and surrendered to the experience. Likewise, businesspeople who are attuned to their jobs, clients, and vision get a wondrous sense of wholeness when everything that has been worked on comes together in a grand crescendo. So to have a sense of wonder, empowerment, connection, and *transcendence* is within reach for anyone who is willing to come back home to his body, passion, and spirit.

> TRANSCENDENCE: Going beyond one's ordinary experience in thinking, perception, creativity, and sense of self.

In modern terms, *transcendence* might be described as "operating closer to full capacity" or "greater effectiveness." This can be achieved through spiritual practice. There is overwhelming evidence that the unencumbered mind can reveal deeper realities of significance when it is able to go beyond the distractions of everyday life to a state of calmness where perceptual clarity emerges. In fact, there are strong indications that we humans are *biologically hard-wired* to experience transcendence—to gain access to deeper realities of our nature that, in turn, reveal our creative, intuitive, and spiritual capacities.

"Being present" is another means to achieve greater effectiveness. By "being present," we mean the ability to focus and concentrate on whatever or whomever you are dealing with, without distraction—focusing all your energies, mental and otherwise, on whatever is happening to you at the very moment it is occurring, which includes not denying or ignoring what you're feeling at that moment. It means staying in the *now*—not in the future and not in the past. A real-life, practical example of higher effectiveness through realistic spirituality and "being present" is evidenced by Ron's observations about working with His Holiness the Dalai Lama:

> I am constantly amazed at how much His Holiness accomplishes among his many responsibilities, primary of which is his work as head of state of the Tibetan government in exile. He wakes at 4 A.M., meditates until 8, does office work and holds personal meetings until mid-afternoon, does some spiritual teaching if called for, and then retires at 6 P.M. As anyone who has met him knows, he is a very attentive listener—always present in the moment, quick to discern the key issues and make wise judgments. He attains closure on each transaction, and avoids being burdened by the past. I have always marveled at his efficiency in the use of mind, energy, and the resources of each moment he encounters.

Imagine the practical impact if you could achieve—even to a limited degree—such focused attention and energy!

If it is true that such potential rests within each person, why is achieving it so elusive? Each form of spiritual guidance, Eastern or Western, has a similar response to that question: the inability to call upon one's spiritual potential is caused by the encumbrances of *past* events, distractions of the *present*, and anticipations of the future. Thus encumbered and distracted, you remain *unaware* of the natural depth and power of your creative potential until you learn to transcend these obstacles through effective spiritual techniques.

In these and many other ways, it is possible for spirituality to lead to enhancements in one's day-to-day, hour-to-hour life and work. The foundation of this book is our conviction that spirituality can have some very *practical results*, such as the following:

- By quieting our internal distractions, we can perceive our surroundings more clearly—including enhanced discernment about the people with whom we interact.
- We can accomplish more with less exertion by having greater clarity as to the appropriate allocation of our energies.
- By becoming compassionate observers, we can see and experience events and people from a broader perspective.

In short, our entire way of being in the world can be proactive rather than reactive.

Spirituality in Business: How Realistic Are the Expectations?

An examination of the commentaries and offerings about "spirituality in business"—in books, the media, seminars, vendor products, and so on—clearly demonstrates that there are a variety of expected outcomes. One is when employees of a company are encouraged to follow a particular belief system or "right practice." (More "religion" than spirituality, this kind of situation often stems from overenthusiastic proselytizing by individuals.)

Another type of expectation for spirituality in business is that the business organization will or should increase its "doing good"—adopting moral behavior, acting in some ways perceived as socially responsible, and so on. This expectation needs to be qualified, in our opinion.

It is understandable that people increasingly look to business to play a more active role in responding to the challenges of today's complex world. This is rooted in a perception that business organizations have greater capabilities to bring about change than government, education, and religious institutions.

Problems occur, however, when the expectation is that "more spiritual" business will automatically divert a significant part of its energies and assets to "doing good"—both internally with its employees, and externally in the local and worldwide community in which it functions.

We share the belief that corporations have the potential to deal more effectively with many of the world's problems; however, we also recognize the tough realities in which businesses operate—and the need for a realistic balance between "doing good" and maintaining the bottom line. In practice, if a business jeopardizes its ongoing viability in the marketplace by excessively focusing on "doing good," its leaders can rightly be accused of neglecting their primary responsibility to the business's shareholders, employees, vendors, and other stake-holders—that of the *survival of the organization.*

Spirituality in business can succeed only if the application of spirituality enhances the effectiveness of the organization and its bottom line, thus creating the ability to *both* remain competitively viable and do good. An appropriate balance between the two is essential.

A strong determining factor is the "self-fulfilling" aspect of applying spirituality to business. To the extent that spirituality is perceived as unworkable—simplistic solutions based on unrealistic expectations—it will have little or no opportunity to be assessed for its ability to enhance—for individuals and organizations—day-to-day effectiveness and the subtle but powerful issues of self-worth, mission, and morality. If, on the other hand, a form of spirituality is perceived as capable of enhancing both the qualitative aspects of a business culture as well as its quantitative bottom-line performance, that form of spirituality has a chance to prove itself.

Business Convolutions Necessitate New Attitudes

Recent events have brought about radical changes for both employers and the employees they depend on to succeed in their business.

On the employer side, organizations are coming to the realization that the accelerating rate of change in technologies and markets increasingly requires a new kind of employee: one who is adaptable, capable of good judgment with minimal training and supervision, and whose self-worth and internal direction enable her to operate confidently in an indefinite and shorter-term employment environment.

On the employee side, there is a greater awareness by individuals that long-term job security no longer exists, leading in turn to the recognition of the need to become more self-aware and self-determined—as with Pragmatic Spirituality or other inward-looking processes. The resulting self-confident and self-directed employee is exactly what the emerging organization needs to be competitive in the new markets; however, these new employees will require a complete change in the organization's employment attitudes and policies.

These changes will be discussed further in later chapters. Clearly, the trends will vary from industry to industry and from one organization to another, but as more and more well-qualified prospective employees become empowered with self-acceptance and self-direction, businesses will inevitably be changed—not for altruistic reasons but simply to compete more effectively in the realities of the market.

Spirituality: A Means of Transcending Compartmentalization

The extraordinary interest in "spirituality in business" may be based on expectations of alleviating a common quandary faced by businesspeople today: they are pulled in opposite directions by their inner voices and their business responsibilities. The natural way of dealing with this dichotomy is to *compartmentalize*, simply ignoring contradictions and conflicts. For generations, managers have attended church or synagogue, keeping separate—with varying degrees of success—their "weekend religion" and their Monday-to-Friday responsibilities. People also compartmentalize and ignore their hunger for more meaning and significance in their life and work. But in today's increased awareness, compartmentalized thinking is more and more difficult to maintain.

We strongly believe that spirituality can have relevance in day-to-day life and work, and can bring new perspective to the difficult trade-offs of the rapidly changing business environment. In order for spirituality to "work" in life and at work, it must transcend compartmentalized thinking and be defined in terms of awareness and attitudes that allow a person to be authentic in all facets of life and appropriate to whatever realities are at hand.

The outcome is to achieve a balance in one's life:

- In an existence preoccupied by *doing* and *having*, spirituality can bring the balancing dimension of *being* (valuing oneself for one's core essence rather than accomplishments or possessions).
- To a person whose life is preoccupied with the *quantitative* aspects of life, spirituality may contribute the *qualitative* dimensions, such as relationships and competence.
- In a world that has become monodimensional and shallow, spirituality offers multidimensional (holistic) significance and fulfillment.

A Pragmatic Spirituality

As a means of achieving the benefits of spirituality, we offer the concept of Pragmatic Spirituality. In accordance with the Eastern belief that there are many paths to "heaven" (God, enlightenment, Nirvana, and so on), Pragmatic Spirituality is one of many ways in which to improve your spiritual balance. We hope that it may provide many enhancements to your life, including

- A form of spiritual practice that transcends differences in definitions between spirituality and religion
- Access to deeper realities of your nature revealing creative, intuitive, and spiritual capacities
- A sense of wonder, empowerment, connection, and transcendence—allowing you to operate closer to full capacity and greater effectiveness
- The ability to perceive your surroundings more clearly—including enhanced discernment about the people with whom you interact
- Greater clarity as to the appropriate allocation of your energies, allowing you to accomplish more with less exertion
- Proactive (as opposed to reactive) decision making
- The chance to become a compassionate observer: to see and experience events and people from a broader perspective
- An enhanced balance to life on a broader scale, extending into the nitty-gritty world of business
- An awareness that allows you to be attuned and responsive to the realities at hand
- The ability to be more present—to be a more attentive listener and to handle your interactions with greater honesty and sincerity

In the next chapter, you can begin the Pragmatic Spirituality process with an overview of its core elements and how they can be applied in your daily life.

3

AN OVERVIEW OF PRAGMATIC SPIRITUALITY

Your vision will become clear only when you can look into your own heart. Who looks outside, dreams; who looks inside, awakes.

—CARL JUNG

IN CHAPTER 1, we examined how developing an Inner Edge can enhance your effectiveness in all aspects of your life by helping you become aware of, and bring into alignment, the inner factors that exert a powerful influence on you—for better or for worse. The technique for developing an Inner Edge is Pragmatic Spirituality, and in this chapter we'll take you on the first step, an overview from two different perspectives: the core elements of Pragmatic Spirituality, and how Pragmatic Spirituality can be applied to your life on a practical, day-to-day basis. Don't be concerned if you don't get everything the first time. Each of the Pragmatic Spirituality elements is thoroughly discussed in subsequent chapters in Section II. For now, just get oriented.

The Core Elements of Pragmatic Spirituality

Figure 3.1 shows how the major elements of Pragmatic Spirituality (PS) relate to each other. Pragmatic Spirituality pulls together proven principles from a number of fields that deal with various aspects of being human: psychology, Eastern meditative practices, and left/right brain studies. PS is *not* a belief system; it can be used either as an adjunct to most religious practices or on its own. And we hasten to emphasize that PS is not a quick fix, although you will notice that its benefits begin to accrue early in the process.

FIGURE 3.1 CORE ELEMENTS OF PRAGMATIC SPIRITUALITY

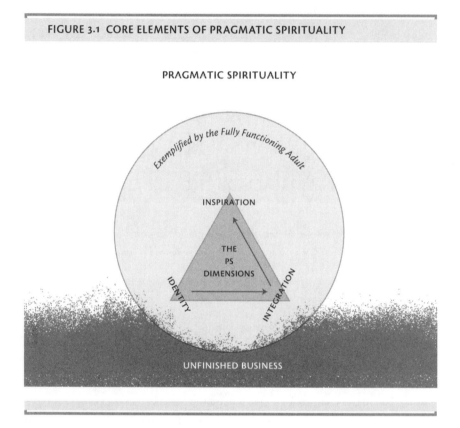

The goal of Pragmatic Spirituality is to enable you to *live more authentically* and *respond more appropriately* to every person and situation you encounter. This is personified by the *Fully Functioning Adult*—an idealized concept.

The Fully Functioning Adult does not exist in real life. It is an ideal—a goal to work toward, an ever-evolving process of growth. Certainly, there are people operating at a high degree of functionality *in their accustomed context*; however, in different contexts, they don't do as well. The purpose of the PS journey is to have the *adaptability* to be authentic and appropriate in *every* situation, whatever the context.

The underlying premise of Pragmatic Spirituality is that each person is hampered and constrained by subtle and powerful inner "scripts" or patterns of behavior, values, and belief systems acquired early in life. This *Unfinished Business* will continue to undermine the person's ability to achieve his potential, and the self-sabotaging and inappropriate actions will continue. Your Pragmatic Spirituality development will involve an ongoing process of *identifying and transcending your Unfinished Business.*

Some people are motivated to address their Unfinished Business out of a commitment to the self-awareness process. Others who are skeptical about Unfinished Business suddenly recognize the need to address it when they fully realize that each time their Unfinished Business is triggered, *they are no longer in control.* That is *not* to say that the person is "out of control," but instead is not able to bring all of her faculties and capabilities to bear on the situation—and thus is less able to be "in control."

These inappropriate patterns—and the fact that their inappropriateness is not recognized by you even as you reenact them—are parts of yourself that need to be revisited and resolved in whatever way necessary. This, by its nature, is not a quick transition—your Unfinished Business has been with you a long time and is very resistant to being identified and resolved. The Pragmatic Spirituality process begins with acknowledging your unlimited potential and then addressing your Unfinished Business, which is focused on in the three Dimensions of each Daily PS Focus.

The Three Dimensions of Pragmatic Spirituality

The three Dimensions of Pragmatic Spirituality—*Identity*, *Integration*, and *Inspiration*—embody complex and powerful concepts. The Dimensions are interrelated and interdependent, like the legs of a tripod. Each Dimension has a specific visualization (these will be covered in greater detail in Section II). When you do your daily application of PS, each visualization builds on the other two—a powerful metaphor of inner stability, strength, and capacity.

Healthy Pragmatic Spirituality develops as you become proficient in each of these interdependent Dimensions:

Identity: The First PS Dimension This Dimension involves all aspects of the core issue: "Who am I?" It includes achieving stability through a healthy sense of self, removing obstacles to achieving your full potential, and accepting yourself for who you are rather than who you *ought* to be.

Your identity is reaffirmed and reinforced every time you do your Identity Visualization.

Integration: The Second PS Dimension Building on the *inner*-focused first Dimension of Identity, the Integration (balance) Dimension focuses *externally*, combining the elements of your life into a constructive whole, allocating your time and energy each day among your own needs and the many factors vying for your attention. The Integration Visualization sets up and prioritizes your day and is focused on answering the question, "How should I best allocate my time and energies?"

Inspiration: The Third PS Dimension As the three PS Dimensions work together, yet independently, the Inspiration Dimension and visualization builds on and refines the first and second Dimensions to create an increasing openness and receptivity to resources and higher powers beyond your normal capabilities. An adjunct to the Inspiration Dimension, the Quantum Decision Making (QDM) process enables you to properly interpret your intuitive *Icons* (the symbols used by your intuitive mind) so that the left/rational and right/intuitive parts of your mind can work together to enhance the quality of your decision making and creative thought. It is the launching pad addressing the question, "What is my destiny?"

The three Dimensions of Identity, Integration, and Inspiration will become the interstitial fabric of your entire PS structure, providing integral feedback and support as you expand your understanding of your behaviors, examine the foundation of your goals, and learn the way to effectively merge spirituality and business as an evolving conviction and integrated aspect of your being.

Daily Application of Pragmatic Spirituality to Enhance Your Life

Now that you have a clear overview of the core elements of PS, the next step is to understand how these can enhance your day-to-day effectiveness and satisfaction in all facets of your personal life and job. This is done with a daily routine—the *Daily PS Focus*, as illustrated in Figure 3.2. The Daily PS Focus enables you to quickly "touch base" with each of the aspects of Pragmatic Spirituality, centering yourself and calling on all of your inner resources to deal with the spe-

---

**FIGURE 3.2 DAILY APPLICATION AND IMPLEMENTATION OF
PRAGMATIC SPIRITUALITY**

Each day at your regular time do a Daily PS Focus (15–20 minutes)

Affirmation

Restatement of Self-resolves

- Self-accountability
- Self-maintenance
- Self-discipline

3D Visualization

- Identity (Compassionate Observer)
- Integration (guilt-free prioritization)
- Inspiration (faith-based or intuitive access)

Start your day with an Inner Edge!

When and if needed during the day do a Quick Re-Focus (30–60 seconds)

3D Review

FFA Cross-Check:

"What would a Fully Functioning Adult do in the current situation?"

(Later) Ask:

"What Unfinished Business was at work?"

---

cific needs of the day. (The *Daily PS Focus* and *Quick Re-Focus* are described
in greater detail in Chapter 9.)

YOUR DAILY PS FOCUS

The Daily PS Focus takes ten to twenty minutes; practice it at the beginning or
end of your day.

- It begins with an *Affirmation* (described later in this chapter).

- Then do a Restatement of Self-Resolves:
  — Self-accountability
  — Self-maintenance
  — Self-discipline

- Next, quickly review the three PS Dimensions by doing a combined visualization for each—called the *3D Visualization*. You orient your 3D Visualization based on what you expect the day to bring: dealing with any Identity issues, using Integration to prioritize (without guilt) your allocation of time and energy, and calling on Inspiration for assistance on specific matters.

Then you can start your day feeling grounded, self-confident, and energized.

QUICK RE-FOCUS

If at any time during the day you find yourself destabilized by unexpected events or need to reorder your priorities, use the following:

- Do a *3D Review*, concentrating on the appropriate PS Dimension to address the situation: Identity to recover your sense of self, Integration (balance) to reprioritize your energies, or Inspiration to call forth intuitive resources.

- Do an *FFA Cross-Check:* ask yourself, "How would a Fully Functioning Adult handle this?"

- As soon as practical, consider what Unfinished Business was at work and decide how you'll prevent a future recurrence.

That's how Pragmatic Spirituality is implemented on a day-by-day basis. As we emphasized earlier, it is not a quick-fix process, since it first requires gaining a familiarity with each PS element and then involves modifying long-entrenched behavior patterns. But you'll start seeing results at an early stage, and the longer you work on your Pragmatic Spirituality, the greater its impact will be.

The Application and Benefits of PS at the Three Levels of Your Life

As symbolized in Figure 3.3, Pragmatic Spirituality applies to all levels of life: personal, work, and organizational. We understand that your primary interest may be how to achieve an Inner Edge in your work. However, it is essential that you first concentrate on the PS process on a *personal* level (emphasized in Section II). Only then should you begin to apply the principles and practices in the more challenging context of your work (discussed in Section III). For those with a desire to carry the PS principles farther, Section IV discusses the potential for, and the likely obstacles to, applying PS to revitalize your organization—thereby achieving true spirituality in business.

Our goal is that you step back and reconsider all the parts of your life, including your organizational roles, with the belief that things can be different— and that you can play a part in making that happen. As you progress through an understanding of Pragmatic Spirituality, don't try to grasp it all during your first go-around. This is an evolving process of increasing self-perception and self-determination. We recommend that you periodically go back and reread the chapters in Section II to gain a deeper level of perception of each of the PS components.

Pragmatic Spirituality offers a conceptual framework, terminology, and techniques that lend themselves to promoting authenticity and appropriateness in a more deliberate manner, with the left/rational part of the brain working in cooperation with the right/intuitive brain for both the individual and the organization.

FIGURE 3.3 PRAGMATIC SPIRITUALITY AT THREE LEVELS OF LIFE

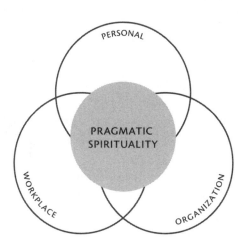

Outcomes on the Personal Level

- A clear and healthy balance between work and the other parts of your life, creating an inner stability and resilience to better deal with anything that arises
- More appropriate responses in your interactions for greater creativity, honesty, effectiveness, results, rapport, and decision making
- Freeing-up of energy that was previously used for your internal maintenance and security
- Greater authenticity from accepting yourself for all your talents, abilities, and capabilities—whatever your shortcomings
- Increased ability to "be present in the moment," resulting in a more profound connection and understanding in all your relationships

Outcomes in the Workplace

- Constructive objectivity toward your work, which enables you to have a clearer perspective of what's going on—and to avoid hanging on after it's time to move on in your career
- More appropriately equipped to look out for your self-interests thanks to Self-maintenance, Self-discipline, and boundaries—guided by an updated perspective of responsibility and accountability
- Greater ability to perceive and respond to the subtleties and needs of subordinates, peers, supervisors, and your organization—unencumbered by your Unfinished Business and well equipped to deal with theirs
- Able to enhance your overall performance—particularly in decision making—by accessing your intuitive resources through QDM

Outcomes for Your Organization

- An organizational environment consistent with PS principles that attracts Fully Functioning Adult–type employees who are (a) objective about their relationship with the organization, (b) stimulated and satisfied with their work, and (c) self-directed and appropriate in discharging their responsibilities—thus enhancing the efficiency and effectiveness of the organization
- Intercompany and intracompany communications throughout the organization occurring more rapidly and accurately, with the resultant improved efficiency flowing directly to the bottom line
- Enhanced creativity and commitment to new ways of doing things

- More effective decisions at every level, with greater wisdom and discernment in the use of resources and awareness of long-term versus short-term implications

The entire Pragmatic Spirituality process begins with you and your willingness to push your own envelope, to suspend investment in your old behavior patterns, and to allow yourself to discover through this book's exercises, visualizations, and concepts a deeper sense of self, capacity, and fulfillment.

The world is poised at the edge of a higher plateau: one of insight and intuition, new portals of resources and creativity, greater sensitivity and compassion in our mutual goals and interactions, and the ability to integrate business and spirituality into a dynamic matrix of potential and fulfillment. *You* are in the vanguard of this momentous time, so let's begin the Pragmatic Spirituality process. The first step? An affirmation of your potential.

Affirmation of My Potential
I have the potential to . . .
reach a higher state of consciousness,
access my full resources,
achieve an enhanced level of authenticity for myself,
and respond appropriately to all situations I encounter.

Take a moment to consider your reactions on first reading this statement. Is your interest piqued? Are you skeptical? Are you ready to embark on a journey that may surprise you, or validate what you already know, or expand your boundaries of understanding and expression? Repeat the Affirmation. Close your eyes and repeat it a number of times so that you begin to integrate it into your sense of who you are. And then think about the process of Pragmatic Spirituality and its benefits and outcomes. What kinds of thoughts come to mind as you repeat

---

YOU MAY FIND IT HELPFUL to follow a CD of this and other imaging exercises. Please refer to Appendix F (page 291) for information about ordering a CD created by Dr. Ronald Jue that includes this Affirmation and the other imaging exercises and visualizations in this book.

the Affirmation? Are you experiencing any emotions? Continue to relax, and don't try to figure out what you are experiencing. Just let the information and sensations move through your consciousness. After a few minutes, open your eyes.

Congratulations! You've just completed your first Pragmatic Spirituality exercise. Did anything surprising come up for you? What emotions did you notice during this period? What are you experiencing now? Whether you had a positive or negative experience, try to remember the details of what occurred (you might want to write this down), because when you complete the entire PS process, you will find it interesting to compare where you were at the beginning of this process with how you've grown and expanded your sense of self, and to note the ways your perspective has shifted concerning your work and the various aspects of your life.

KEEPING A JOURNAL is one of the easiest methods for tracking your progress, for freely expressing your thoughts in safety and privacy, and for remembering important ideas, thoughts, and events. It is another way of seeing within yourself—a way of creating an emotional historical map that shows you a larger perspective of your life's terrain. You'll discover insights about who you are and understand more clearly your needs and aspirations. It is a window into your inner being.

Now that you've had a summary overview of the core elements of Pragmatic Spirituality and how they are applied on a daily basis, it's time to move on to Section II for a detailed examination of each of the PS elements and how they interact together.

PRAGMATIC
SPIRITUALITY AT THE
PERSONAL LEVEL

II

4

UNFINISHED BUSINESS: ITS NATURE AND RESOLUTION

No one can shut out unfinished business. No one can close the
book on the incompleted sentence, the partial paragraph. The
book, I say, will reopen itself. Its pages will blaze forth
instruction—then quietly close when the lesson is learned.

—Doris Kerns Quinn

The Pragmatic Spirituality journey begins by traveling *down* and *back*—to find and deal with issues that are constraining your energy and potential, issues we call *Unfinished Business*. Discovering your Inner Edge, as we mentioned earlier, allows you to access and use your talents with maximum effectiveness. And again, each person's effectiveness—at work and in all aspects of life—is strongly influenced by patterns from the past. Some of these patterns continue to be useful; others are actually obstructing your ability to move forward in life.

Why Do Smart People Do Dumb Things?

Think back for a minute to a situation in which someone you consider rational and intelligent did something that really worked against that person's best interests. Perhaps something like one of the following:

- You see a coworker reacting to the boss in a way that makes you think, "Uh-oh! She's asking for trouble."
- In a normal conversation, someone suddenly responds in a manner that seems completely "out of left field."

- In the critical stage of a multimillion-dollar negotiation, one of the participants loses his temper and blows the deal.

And—truth be told—there have probably been times when *you* have responded to a situation in such a manner that you later wished you could turn the clock back and do it all over again.

It is all too common to respond to situations inappropriately, and then in hindsight say, "What's going on? Why did I do that?" This kind of occurrence is very disturbing, especially for people who have invested a lot of time and money in the training and preparation of their rational mind, because *you want your rational mind to be in control*!

The truth is that a large part of everyone's day-to-day, hour-to-hour living takes place without much input from the rational mind, but tends to operate according to "inner scripts."

WE LIKE THE TERM *Unfinished Business* for two reasons: (1) it is neutral, so it could relate to any kind of experience, positive or negative, and (2) it is a reminder that there is something unfinished—something that needs more attention and work to be resolved.

Your Inner Scripts

There is a lot going on beneath your awareness. The fields of psychiatry and psychology have many complicated concepts and names for all that stuff. We use the term *Unfinished Business* as a catchall for those subconscious happenings that are capable of reducing your overall effectiveness or the appropriateness of what you say or do in a particular situation.

What happens to distort and even sabotage the intent of your rational mind is that your *established behavioral patterns* take over. These patterns are pre-programmed scripts you learned early in life about the "correct" way to respond to situations. These scripts can be very useful as you go through your day-to-day life—like being on automatic pilot, so you don't have to stop and think about everything you do. But problems arise when these automatic responses are *not appropriate* to the situation at hand. That may be so because the inner script is *out-of-date* (you learned it from your parents, who learned it from their parents). Or maybe the script relates to a different context (as in going from one culture to another). Or maybe it was never valid in the first place (as with prejudices or phobias).

Whatever the reason, if your reaction to a situation is determined by an out-of-date inner script, your response is not going to be as appropriate as it could be. And, more important, you are not going to be fully aware of your lack of appropriateness. Instead you will probably rationalize the problems as being the fault of the person or group you are dealing with—and the miscommunication will escalate.

Ironically, the individuals who are most resistant to acknowledging the existence of inner scripts and Unfinished Business are usually the ones who place the greatest importance on *always being in control*. When your response to a situation is determined by out-of-date scripts, *you are not as in control of that situation as you could otherwise be*. Those inner scripts have power over you—even greater power because you are unaware of them, or in denial that they exist.

Here are some examples of inappropriate inner scripts at work and a look at how Unfinished Business played a role.

Bob

The Inner Script at Work

Bob arrived home from a very tough day at the office to learn from his wife that their eleven-year-old son had brought home a report card with several near-failing grades. Bob went to his son's room for a talk, but soon found himself screaming at the boy, whose face registered genuine fear. Drawn by the noise, his wife pulled Bob down the hall and confronted him with blazing eyes: "How can you talk to your son that way?" Bob—coming out of the near trance he had been in—was appalled at what he had done, and had no answer for her.

The Unfinished Business Beneath the Inner Script

Bob had gone to his son's room with a sincere desire to help the young man do better in school. But his son's initial reaction, which seemed to Bob like a lack of motivation, suddenly triggered some old scripts between Bob and *his* father: "If you don't try your very hardest, you'll dishonor the family and waste all the hard work of your parents and their parents before them." And before he knew it, Bob was yelling at his son, hooked by the old patterns he got from *his* dad so many years earlier.

ESTELLE

The Inner Script at Work

Estelle, an attractive sales rep, did very well in signing up new accounts and quickly earned the reputation of being a diligent worker. When she first joined the company, she was rather accommodating, but as she became more comfortable with her coworkers she began making demands. At first, this was perceived as exercising her rights: she didn't want to take notes for meetings or get coffee for male workers. Eventually, people became annoyed at her quickness to take offense at perceived sexist implications of customary language usage. They found her behavior disruptive and a waste of time. When confronted by her supervisor about her viewpoint and behavior, she reluctantly stepped down from her position, her resentment quite obvious.

The Unfinished Business Beneath the Inner Script

Estelle came from a family of mostly boys. Her father made it clear that he believed women were inferior and should remain "in their place." She considered her mother weak and passive. Growing up, she vowed never to be like her mother and to excel at whatever she did. Even though her self-esteem was supported by high intelligence and an excellent academic record, she still harbored a great deal of resentment about how she was treated while growing up, as well as later instances of sexual discrimination. Her resentment was now being acted out at work in the role of self-appointed censor for politically correct sexism.

ART

The Inner Script at Work

Art's success in sales was largely due to his ability to communicate with a prospective client in a very empathic and articulate manner. When he made a presentation, the right words just seemed to come to him. Then a new sales manager, Bill, was appointed. In their first meeting Art's mind froze and his tongue wouldn't work properly. Bill proposed some changes that Art strongly opposed, but for some reason he couldn't articulate his points. Afterward, Art was trying to figure out what happened—it was as if he had been paralyzed. But why?

The Unfinished Business Beneath the Inner Script

Why did Art, the master salesman, become tongue-tied with Bill? Because deep down, Bill's mannerisms brought forth a recollection of an uncle whom Art was terrified of, for reasons unremembered. That memory below his awareness was powerful enough to submerge Art back into the fear pattern of his childhood and completely disrupt his reasoning and communication abilities.

Bob, Estelle, and Art were intelligent, talented people, yet they found it impossible to react to particular situations as their rational minds wished. These, and countless similar examples, attest to the insidious power of Unfinished Business to influence *everyone's* day-to-day existence.

Highly Charged Holograms from the Past That Influence the Present

During every moment of life, each person travels with extensive memories of the past embedded in various levels of his consciousness, played and replayed in many variations. They have extremely powerful nuances of meaning and emotions compressed into a few images. These memories are like emotional holograms, strongly influencing one's perception of the world and affecting every action.

The roots of your Unfinished Business relate back to very early chapters of your life. And the reason these roots are so powerful is that they date back to your infancy, a time of dependency and survival. In that place of vulnerability, you instinctively sought and developed patterns of survival, interacting with your parents and all the members of your family of origin who were your sources for getting your needs met. In time, this evolved into a family emotional matrix, a kind of "dance" in which each person had a role to play.

Out of that emotional matrix you developed techniques of accommodation and other behavioral patterns that worked for getting what you needed. Depending on the climate of your family situation—the degree of giving or withholding—you developed ways, inappropriate or appropriate, of dealing with your needs.

Jason

The Inner Script at Work
"Jason, this damned entitled attitude of yours has got to change immediately or you're out of here!" Jason couldn't believe his ears. Hadn't he been recommended for this job by a very important client of the company? His boss continued speaking, citing examples of Jason's negative impact on the workplace. His head reeling after the meet-

ing, Jason was convinced that he was the victim of a personal vendetta; however, when he sought consolation, his close friend sided with his boss: "Let's face it, Jason— you're hopelessly entitled."

The Unfinished Business Beneath the Inner Script

Jason was referred to Ron, who readily identified the problem. Jason had grown up in an affluent family, gone to the best schools, and never lacked for anything. The problem was that he had never developed commonality or empathy with others. Jason acted as if he did not have to play by the same rules as everyone else. This was not surprising, since his family situation had enabled him to avoid many of the realities and accountabilities of normal life (including one minor infraction of the law that was glossed over thanks to his parents' influence).

Jason's Unfinished Business gave him behavior patterns of entitlement and lack of accountability. Understandably, these caused big problems with coworkers and clients. In spite of extensive counseling, it took Jason several lost jobs and failed relationships before he was able to make substantial progress in finishing up this Unfinished Business.

JAN

The Inner Script at Work

Jan was one of the first women graduates from her alma mater to go on to obtain an M.B.A. She became a successful executive in a very demanding industry. Her coworkers called her "the Steel Butterfly" because of the emotionless manner in which she hired and fired, confronted difficult clients, and negotiated deals. Jan sought help after she became aware that her business persona served her financial interests well, but interfered with her personal life. In relationships with men, she could not let her guard down, always seeking to be in control. This had been the undoing of relationships with several very special men, and she was starting to despair.

The Unfinished Business Beneath the Inner Script

Jan's background quickly yielded the relevant Unfinished Business. Growing up in an alcoholic environment in which family members were not emotionally accessible, Jan learned early in life to monitor her behavior in order to minimize her father's angry outbursts. She developed a wall of numbness. Her defense was not to feel, but rather to use her cognitive abilities and intelligence to handle difficult situations and to stay in control emotionally. These highly adaptive, stoic attributes helped her to gain admission and do very well at a prestigious college.

Once Jan understood the ramifications of her Unfinished Business, she realized that to find significance and emotional fulfillment, she would have to dismantle those compensatory behaviors of denial and emotional avoidance in order to reclaim her capacities to experience herself as a woman. This was a difficult process, because she not only had to deal with her control issues, but also reexamine her perceptions about being a woman (the attraction of fulfillment, as well as the negative image of her mother as a "doormat" to Jan's father). Jan used her tenaciousness to work through the issues, which led to a very satisfying relationship with a wonderful man. And her chronic back pains, which were probably related to stiffness in her movements from holding back emotions, disappeared.

Reenacting Past Scenarios in Your Present Life

As illustrated in these mini-cases, people tend to replicate the patterns found in their family of origin. They not only filter and reformat their perceptions of current day-to-day reality according to their inner life, but they also attract to themselves the needed elements—people and situations—to reinforce and recreate the mandates and expectations that were internalized so many years ago. Thus, Unfinished Business restages or reenacts emotional scenarios of the past in the present moment.

Reenactments are done repeatedly, in one situation after another, by people seeking a solution to their Unfinished Business. An example is a woman who never got the love she wanted from her distant, emotionally inaccessible, alcoholic father. Throughout her life she finds herself consistently drawn to distant men, often with drinking problems, attempting to find the love she never realized with her father.

Everyone has witnessed countless reenactments, probably without being aware of what's going on. When the boss is in a bad mood, when two department heads go at it yet again, when the office mimic entertains a circle of coworkers with unflattering stories about managers—these are all reenactments, fruitless and unconscious attempts to resolve Unfinished Business.

In business situations, the most destructive reenactment patterns are those involving approval, intimidation, and unresolved anger—with subordinates, superiors, and colleagues. When these patterns are played out, there is a déjà vu feeling. If the situation is an emotion-laden one, it may play out in a highly melodramatic manner.

The sad fact is that reenactments never resolve Unfinished Business; they only perpetuate it. However, reenactments can be one of the paths to discovering and exploring Unfinished Business. And often it is the aftermath of a particularly dramatic reenactment that moves a person, either on his own or at the encouragement of others, to seek out the reason for his inappropriate and destructive behavior.

INDIVIDUALS ENTRENCHED IN THEIR PATTERNS often seem automated and predictable as they once again perform the reenactment. Witnesses to the reenactment feel enervated and frustrated because there is no closure, or even an interest in seeking solutions.

Everyone has Unfinished Business. The bad news is that it's not all that simple to identify your particular Unfinished Business and begin to deal with it. The good news—in fact, *very* good news—is that resolving Unfinished Business can unleash energies bound up by old patterns to achieve higher levels of potential and functioning.

Several of the mini-cases in this chapter illustrate how some aspects of a person's Unfinished Business can work in her favor. Dealing with Unfinished Business is not about eliminating the behavior, but *finishing* it—resolving the issue that has been unresolved for so many years. In that regard, we can think of Unfinished Business behaviors as immature forms of our potential: when they are finished, the way is clear to move ahead!

You may be wondering if you must deal with *all* of your Unfinished Business before you can begin working on the other aspects of the Pragmatic Spirituality process. The answer is *no*—just make a commitment and begin the process. Sorting through and transcending Unfinished Business is *ongoing*. The Pragmatic Spirituality process is synergistic: as you deal with Unfinished Business, the way is opened for growth, which, in turn, affirms and enables further progress on your Unfinished Business.

Exactly how do you deal with Unfinished Business in order to clear the way for the PS process and achieve your Inner Edge? It need not involve therapy or counseling; it is completely feasible for most people to learn to deal with their Unfinished Business without professional help. In practice, though, many people become so intrigued with the prospective benefits that they choose to accelerate the process (or get help with particularly complex issues) by working with a professional therapist or counselor. The *Four Rs* give you a technique for dealing with Unfinished Business on your own within the context of your regular day-to-day activities.

Dealing with Unfinished Business — the Four Rs

Let's stress again that dealing with Unfinished Business is a slow process that involves digging up and modifying lifelong habit patterns, so begin with realistic expectations. Once the process is begun, however, it gets easier as you progress.

The Four Rs for dealing with Unfinished Business are as follows:

1. **Recognition:** Become aware of a behavior pattern.
2. **Responsibility:** Own the pattern.
3. **Research:** Uncover the underlying Unfinished Business dynamics.
4. **Retrofitting:** Modify an outdated behavior pattern to fit an existing situation.

THE FIRST R: RECOGNITION

The first element in dealing with Unfinished Business is *Recognition*: developing the ability to recognize when one of your Unfinished Business patterns is triggered. As we've discussed earlier, Recognition is much more elusive than it would seem. After all, if you were aware at the time that you were doing something inappropriate, you probably wouldn't have been doing it, would you? The unawareness is completely understandable: this is a behavioral pattern that dates *way back*, and one that feels completely natural—until the day that you start to become aware of its fallout and inappropriateness.

As soon as you acknowledge the fact that you, like everyone else, have Unfinished Business and inappropriate scripts that need to change, you are much more likely to recognize inappropriate behavior when it occurs. Here are three ways you can accelerate the process.

1. Find some quiet time and think back to past situations when you haven't handled a situation as well as you would have liked. These are often memorable because they are characterized by retrospective "I should have done

thus-and-thus instead" thoughts or self-recriminations. Write them down. What are the similarities: the circumstances, participants, topic, transaction? Once you identify a common denominator, you are close to recognizing an Unfinished Business pattern.

2. Be alert to your inner signals that something's amiss. Normally one's feelings give a warning just before Unfinished Business surfaces (such as a voice inside that says, "Something's wrong with this situation," or an uneasy off-center sensation). However, many people have become quite good at ignoring their feelings, especially those related to Unfinished Business. Learn to listen to your feelings—they are like warning lights on a pilot's instrument panel.

3. Another method of improving Recognition is to enlist people who are willing to alert you when some Unfinished Business affects your behavior. This person could be your spouse, close friend, or coworker; someone you feel comfortable with. Since these are people who may very well have become adept at turning a blind eye to your inappropriate behavior, it's your job to convince them that you really want their candid input. If you are successful in this, the results can be very useful. As one person put it, "Ever since I asked my wife to alert me to this kind of behavior I'm trying to change, it's amazing how much more perceptive she's become."

THE SECOND R: RESPONSIBILITY

Once you have Recognized an inappropriate behavior that is likely connected with Unfinished Business, the next step is to take *Responsibility* for that behavior—to *own* it. Do this by making the statement, "I recognize that I have a history of [name the inappropriate behavior], and I want to change that. I vow to uncover and resolve the Unfinished Business that causes this behavior."

THE THIRD R: RESEARCH

The next step is to do the necessary *Research* to uncover and defuse the Unfinished Business. Here are three ways of doing this on your own.

1. Go back to those people you enlisted for help in Recognition. Say to each, "I've become aware that at times I have a tendency to [describe the inappropriate behavior]. I'd appreciate hearing your perceptions about the cir-

cumstances that contribute to that happening." You may hear some very useful insights. Examples of such feedback include:

— "It seems to me that most of the time that happens when you're feeling like you're being criticized."

— "When you're focused on a task, you don't deal well with any kind of interruptions. I'm not offended by your brusque manner on the phone when I call, but others very well may be."

— "I've never understood how you can be so patient when you're teaching your pupils, yet when you're explaining something to an adult you become exasperated if the other person doesn't get it immediately."

— "It seems to me that the common denominator for when you become really angry is a situation where you feel that something isn't being done 'the right way' or someone isn't behaving 'the way she should.' Whenever I hear that judgmental tone in your voice, I know there's trouble ahead."

With this input, you can consider what kind of Unfinished Business is being triggered by considering what event in your early life the "triggering" circumstances might be recalling.

2. A related Research technique is to ask yourself some questions:

— "Is what I'm doing similar to or reminiscent of something that was done to me?"

— "Does this pattern reflect what was done in my family?"

— "What kind of feelings do I associate with this behavior?"

— "Whom am I addressing in this situation?"

Some examples of the realizations that may come in response to such questions:

— "When there is a confrontation, I find myself going into my 'cave.' At an early age I learned that my room was a safe place of retreat whenever the chaos level in our house got too high."

— "When anyone raises his voice, I expect criticism. That goes right back to my parents. I learned to close my ears, space out, and hear nothing. And I'm still doing it, in one form or another."

— "In my family of eight siblings, if you didn't fight for your needs, you would end up with nothing. I feel I have to do this now in order to survive and be respected by my coworkers."

— "When I encounter an authority figure I perceive as opinionated, rigid, and overbearing, I react to that person as if he were my father."

— "I always feel cautious and mistrustful when I am with people I don't know. My parents fled from turbulent times in the old country, and they instilled in us that we should never trust strangers."

Using these techniques, you can look back into your early upbringing for experiences and Unfinished Business connected with the inappropriate behavior. The visualization you'll be doing shortly may help in that process.

3. Another way of finding out more about what's behind the inappropriate behavior is to use visualization techniques, because many of the injunctions behind Unfinished Business come from the *nonverbal* behavior of one's parents and other authority figures.

The "What Were Your Early Injunctions?" visualization allows you to focus on those influential figures in your life. Use this visualization to further your Research.

You may wish to go back and repeat the visualization with your father or another important authority figure as the focus. In each case, write down the injunctions necessary for you to feel accepted and safe with your parent. The following is a list of the types of injunctions derived from the visualization that might be the basis for Unfinished Business.

— "Never trust your feelings or instincts."
— "Don't express your feelings or thoughts."
— "Don't think you're smarter than I am."
— "Be perfect in terms of what is expected of you."
— "You are responsible for the happiness and well-being of your parents."
— "Your parents know better than you what is good for you."
— "Do as I say and not as I do."
— "Your self-worth lies in loyalty to the family."
— "Show respect for authority."
— "Be worried about what others think."
— "Don't see too much."
— "You have no rights unless they are given to you."
— "Take before you get taken."
— "You have to work twice as hard as others to be accepted."

As you read through this list of childhood injunctions, quite likely one or more gave you a tingle from a very deep place in your being. And it is easy to see how injunctions like these become generalized into *social* injunctions that powerfully influence your adult life. The power of such injunctions, whether internal or socialized, stems from the fact that they bypass your rational screening: thus you think and act as if these injunctions were intrinsically true.

These injunctions affect all parts of your life and distort your sense of self—you tend to associate with people and situations that reinforce these injunctions, which become even more deeply embedded in your consciousness. And, most significant, these early-life injunctions can continue into adult life to dominate your sense of self as Unfinished Business.

When you are able to "get into the moment" of these injunctions, you can quickly see how they became Unfinished Business that has influenced your life ever since. You may be surprised at the degree to which they are either irrational

---

SUMMARY VISUALIZATION: WHAT WERE YOUR EARLY INJUNCTIONS?

After "setting the stage" (quiet environment, phone off the hook, comfortable chair, etc.), relax and concentrate on your breathing—each inhalation bringing in relaxation, each exhalation breathing out stress.

As you gain awareness of your internal space, allow your mind to go back to the house of your childhood. See yourself as a child of prepuberty age in the presence of one of your parents—for example, your mother. Experience the scene: remember the feelings of the environment, the smells, sounds, and so on. See your mother doing her normal routine. Begin to feel the "emotional atmosphere" that filled your home, concentrating on the dynamics of your relationship with your mother.

You instinctively sense, as you did as a child, that *in order for you to remain accepted by your mother* there are certain things (behaviors and attitudes) that are expected of you, some that are tolerated, and others that are unacceptable. Take time to recall those injunctions by your mother, and then write down your impressions of what was important in order for you to be safe and accepted by your mother.

or self-destructive. They are like chains that have bound you tightly all of your life, their power demonstrated by the anxiety they arouse in your present day-to-day life when you are on the verge of disobeying them. It is this anxiety that gives such power to Unfinished Business, limiting the extent to which you are "allowed" to become successful or to realize your full potential.

Now that you more fully understand the source of the Unfinished Business underlying your inappropriate behavior, you are well on the way to resolving the problem by using the Fourth R: *Retrofitting*.

The Fourth R: Retrofitting

Once you have Recognized the inappropriate behavior, taken Responsibility, and done the Research to find the underlying reason, you are now in a position to take action—to *Retrofit* your behavior to a form that is appropriate—thus "finishing" the related Unfinished Business.

The secret to successful Retrofitting is to learn to discern when the inappropriate behavior (related to Unfinished Business) is *about to be triggered*, so that you can take control by reinterpreting the Unfinished Business. Consider this analogy: a person with a skin condition that at times produces a strong itching feeling instinctively responds by scratching. But when the dermatologist points out that scratching is inappropriate because it aggravates the condition and intensifies and prolongs the itching, the person is able to refrain from scratching. The automatic behavior was brought to a level of awareness and recognized as being contrary to the person's best interests.

Another Retrofitting technique is to set up a feedback loop that attends to the underlying needs that create the situation, so that the inappropriate behavior is "short-stopped." To avoid the automatic knee-jerk reaction, when you become aware that some Unfinished Business is about to be triggered, you can create a *different focus* on the situation by asking the question, "What would serve the best interests of this situation?" It is a simple cognitive question that redirects your attention and energies into examining the situation from a different perspective, thus increasing the likelihood that you may respond to and handle the situation differently than in your usual (inappropriate) manner.

A third Retrofitting technique is to modify the *environment* in which the Unfinished Business behavior plays out. When you examine your inappropriate behavior, quite often you will see that some particular set of circumstances triggers or reinforces it. With this awareness, you can modify or avoid those circumstances and achieve a successful Retrofit. Following are some examples of how this might be done.

In Your Life Context

- Recognize how individuals who represent (remind you of) your family of origin tend to reinforce your self-defeating patterns, and take steps to disengage yourself from those kinds of relationships.
- Learn a new response pattern that addresses the emotional trigger. Response patterns that involve a humorous attitude are often very effective at depersonalizing a situation.
- Depersonalize a pattern by focusing on understanding the other person's context for doing what she is doing (which triggers your response). Recognize that you are *not* the "target" of the other person's displaced negativity.

In the Work Context

- Don't work for a person who represents or triggers your worst fears.
- Don't choose a company environment that replicates your family of origin.
- Do choose a work environment and supervisory situation that supports and reinforces your values, which in turn support your personal best.
- Do choose a work situation that brings out your best, offers professional growth opportunities, and enhances your well-being. Money should have a lower priority than your values.

Many of the admonitions of the past are constricting. Even the positive ones limit your capacity to respond spontaneously to each life situation you encounter, and the negative ones actually sabotage your attempts to be successful. To deal with them, apply the Four Rs and increase self-awareness. Increasingly, your responses to the life situations you encounter will be spontaneous and appropriate, based on an aware openness rather than old scripts of admonitions from the past.

Examples of Successful Use of the Four Rs

Here are some examples of how people have used the Four Rs to deal with Unfinished Business and change old, inappropriate behavior patterns.

KEN

Ken was finally forced to recognize his tendency to interrupt people, which was off-putting to those close to him and brought negative feedback at work. Over a weekend, Ken arranged for some uninterrupted time, took the phone off the hook, and sat quietly. He visualized himself interrupting others, and then asked himself, "Does this remind me of the patterns in my family?" Quite vividly, he recalled his father and mother talking—his father interrupting his mother and his mother complaining about it. "Why did Dad do this?" he asked, and he had a sense that his father used the technique of interrupting as a means of assertiveness, of controlling a situation.

Ken reflected on the parallels with his own life, coming to the conclusion that he doesn't have that much of a need to control now, but that the pattern may have begun when he did have a need to be more assertive. With the awareness gained from this visualization, Ken vowed to change this behavior pattern. He developed several Retrofitting techniques, including learning to identify the early warning "tickle" when he was about to interrupt. To his gratification, communications went much more smoothly—as did his relations with his fellow workers.

JOHN

Input from several people, including his boss, forced John to recognize that he had a tendency to lie about minor and major aspects of his life—from claiming he had seen first-night movies to exaggerations about accomplishments in past jobs. He was oblivious to the fact that coworkers and friends were aware of his looseness with the truth. Finally, after his wife confronted him and threatened divorce, John fully understood the impact of this behavioral pattern. He did some inner work, including discussing it with several close friends and doing several visualizations, which gave him the realization that his lying stemmed from his feelings of not being OK just as he was—and thus having to embellish things. He saw clearly for the first time that this behavior only created greater inadequacies and jeopardized his relationships as well.

Realizing that his life was at a critical juncture, John accepted responsibility for changing his behavior and started working on new ways of communicating with others and enhancing his sense of self-worth. Whenever tempted to stretch the truth, he asked himself, "What would serve the best interests of this situation?" His feelings about himself began to improve, as did his relations with others. Inevitably there were setbacks with knee-jerk lies, but he forced himself to go back to apologize and state the truth. His self-esteem and reputation continued to improve.

JANET

Janet relished her reputation as critic and clown among the people she knew. She was unaware that her behavior was a serious impediment to close relationships. Her verbalizations seemed to come from a loose cannon spewing out sarcastic remarks about anyone she chose as a target. When her boss told her in her annual review that she had been considered but rejected for a promotion, the realization hit her of how offensive and inappropriate her behavior had become. Whereas in the past she had shifted the blame to others, this time she accepted Responsibility.

Janet began a process of self-reflection that led to unpleasant memories of humiliation when her mother frequently teased her in front of her friends. She realized that she was reenacting the scenario as her parents, who used humiliation, sarcasm, and criticism to control behavior in the family. With this Recognition, Janet was able to create a self-discipline, using several of the Four Rs techniques, to reduce her need for control and learn new forms of more appropriate behavior.

The Shadow

In speaking about Unfinished Business, we are extending the idea of the *Shadow*, a term originally defined by Carl Jung. The Shadow is something that personifies everything that a person refuses to acknowledge about himself. In thinking about their Shadow, most people tend to focus on undesirable character traits.

Our perspective of the Shadow is much broader. It encompasses not only unresolved issues, but also incomplete perceptions and judgments that cause a person to avoid examining certain issues that need to be addressed. We see the Shadow as also including the spiritual nature of our essence.

The message of the Shadow is that, much as we may try, we cannot avoid our past Unfinished Business, *because the dynamics of the things we avoid become projected into our lives*—the same themes and issues come back over and over again until we bring them to conscious resolution.

The conscious resolution of Unfinished Business is the task of Pragmatic Spirituality. We'll discuss the Shadow in greater detail in Chapter 9.

On to the Next Part of the Pragmatic Spirituality Process

We hope that after reading Chapters 3 and 4 you have become comfortable with the concept of Unfinished Business, aware of its disruptive and insidious power, and open to the idea of seeking out and working through the Unfinished Business that is holding *you* back. With that preparation firmly in place, you are ready for the next step in the Pragmatic Spirituality process.

Chapter 4 Highlights

Smart people do dumb things because out-of-date behavior patterns are triggered, causing them to respond inappropriately.

You want your rational mind to be in control, yet a large part of your everyday living comes from old scripts—some appropriate, but many connected with Unfinished Business.

Unfinished Business consists of old, inappropriate scripts that subtly but powerfully limit your potential and cause you to respond inappropriately to situations. Ironically, the people most resistant to acknowledging the existence of Unfinished Business are those who most want to be in control.

The roots of Unfinished Business go back to your early life. They are highly charged holograms from the past that influence the present.

Resolving Unfinished Business can unleash energies bound up by old patterns to achieve higher levels of potential and function.

The Pragmatic Spirituality process is synergistic: as you deal with Unfinished Business, the way is open for growth, which enables further progress in working on Unfinished Business.

The Four Rs for dealing with unfinished business are Recognition, Responsibility, Research, *and* Retrofitting.

The Shadow *personifies everything that a person refuses to acknowledge about herself. We cannot avoid Unfinished Business because the dynamics of things we avoid become projected into our lives.*

The task of Pragmatic Spirituality is to bring conscious resolution *to Unfinished Business.*

5

YOUR SELF-RESOLVES: SELF-ACCOUNTABILITY, SELF-MAINTENANCE, AND SELF-DISCIPLINE

People often say that this person or that person has not yet found himself. But the self is not something that one finds. It is something that one creates.

—Thomas Szasz

The previous chapter emphasized how Unfinished Business can keep people from living a fulfilled and productive life. The old, inappropriate behaviors of Unfinished Business scripts are particularly powerful because they work from a subconscious level, leaving their owner unaware of their effects.

In the coming chapters you will learn how to use the techniques of Pragmatic Spirituality to achieve your Inner Edge, opening the way toward achieving your full potential and effectiveness in your day-to-day life. But first, in this chapter, we need to go over some preliminary concepts.

The Three Self-Resolves

Inevitably, as you explore your Unfinished Business, you will encounter the memories of people in your past who intentionally or unintentionally contributed to the limiting of your options and the curtailment of your abilities. At that point you have two options:

1. Focus on blaming the other person for your unfortunate state.
2. Forgive the person and move ahead by modifying the old behavior patterns.

Some of today's "self-discovery" practices seem to favor blaming others. Pragmatic Spirituality is grounded in Self-accountability, asserting that the grip of Unfinished Business's old memories and old patterns can be loosened only by accepting *full accountability for yourself*, thus opening up the prospect (both attractive and terrifying) of determining your destiny.

> **SELF-ACCOUNTABILITY** has to do with deciding to sort out Unfinished Business rather than dodging the issue by blaming it on people in your past.

Once you accept the first self-resolve of *Self-accountability*, the second two—*Self-maintenance* and *Self-discipline*, which are intrinsically entwined with each other—will help you stick to the Pragmatic Spirituality process no matter what may occur in your personal life or at work. Self-maintenance involves taking care of yourself as responsibly as you take care of your automobile and other possessions you depend on. Most people understand how important it is to maintain their car (oil changes, checkups, and so on) and take care of their physical welfare (eating well, exercising, brushing teeth, going to the doctor, and so on). However, a surprising number of people never learned to take care of their *mental* and *emotional* self, which is absolutely essential for any kind of growth or renewal.

> **SELF-MAINTENANCE** has to do with the appropriate level of taking care of yourself. **SELF-DISCIPLINE** has to do with accepting responsibility for making good on your commitments to others and to yourself.

Once the importance of Self-maintenance has been embraced, a well-honed Self-discipline is needed to make it happen. Self-discipline means making good on the commitments you have made to others, as well as the Self-maintenance commitments you have made to yourself. Don't allow the latter to get pushed aside.

Both Self-maintenance and Self-discipline are based on an intrinsically *healthy* tendency to nurture and honor oneself. Any difficulty in accepting the legitimacy of these tools, or in mastering them, *signifies that there are related Unfinished Business issues that need to be addressed.* As we've mentioned before, the Pragmatic Spirituality process is self-reinforcing: increased awareness of self-defeating Unfinished Business issues leads to a strengthened ability to transcend and neutralize them.

The three Self-resolves—Self-accountability, Self-maintenance, and Self-discipline—may be familiar to you, or not. The reality is that a large percentage of people come into adulthood with little or no awareness of these concepts. It is as if a large part of the population continually misses the class "How to Deal with Life."

Why Were These Important Tools Omitted from the Usual Life Lessons?

The reason so many people failed to learn the three Self-resolves from their parents is that most parents were prevented from learning these concepts as they grew up by a variety of cultural and social influences, as well as family dynamics.

- **Self-accountability:** This concept may have been thought to be self-evident in earlier times. The idea of dodging responsibility by blaming someone involved in one's upbringing is a relatively new mentality.

- **Self-maintenance:** Many factors in our cultural conditioning have mitigated against "looking out for yourself." Among these are the ideas of self-sacrifice, consideration for others, "not tooting your own horn," and the economic and social realities that prevent taking a proactive part in one's work or life.

- **Self-discipline:** Our society places a high value on discipline of *external* factors (the law, one's work, and so on); however, when it comes to *Self-discipline* (setting commitments for oneself and sticking to them) these can run afoul of the same cultural prejudices that inhibit Self-maintenance.

Because of such social and cultural attitudes, many people are in a catch-up mode regarding these "look out for yourself" concepts. If your growing-up process did not give you a strong proficiency in Self-maintenance and Self-discipline, read on!

Self-Maintenance

Everyone who owns a car knows that it is important to *maintain* the car: change the oil, check the coolant and the tire pressure, and so on. Do that, and the car is ready at any time. Neglect the maintenance, and the car may not perform when you need it.

It is true that a significant number of drivers cut corners in maintaining their vehicles. Given the fairly straightforward cause-and-effect of car maintenance, it is puzzling why these people jeopardize their financial investment and, more important, the reliability of their vehicle. This probably explains why even more people do such a poor job at the much more important task of Self-maintenance.

Self-maintenance means *responsibly* taking care of yourself on all levels: physically, emotionally, and spiritually. (It is worthwhile to add here that in order to initiate that responsibility, you need to be *aware* of yourself on all these levels.)

WAYS TO TAKE CARE OF YOURSELF
- Make time in your busy schedule to exercise your body: for example, get up earlier for a session at the gym, or take the stairs rather than the elevator.
- Give yourself a self-honoring "gift" each day, even if it is only a brief soak in the tub, a small bouquet of flowers along with the takeout from the salad bar, or reading a chapter of your bedside book before retiring. Consciously see yourself presenting this special treat to *yourself.*
- Proactively make time to be with friends who support you in affirming your sense of values and your sense of essential self.
- Get involved in yoga or some physical activity that allows you to more fully be "in your body."
- Set boundaries so that you can be fully present in each moment, with each person, and for each situation. (You'll read more about boundaries in Chapter 7.)
- Create a place of sanctuary where you can reflect on the process of the day.

Growing up, most people learn to take care of themselves physically, but far fewer people learn to take care of themselves emotionally and spiritually. Effective Self-maintenance—on all levels—is an essential part of the Pragmatic Spirituality process. If your Self-maintenance training was deficient (or if you're out of practice), get those muscles toned up by learning this affirmation and saying it every day:

It is my responsibility—a very important responsibility—
to do effective Self-maintenance by taking care of my
physical, emotional, and spiritual well-being
regularly and thoroughly.

It may take a while to become proficient in Self-maintenance, but it's well worth the investment of your time and energy.

Self-Discipline

One kind of Self-discipline is related to *external* commitments—you make a commitment to do something, and Self-discipline ensures that you do it. If you fail to perform, there will likely be external consequences of a negative nature involving other people or events.

The other kind of Self-discipline is related to commitments you make to *yourself*. This internal Self-discipline is the complement to Self-maintenance. You decide on a course of action to benefit you in some way, a course of action that probably involves changing certain habit patterns. Whether or not that commitment is honored, the course of action carried out depends on the effectiveness of your Self-discipline.

It is not unusual for people who are perceived as highly disciplined to be very good at fulfilling their external commitments and extremely poor at honoring their commitments to themselves. For example:

- The successful executive who repeatedly has tried to give up smoking without success
- The conscientious and reliable employee who knows that she is in a dead-end job, but never has the energy to look for more fulfilling positions
- The "supermom" whose resolve to get back to the pleasure of gardening always gets pushed aside by the demands of looking after her family

Our society has a halo for those who put others' interests ahead of their own, but lack of Self-discipline precludes the ability to better oneself.

DONNA

Donna was the head of an adoption agency. She prided herself in the service she provided childless couples. Her dedication to her agency and its clients was obvious, but her friends were concerned about her exhausting and compulsive work habits. She could not see that her work was driven by the Unfinished Business of abandonment by her own parents and that she was acting out a compensatory pattern of taking care of abandoned children.

BRYAN

Bryan was a vice president whose primary duties were to take care of the president of the corporation, a brilliant man who lacked interpersonal skills. Bryan was very good at getting the necessary people to support the president's projects. In fact, Bryan enjoyed the role of "professional rescuer," not only for his boss, but for his entire family. Although he got many accolades, Bryan never attained an influential role in the corporation, because the rescuing got in the way. He never realized that it stemmed from Unfinished Business dating back to his childhood, where he had learned that being a rescuer brought him approval and love.

If you are better at honoring your commitments to others than your commitments to yourself, it is essential that this behavior pattern change. Envision the necessity for this change from a spiritual perspective: the necessity of giving respect, honor, value, and self-esteem to yourself in ways that enhance your capacity to be creative and fully functioning. Make this commitment to yourself *now*! Sit down and figure out some techniques for improving the reliability of your Self-discipline for commitments you make to yourself. Some possibilities include

- Tell someone close to you about your commitment, and—with that person's agreement—give him specific tasks to help you move toward it (periodic reminders, for example).
- Mark your calendar each day with a step toward accomplishing the commitment.

- Write a letter of support and accountability to yourself—and mail it to yourself.
- Listen to music that lifts your spirit.
- Make use of your physical abilities to enliven your sense of self such as yoga, tai chi, aerobics, dance, swimming, bicycling, walking, and so on.
- Create a physical space that functions as a place of sanctuary, wherein you may reaffirm your commitments to yourself.
- Set boundaries (see Chapter 7) in order to maintain a sense of integrity—emotionally, mentally, physically, and spiritually.
- Learn to be quiet so that you can listen with your heart, mind, and spirit, rather than listening to the chatter of your conditioned mind.

TELLTALE SIGNS OF LACK OF SELF-MAINTENANCE AND SELF-DISCIPLINE

Do any of the following describe you in your personal or work life?

- A feeling of burnout, running on empty, overextension of all internal resources
- Boredom; inability to relate to your responsibilities, people, or the environment
- Psychosomatic symptoms such as recurring headaches, colitis, ulcers, lower-back problems, or lethargy
- Low productivity, inability to concentrate, high incidence of mistakes
- Compensatory behaviors such as long breaks, computer escapism, or excessive use of the workplace to satisfy social needs
- Mechanical or robotic behavior to give the appearance of work, but with a lack of awareness and prioritization
- Playing blamer or victim when things are not getting done
- Absenteeism and tardiness
- Not connected to the overall picture of what needs to be accomplished; poor work boundaries
- Frequent rationalization as to why things are not getting done; poor accountability

If any of these fit, it's a strong message that you need to address how well you are looking after yourself.

Where Are You on the Continuum of Self-Interest?

So far, this chapter has been focused on those people who don't spend enough time and energy looking after their own self-interests. However, there are also people at the other end of the spectrum, people who are overly preoccupied with their own interests. The healthy position is the midpoint of the spectrum.

Insufficient Self-interest ←———————————→ Excessive Self-interest

Excessive self-interest is not a normal or healthy condition. Self-absorbed people cannot constructively interact with others or perform effectively in any group effort. Their excessive self-interest cuts them off from the world. Most likely, this weakness is due to some heavy-duty Unfinished Business in the person's history.

Unfortunately, the growing degree of impersonal communication technologies (such as the fax and E-mail) have legitimized, and even glorified, a detached type of interpersonal interaction. It may be that the highly self-absorbed person may not immediately recognize the benefits of the Pragmatic Spirituality process, including greater authenticity to self and appropriateness to others—in short, the *Inner Edge*. However, we believe that ultimate fulfillment must involve constructive human interaction, so the highly self-absorbed person will benefit greatly from following the Pragmatic Spirituality process.

Where do you stand on the self-interest continuum?

Now you have a grounding in the three self-resolves—Self-accountability, Self-maintenance, and Self-discipline—as well as Unfinished Business. Let's get on to the three dimensions of Pragmatic Spirituality—Identity, Integration, and Inspiration!

Chapter 5 Highlights

The three Self-resolves are essential in using Pragmatic Spirituality techniques to achieve your Inner Edge.

Self-accountability *is consciously deciding to address and resolve your Unfinished Business rather than dodging the issue by blaming it on people in your past.*

Self-maintenance *is taking care of yourself in an appropriate manner.*

Self-discipline *is accepting responsibility for making good on your commitments to others and to yourself.*

The three Self-resolves are healthy tools that some people learn as they grow up; however, many others do not acquire them because their parents never learned them and/or because of Unfinished Business.

Self-maintenance is discouraged by cultural conditioning and ideas about self-sacrifice, consideration for others, "not tooting your own horn," and so on.

Our society places a high value on discipline related to external *factors (the law, one's work, and such), but Self-discipline can run afoul of the same cultural prejudices that inhibit Self-maintenance.*

Insufficient self-interest and excessive self-interest should be avoided. The healthy position on the continuum of self-interest is the midpoint.

6

IDENTITY: THE FIRST DIMENSION OF PRAGMATIC SPIRITUALITY

He who knows others is learned; He who knows himself is wise.

—Lao-tzu, *Tao te Ching*, 6th century B.C.

THE ESSENCE OF THIS CHAPTER is to explore the question, "Where is the locus (center) of your identity?" A healthy identity has an *internal* locus, but because few people have learned this "identity wisdom" while growing up, it is often necessary to acquire it later in life. This is why *Identity* is the first of the Pragmatic Spirituality Dimensions.

> **RECALL THAT PRAGMATIC SPIRITUALITY** has three Dimensions, each representing an aspect of being human. Maximum fulfillment and effectiveness come when each of these Dimensions is whole and balanced with the other two. That is the goal of the Pragmatic Spirituality process—to achieve your Inner Edge.

If your locus of identity depends on *external* factors—expectations of others, how well your most recent performance has gone, value of material possessions, job title, club membership, and so on—you are in a very precarious and vulnerable situation. When your sense of self depends on factors *beyond your control*, inevitably there will be a reversal in one or more of those factors. For example:

- Your physical prowess or beauty starts to decline.
- Your children change from "perfect darlings" to complete strangers.
- You blow a big presentation or important deal.
- You are terminated from your job because of a merger or for some other "no-fault" reason.
- You must financially downsize because of a reversal of your fortunes.
- You fail to be reelected to a very prestigious position or office.

Your identity—your *sense of self* operating well below the level of your conscious awareness—is the most significant factor in how you function and succeed in life. It may be referred to as *self-worth* or *self-esteem*, but whatever the label, it answers for each person the vital question, "Who am I?" It has a powerful but subtle impact on what you do day-to-day and minute-to-minute. It can both inspire you to exceptional performance and undermine you and cause failure. Identity determines your happiness and your sense of fulfillment and satisfaction. Given the profound influence of identity, it is disconcerting to realize that it is programmed with all sorts of erroneous and misleading data!

Sources of Identity

Your identity is derived from many sources.

FAMILY-ASSIGNED IDENTITY
One of the most powerful determinants of identity is the one projected onto you by parents and those with whom you identify strongly. This type of identity can entirely dictate the social groups you join, the schools you attend, whom you marry, and your station in life.

> Scott was born with a privileged name and pedigree. His great-grandfather had been a respected philanthropist, a tradition continued by successive generations. From his first recollections of childhood, Scott was aware of the high expectations for him— levels of achievement, station in life, and social circles. Acting contrary to those expectations would be a betrayal to the traditions set by the family.

SOCIALLY ASSIGNED IDENTITY
When a certain set of values are strongly held by a community of individuals, there are intense pressures on each member of that community to accommodate

HOW YOUR SENSE OF IDENTITY EVOLVES

As with every child, you were one with your mother during pregnancy. After birth, your identity remained focused on your parents or caregivers for the first six years, prior to the socialization process of schooling. One of the key steps of development was when an instinctual part of you began to realize that you were, in fact, *distinct*—that is, you had an *identity* apart from your adult caregivers. This exciting awareness was quickly coupled with more complex feelings, because you were still dependent on those adults for your total existence. Thus, as the realization of your "apartness" grew stronger, so did the terror that it might cause them to abandon you.

As discussed in Chapter 4, in the early years of development each child begins to internalize the expectations and attitudes of important caregivers in his life. The child develops an accommodating persona to handle the demands and attitudes of the outside world comprised of parents, siblings, close relatives, and friends.

Shortly after birth, every child becomes an expert at discerning the mood of mother, father, and other caregivers, and at developing an array of behaviors to influence—by deflecting, mollifying, or distracting—the adults who control the child's life. This is not a problem at first, because the child's expectations and desires exactly mirror those of the caregivers. Gradually, however, a split develops (*dissonance* occurs). The child wants one thing—the adult wants another. As with the realization of one's apartness from one's parents, this divergence of wants and expectations is an experience both exciting and terrifying to the child.

Obviously, the child is not aware of these experiences on a rational basis; however, the experiences are recorded as feelings and emotions that permeate and imprint her entire being. As the child becomes an adult, these embedded experiences continue to influence present-day behavior patterns.

and reinforce those values in order to retain acceptance by the group. Minority groups, whether by gender, race, or political or religious affiliation, often encounter situations where peer-set values govern acceptance into a group. When a person joins a company, she quickly learns what values and behaviors are necessary to get ahead in the organization.

Jonathan had been raised in the Midwest with an Asian background. When he joined a company on the East coast, he was welcomed as a fresh addition to the company. His performance was excellent and his talents were praised. However, as time passed, he gradually realized that he would never make it into the upper-management team. He had plenty of talent, but he did not fit the socially assigned identity that the company had created for its executives: Anglo-Saxon origins, enthusiasm for golf, Ivy League schooling, and involvement in local social circles.

Self-Assigned Identity

Beginning the process of disassociating with one's "hand-me-down" identity and seeking a locus of identity that is truly one's own is a positive step. This sense of identity emerges from one's own growing self-awareness, *influenced but not unduly encumbered* by other sources of identity.

Carrie was a maverick, encouraged by her parents, who emphasized individual thinking and independence. She traveled a lot, learned about different worldviews, and became reasonably proficient in several languages. In time, she settled down, and—relying strongly on her own instincts—built her own company. It succeeded, achieving her intuitive goal of being self-reliant and self-sufficient in the world.

In each of the examples we've cited, the person was profoundly influenced by his or her identity—for better or for worse. The distinctions between the three sources of identity are not clearly delineated. The important thing is to choose at some point to move toward a self-assigned identity.

Examples of Undeveloped Identity

Following are a few generic examples of adults whose identities are still tied to an earlier place and time in their life.

- Some men remain emotionally immature, holding on to their childhood fears and adolescent dreams. Social and psychological commentators have observed that in modern cultures males have a prolonged stage of adolescence, deferring—and in some cases never achieving—the mature posture of autonomy, responsibility, accountability, and stewardship in their relationships and family. In social mythology, this is known as the *Peter Pan syndrome*: the boy/man who never wants to grow up.

- There are women who look for "Prince Charming," waiting for their knight in shining armor to save them and provide for all their physical and emotional needs. Thus, they never achieve a sense of autonomy or independence, and are unable to fend for themselves out in the world.

- The *dependent personality* has an excessive and pervasive need to be taken care of that leads to submissive and clinging behavior. This can lead to fear of separation, difficulty in making everyday decisions, needing others to assume responsibility for most areas of one's life, and—in extreme cases—an excessive helplessness and unrealistic perception of not being able to care for oneself in any environment.

- A *co-dependent* personality differs from the dependent personality in that both parties in a co-dependent relationship are blindly responding to and enabling each other's behavior. A classic example is the relationship between a spouse and an alcoholic partner. Unwittingly, the spouse and alcoholic partner promote, maintain, and justify each other's behavior through fear, insecurity, low self-esteem, and addiction. This co-dependency can be so great that if the alcoholic partner ceases drinking, the relationship may be jeopardized unless the spouse can adapt.

- The *derived identity* describes someone so insecure about their own identity that he seeks to find it in external, socially assigned status symbols: cars, houses, clothes, or memberships in churches, charitable causes, or exclusive country clubs.

People with underdeveloped identities are not always easy to spot. In fact, they are often quite proficient at compensating by becoming very competent in particular activities and roles. It is the lack of appropriateness of their interactions with others and their low level of *comfort* with themselves that reveal the inner problems. The other reason such underdeveloped identities evade our attention is that these characteristics have become so stereotyped and ingrained in our society as to become commonplace and, at times, supported and/or praised.

Inevitably, the underdeveloped identity self-destructs. You can probably recall someone you admired because he seemed to have it all together. Then, suddenly, his world fell apart, leaving friends and acquaintances dumbfounded. For example, an "ideal couple" endures a bitter divorce; a respected minister is discovered in a sordid affair; a brilliant top executive is fired for lying about his credentials; a successful politician is indicted.

These and other similar life tragedies stem from a life lived without one's own authentic identity. The essential aspect of the Identity Dimension of Pragmatic Spirituality is that your sense of self—your identity—must be *yours*, not a "hand-me-down."

Two Reference Points for Identity: Doing/Having Versus Being

A good way to maintain a healthy sense of self is to recognize that there are two reference points for your sense of identity:

- Doing/Having (externally based)
- Being (internally based)

The *Doing/Having* identity derives its sense of self from accomplishments, possessions, and affiliations. Western cultures tend to fall into this category. The U.S. advertising industry has developed a highly effective expertise at manipulating the consumer's sense of self—that a particular product is essential for "you being you." The world of business, with its emphasis on titles and bottom-line results, is permeated with the implicit message "You are what you do and have."

BECAUSE OF SOCIO-CULTURAL PATTERNING, it is inevitable that virtually everyone arrives at adulthood deriving most or all of his identity from Doing/Having. One's opinion of a person is strongly influenced by the person's accomplishments, position, or wealth. When meeting for the first time, an early question from both individuals is, "What do you do?"

Additionally, our lives are subjected to inescapable commentary of the "best," "thinnest," "best dressed," "most successful." At a very early age, our children get the message that they are nothing if they don't have "the latest" clothing or toy. "Acquiring" takes on greater attraction and power by its association with beauty, power, and other attributes of success.

In every facet of life, the pressure to base your identity on *doing* and *having* is pervasive.

The *Being* identity derives its sense of self from "just who I am"—intrinsically, transcending what you do and what you have. It relates simply and clearly to your essential existence. Identity based on Being states in simple terms, "I am comfortable with myself and I accept myself just as I am."

The problem is not with Doing/Having, but with a *lack of balance* with the other essential element of identity: Being. Our culture too often falls into a dichotomous thinking: black or white, right or wrong. Thus, a person is either a "spiritual" type or a "practical" type. Far more healthy is the Eastern way of thought, which accepts—and even values—the ambiguous, the paradoxical, the "gray areas." The healthiest sense of identity comes from a balance of Doing/Having and Being.

Most will find that an increased awareness of Being as a source of identity tempers and complements the Doing/Having source, transforming the Doing/Having into a *means* rather than an *end*. Having possessions, being ambitious, is not the problem. The problem is when these become the sole source of identity.

Take Charge by Reestablishing the Locus of Your Identity

Pragmatic Spirituality moves the locus of your identity to within yourself. That may seem an obvious concept. However obvious, it is definitely not simple to do, because it involves changing many years of habits. But, as many people have proven, it *can* be done.

The first step in moving the locus of your identity within yourself is to acknowledge the existence of your Unfinished Business obstacles and begin to identify them. As they are brought to light, your various items of Unfinished Business begin to lose their power.

Next, bring your Identity Dimension into proper balance and reestablish your locus of identity with the following techniques:

- Practicing self-acceptance
- Developing your *Compassionate Observer*
- Doing the *Identity Visualization*

Self-Acceptance

The essence of self-acceptance is fully embracing and loving yourself, just as you are—the good and the bad. It is a means of developing the Being aspect of your sense of identity, and reducing the preoccupation of your sense of self with Doing/Having.

Most people are totally unfamiliar with the concept of self-acceptance, having never encountered such "unconditional love" in their growing up. Moreover, it strikes against the underlying tenets of our society, seeming to imply "something for nothing" or a complacent willingness to accept a lower standard of performance. As one person put it:

> When I first encountered the idea of self-acceptance, I could feel that a part of me was extremely attracted to it—that was a very deep, inner part of me. However, there was another part of me—the parent voice that I knew so well—that said, "If you accept yourself, it will condone laziness and slack behavior, and compromise the high standards you need to set for yourself." The idea of self-acceptance was seductive, but appeared contrary to the work ethic.

There is no doubt that "high self-expectation" can be a very effective motivator, and in fact it is an essential part of the American work ethic. However, unreasonably high self-expectations can have negative implications on a healthy identity and self-worth if they result in an inner game you can never win. All too often the good intentions of parents to motivate their children linger on, years afterward, in the child's Unfinished Business related to "I'm not good enough" issues, which in fact work against achieving and maintaining high performance.

Because a healthier sense of identity leads to greater productivity, it is your responsibility to do everything possible to develop the Being aspect of your identity by working on your self-acceptance. One way to do this is to practice the "I Accept Myself Completely" affirmation. Say to yourself:

Whatever my track record,
whatever my imperfections,
I accept myself completely—
without reservations.

Then do the following:

- Notice how saying the affirmation feels. The *unconditional* nature of the statement can help move you to a place of self-acceptance. It is something that you would say to someone you love very much.
- Compare this statement with your customary internal dialogue, which most likely is full of self-criticism, focusing on how you have failed to live up to an expectation.
- Promise yourself that you will practice this affirmation regularly, and do it and believe it!

The first time you say the affirmation, your initial reaction may be, "That's crazy! How can I accept myself *without reservations*?" That reaction is completely normal. That's your "truth of the moment," so accept it. But don't let it deter you. The affirmation statement goes strongly against the grain of many of your imprinted messages and patterns, so some resistance is to be expected. In time you'll be able to say it readily—and believe it completely.

Your Unfinished Business's Resistance to Change

At some point after you begin the Pragmatic Spirituality process—quite possibly after you start the "I Accept Myself Completely" affirmation—your Unfinished Business will realize that you are serious about changing old patterns. From then on, you will encounter resistance in some clever and devious defense tactics. You will begin to hear all sorts of inner arguments against the process. For example:

- "This will make you soft and less effective (lose your competitive edge)."
- "You are betraying your responsibility to maintain standards."
- "This is a lot of silly gobbledygook."
- "There are better ways of using your time."
- "You've tried and it's not working, so give it up."
- "All that 'self-help' work and you still lose your temper like that. You'll never make it!"

Your Unfinished Business will distract you from keeping your appointments with yourself for visualizations and other reinforcement techniques. It may create diversions or complications in various aspects of your life to distract you.

Accept that this is part of the process, like "three steps forward, two steps back"—and some days you will actually lose ground. But don't lose heart. Gradually, you will detect a definite change in the way you feel about yourself, the way you interact with others, and the way you function.

Balancing Your Perspective with a Compassionate Observer

Another technique to help you along in this process is to work with your *Compassionate Observer*. You're well acquainted with the inner critical voice that does the play-by-play running commentary on your behavior. As we have discussed, that comes from Unfinished Business related to poor self-image and unreasonably high standards for yourself. This voice is related to the Doing/Having source of identity.

Let's call this voice the *Critical Judge*—the inner voice who, for as long as you can remember, has held you to high standards, focused on the test questions you got wrong rather than the ones you got right, and motivated you by putting you down. It's the voice inside that says, "That was a stupid thing to do!" or "Pay attention so you don't screw this up like you did the last time!" or "OK, that went pretty well, but don't get complacent!"

A running critical commentary from your Critical Judge can be devastating to self-acceptance. However, the Critical Judge also serves a valid motivating function. Truth be told, you probably owe the Judge a lot of credit for helping you get to where you are today. So it is not a matter of trying to eliminate this inner critic (which would be virtually impossible to do anyway), but to *counterbalance* it with another inner voice—that of a Compassionate Observer.

> *Your goal is to develop the Compassionate Observer so that it becomes an effective neutralizer and complement to your Critical Judge.*

THE COMPASSIONATE OBSERVER is like a caring friend, very interested in your well-being but without any patterned "should/ought" expectations. If you do something wrong, the Compassionate Observer would note what happened and move toward taking corrective action in a caring manner.

The important distinction is the difference between being *reactive* and being *responsive*. You can't always control your external circumstances, but you always have the option of controlling your *response*—and developing discernment. The Compassionate Observer helps you to become aware of judging, forestalls your usual automatic reaction, and advocates a more reasoned, balanced response.

Here's one example of the compensating function of the Compassionate Observer:

Scenario One: Your Customer Places a Big Order with a Competitor

Critical Judge: You really screwed up! If you had been on top of the situation, that would never have happened. Wait until the boss hears about this. You've lost your touch.

Compassionate Observer: You lost the business, at least for now. That's not good, but it's not the end of the world. Quite likely you did—or didn't do—something that contributed to this. Now's the time to learn more about what happened and be in a position to get the next order.

See the effect? The Compassionate Observer counterbalances the reaction of the Critical Judge and helps keep things in proper perspective.

On the other hand, the Compassionate Observer is not a namby-pamby apologist. At times it may not approve of something you do.

Scenario Two: You Upset Your Sister

Critical Judge: How could you have done that to your very own sister? Whenever you are sick or down in the dumps, she is there for you, and now you have hurt her over something trivial. You don't deserve to have a sister—or any relatives. You are an ungrateful, selfish person.

Compassionate Observer: Clearly, what you did has hurt your sister a great deal—much more than you expected. Maybe you overreacted, or perhaps she's not in a good place. Since you created the situation, it's up to you to make it right.

In time, the Compassionate Observer and the Critical Judge will learn to work together to support you with their input without diminishing your self-acceptance.

Each day, make a conscious effort to give your Compassionate Observer equal authority with your Critical Judge. In time, it will soon become clear—even to your Critical Judge—that your performance level has *not* decreased, it has improved! In fact, you are more effective and more highly motivated because you have reduced the amount of energy wasted on negativity and inner conflict.

The following visualization will get you started with your Compassionate Observer:

ESTABLISH YOUR COMPASSIONATE OBSERVER

- Visualize your Critical Judge. Locate it somewhere in your body—for instance, on the right side of your solar plexus. See your Judge clearly. Honor its useful contributions toward getting you where you are today.
- Now visualize a second figure in your body next to the Critical Judge, possibly to the left side of your solar plexus. This is your Compassionate Observer, whose function is to counterbalance the Critical Judge to keep things in proper perspective.
- Introduce the Compassionate Observer to the Critical Judge, explaining that you have come to the realization that it is very important for you to achieve greater balance between *high expectations* and *supportive compassion* for yourself. The Critical Judge has done a great job on the expectations side, and now you want the Compassionate Observer to moderate things.
- Your Critical Judge will not be pleased. Acknowledge the good service the Judge has given over your lifetime, and make it clear that this is a decision completely within your rights to make in order to enhance the quality and duration of your life.
- Set up the ground rules: whenever the Critical Judge feels it's necessary to issue a critical judgment, the Compassionate Observer will have equal time to make an observation.

Having learned to reestablish your locus of identity with the "I Accept Myself Completely" affirmation and with your Compassionate Observer, now let's move on to the first of the three PS Visualizations.

The Identity Visualization

Each of the three Dimensions of Pragmatic Spirituality has a visualization. The *combined* visualizations are the basis for the 3D Visualization in your *Daily PS Focus*.

A summary of the Identity Visualization is included here; the full visualization is contained in Appendix A. We encourage you to record the visualization or order the CD version (see Appendix F) so that you may turn the guided narrative on and off during the course of the visualization.

YOUR IDENTITY VISUALIZATION

As in all the visualizations, begin by *setting the stage*. Concentrate on your breathing, and then gradually turn your focus to a point just behind your navel—see this as the *center of your being*. Say the "I Accept Myself Completely" affirmation, feeling the effect. Then see a confluence of brilliant multicolored rays (each representing one aspect of your identity), which form a shining hologram of your identity around your center of being. Some of the rays are Unfinished Business (identifiable by their dull luster). Remove these—and your Identity hologram gleams more brilliantly. Celebrate the multicolored and shining image of your identity, with particular healing attention to any items of concern or special challenge. Feel the self-acceptance. Make sure your Compassionate Observer is paired with your Critical Judge. Now you are ready for the day.

Note: When you do the Daily PS Focus, the Identity Visualization will segue into the Integration Visualization and then into the Inspiration Visualization . In the learning phase, it is helpful to practice each one separately.

Other means of enhancing your identity include some of the following techniques.

- Get back into your physical body through meditation, yoga, dance, music, sports, martial arts—anything that reconnects your senses.

- Be sensitive to your inner sense of *resonance* and look for ways to bring into your life things that provide you with personal significance—meaningful things that touch you deeply. This can apply to your job life, finding work that gives you a sense of mastery, challenge, and self-awareness.

- Start to unclutter your life of things that don't bring you any sense of significance—clutter takes up space and distracts you from your sense of identity. Insignificant clutter can also give a sense of false identity. Get rid of the insignificance in your life and allow your own inner resonance to be your guide in discovering what is significant. When you have a world of significance, you will then understand your passions, loves, and your own sense of identity. Then "having" is no longer an addiction, but becomes one of the ways of affirming who you are.

Get Started Now!

In this chapter, you have considered the first Pragmatic Spirituality Dimension, Identity, and learned some practical techniques for enhancing your sense of self. Most readers will have a tendency to say to themselves, "I'll come back and start on that later." The choice is certainly yours, but we'd strongly suggest that you take a little time right now to try an Identity Visualization exercise—however short.

Try not to set up any expectations for yourself; just let the process work. (For most people, this is a difficult thing to achieve, but avoiding expectations comes more readily with practice.) As we mentioned earlier, there will be frustrations and setbacks, but once you get started you will perceive yourself and your surroundings with different eyes.

In the next chapter, we'll move to the second Dimension of Pragmatic Spirituality, *Integration*.

CHAPTER 6 HIGHLIGHTS

Identity *is the first of the three PS Dimensions.*

The locus of your identity should be internal, not external.

Typical sources of identity are family-assigned, socially assigned, *and* self-assigned. *Your goal is to work toward a self-assigned identity.*

Your sense of identity develops early in life.

The two identity reference points are Doing/Having *and* Being.

Establish the locus of your identity by practicing self-acceptance, developing your Compassionate Observer, and doing the Identity Visualization.

7

INTEGRATION: THE SECOND DIMENSION

If I am not for myself, who will be for me?
If I am only for myself, what am I?
If not now—when?

—HILLEL, ancient Jewish sage

THE FIRST DIMENSION OF PRAGMATIC SPIRITUALITY, *Identity*, which we considered in Chapter 6, is the foundation for the second Dimension, *Integration*—as in "wholeness." Identity has to do with *internal* focus, whereas Integration deals with (a) the self-maintenance aspects of body/mind/spirit within yourself, and (b) the world outside yourself. In other words, Integration focuses on how to best allocate your time and energies among the many external demands competing for your attention, while maintaining a sense of inner balance and centeredness.

By their very nature, the external demands in each person's life are intrusive. At times they can become overwhelming, coming from all directions:

- Parents
- Children
- Friends
- Job
- Religious affiliations
- Charities
- Service commitments
- Family members
- Colleagues

The day does not have enough hours to deal with them all! And, all too often, what doesn't get done turns into a big guilt trip. The Integration part of the Pragmatic Spirituality process offers a means for contending with all of this as a part of achieving your Inner Edge.

Neutralizing External Demands

The essence of the Integration Dimension is to (a) neutralize and (b) prioritize the external demands in your life so that you can *allocate your available time and energy appropriately* between external demands and Self-maintenance. Prioritizing is something you are familiar with: it is very common within a business context. It is what you do when you allocate a finite amount of money among competing demands, whether it be a million-dollar project or the monthly bills at home. So why is prioritizing one's time and energy so much more difficult?

The answer to that question is contained in our earlier discussions about Unfinished Business and its impact on identity and function. One of the big differences between prioritizing demands at work and prioritizing external demands on your personal time and energies is that many of those external demands have very powerful and subtle influences on you. These influences are rooted in old behavioral patterns, and the "hook" is set very deep at a nonrational, subconscious level. In order to realistically balance and integrate all of the external demands, it is first necessary to *neutralize* the ones with these "hooks" so that an objective prioritization can be done.

Figure 7.1 shows a few examples of external demands with "hooks" based on Unfinished Business, along with the freeing awareness that can get you unhooked.

The first step in neutralizing these "hooks" is to examine your Unfinished Business to determine exactly how each of your external demands claims preferential treatment. Bear in mind, the hooks date all the way back to a childhood context in which, in order to win the love of parents and to emotionally survive in the family, it was necessary to embrace certain assumptions. Once you are able to get in touch with the source of the hooks and scrutinize them, it will become clear that—under present-day realities—the claim by these particular external demands to preferential treatment is no longer valid. From then on, those external demands—parents, children, religious affiliation, or other very important factors in your life—will have only the priority on your time and energy that *you* assign them on a day-to-day basis.

FIGURE 7.1 EXTERNAL DEMANDS WITH "HOOKS" BASED ON UNFINISHED BUSINESS

EXTERNAL DEMAND	"HOOK" OR INTERNALIZED INJUNCTION	NEW AWARENESS
Respond compulsively to the "underdog."	You must be a "rescuer."	You can be supportive without rescuing.
An injustice needs to be confronted, but isn't.	Avoid confrontations for fear of rejection.	You need not reject yourself and your principles.
Work harder.	Only hard work brings results.	Working "smart" is equally as important as working hard.
Loyalty to work comes first.	Loyalty to authority makes a good person.	Loyalty to one's integrity comes first.
The one with the most "toys" wins.	Accumulation of assets is a measure of personal worth.	True success is internal.

The technique for neutralizing the power of certain external demands is to recognize that each has two parts:

- Its *historical* connotations to your identity
- Its *current* context as an external demand in your life

Note that the first part, the historical aspect of identity, has no relevance to your current existence—other than whatever influence you allow it to have over you as Unfinished Business. Only the second part is truly relevant to your life now. Or, to state this in terms of the Identity Visualization, the second part (current context) of each aspect of your identity forms the vivid and colorful rays in your

ANOTHER REASON FOR UNDUE INFLUENCE by some external demands is that they make up a significant part of your identity. Remember the Identity Visualization's hologram made up of rays from many sources? Many of those rays are external demands, and many of those (the dull ones) involve Unfinished Business. Examples include the following:

Parent: "You need to seek perfection in everything you do in order to gain respect."

Parent: "A good child honors her parents by being obedient and respectful."

Religion: "Redemption is found only by respect for the authority of the church."

Friends: "If you are a true friend, you must be loyal without question."

Society: "Looking good is everything."

Identity hologram, whereas the historical part forms rays that are dull and lusterless—*detracting from* rather than *contributing to* your identity.

One very common example of an external demand with a deeply set hook is the interaction of parents with their adult children. Careful consideration, through both rational processes and visualizations, will enable the adult child to sort out parent-related external demands into two categories:

1. **Historical connotations:** "My parents raised me as well as they could, always trying to do what was best. They spent a lot of time and money on me. In general, I was a good child, although there were problems when I wanted to do my thing earlier than when they were ready to let go. I ended up with some pretty heavy Unfinished Business related to them, but that was because they didn't know any better. That chapter of my life is finished, and I am an adult."

2. **Current context:** "My parents are getting old, and that frightens them (and me). For the time being, they don't have any major health problems, and they have several good acquaintances and activities. They are OK financially. They complain that I don't spend enough time with them, and I understand that. However, the time I spend with them is conditioned by all the other demands in my life, and at times I probably give them a

higher percentage than I should—which makes me resentful, feeling like I'm still a child."

See how helpful this can be? The person in this example, in fact, seems to be giving an appropriate amount of attention to his parents. The feelings of guilt stem not from the current situation, but from old patterns. The objective of the Integration Dimension is to sort out these residual factors to enable the prioritization to be done more rationally.

Key Tools: Self-Maintenance and Self-Discipline

In allocating your time and energy each day, your own needs should be given appropriate priority. Too often, one's own needs are shoved aside by external demands: the annual physical is skipped; the daily exercise regimen is neglected; the day ends and the "my list" has again been preempted. Leaving oneself for last is all too common, and the reason is simple. As discussed in Chapter 5, many people never learned the concepts of Self-maintenance and Self-discipline, essential tools for properly processing the Integration Dimension.

SOME PARTS OF OUR SOCIETY, secular and religious, set a high value on "putting others before self." There is a fear of being judged as selfish if one doesn't think of others before oneself. If you recognize that as a hook/internalized injunction, you can process it with Self-maintenance into a new awareness of balancing others and yourself, which is the essence of the Integration part of the Pragmatic Spirituality process. This leads to clarity about an important distinction: "selfish" is thinking of oneself without any consideration for others; however, it is *not* selfish to take care of yourself in ways that release more nurturing and creative energies for yourself and others in your life.

Boundaries

Another common root cause of difficulties dealing with external demands, and with other people in general, is a lack of *boundaries*. Defining boundaries is a behavior and mind-set that some children acquire as a normal part of growing up; however, many children do not learn this because their parents never learned it from their parents. The failure to acquire a proficiency in boundaries, as well as Self-maintenance and Self-discipline, is a form of "family curse" in which a type of inability to cope is passed from one generation to another.

A person with healthy boundaries has a clear understanding that there is a space from the center of his being out to a certain distance over which he has inalienable rights. The perimeter of this psychic space is that person's *boundaries*, which he controls. It is a natural tendency for a child to try to gradually establish his boundaries. The key factor is the degree to which the parents *honor* those incremental attempts at boundary-building. If the parents understand the importance of boundaries, the child will be allowed and encouraged to develop her boundaries as a part of the process of separating from parents and becoming a unique person.

WE LIKE THIS INTERPRETATION OF BOUNDARIES, which is adapted from the images of John Bradshaw, author of *Healing the Inner Child.*

Healthy boundaries: These are like a picket fence, high enough to keep people out of our space but low enough for us to speak with people on the outside. The picket fence has a gate with the handle on the *inside*, so only we can decide whether to let the person inside our boundary.

Inadequate boundaries: Unfortunately, most people never learned about boundaries as part of their growing up. So they have few boundaries, and are increasingly frustrated by people invading their space. This brings about a sense of diminished self, as well as inappropriate interactions when the long-suffering gives way to anger.

Isolating boundaries: Tired of having their space invaded, people build "ten-foot walls" to protect their space. These do keep others out, but they also isolate the individual, preventing any constructive interaction with others.

Every day you encounter examples of the various types of boundaries. Consider the following examples:

- The vulnerable person ("too nice," "overworked," "overly conscientious," "exploited") who can't say no, gets stuck with the dirty work, and periodically blows up and then apologizes ruefully, "I don't know what came over me" (inadequate boundaries)

- The isolated person ("defensive," "aggressive," "surly," "guarded") who never lets his guard down and has few, if any, close friends (isolating boundaries)
- The constructive person ("has her act together," "a pleasure to deal with," "great at sorting out situations," "gets along with everyone") who is very proficient at maintaining appropriate boundaries so that people only get as close as she wishes to allow them (healthy boundaries)

Establishing Effective Boundaries

There are two basic elements to establishing boundaries. The first is being aware that it is not only appropriate to have boundaries, but that it is your *responsibility*—a very important one, at that. The second is recognizing that any difficulties you have setting boundaries, either in general or for a particular person or situation, is most likely caused by Unfinished Business.

Here are the basic steps:

1. Be aware of the appropriateness of boundaries.

2. Affirm that the establishment of boundaries is completely appropriate and that it is *your* responsibility to institute them.

3. Note where your boundaries are weak:
   — Typically, what are the circumstances?
   — How does the lack of a boundary affect you physically? emotionally?
   — What could you do to correct the situation? (What kind of boundary is needed?)
   — Why don't you do it? When you try, what happens?

4. Take some quiet time to reflect on the Unfinished Business at work in your situation.

5. Once you have realized that you are contributing to the situation (actively or passively) because of Unfinished Business, decide on an appropriate course of action. Some examples include
   — Discuss it with the person involved. If he has been unaware of violating your boundary, you can describe how you would like the interac-

tion done in the future. If the other person is a "bully" or "type A" personality who invades boundaries frequently, this discussion will alert him that you are aware of what has been happening and are determined to change the interaction.

— Make changes in your physical layout, timing, and other factors that augment your boundaries. If a coworker intrudes by sitting on your desk, reconfigure your desk to eliminate the "seating area." If someone is in the habit of interrupting you on the phone, get a headset and signal that you're busy. Change your route or your schedule to avoid encountering certain people in certain circumstances.

6. Prepare a "script" to use in identifying and enforcing your boundaries. Work on it until you're comfortable. Tape it to your bathroom mirror. Memorize it. Practice it on your friends. Then when someone starts to invade your boundary, say it! Consider the following examples to get you started.

— "Excuse me, but I'm uncomfortable with your standing so close to me. Besides, I can see you more clearly if you stand a little farther away. Thanks."

— "I'd be happy to help you as soon as I finish this. Shall I call you, or would you prefer to come back?"

— "So that I understand this new assignment properly, let's make sure we're clear about when it is due and how that will affect the other projects I have been working on."

— "Honey, tomorrow my day is very full, so I won't be able to do any errands for you. Maybe we could do them together this weekend."

7. Enlist the help of others. Discuss it with friends and get their input. Or, if you know someone who deals with your "problem person" effectively, talk with her about how she does it; you may get some good pointers.

8. Finally, and most important, do your Integration Visualization regularly.

The Integration Visualization

A summary of the Integration Visualization is included here. Just like the Identity Visualization (Chapter 6), the full Integration Visualization is contained in

---

YOUR INTEGRATION VISUALIZATION

To begin, segue from the end of the Identity Visualization, or set the stage as in other visualizations. Reenvision your Identity hologram around your center of being (behind your navel). Some of the rays leading into the hologram are ropes that lead outward—each connected to one of your external demands. These external demands are arrayed in a circle around you, each vying for your time and energy. Swing your attention around the circle, honoring each one of them. As you do, note how each one weighs you down to varying degrees. Envision a brilliant flame springing up around you: the flame burns through each rope, severing the connection. As the ropes burn through, send forgiveness to each external demand. Thus freed up, you can now do a realistic prioritization of your time and energies for the day among your Self-maintenance needs and the external demands you choose. Tell all the external demands that your prioritization choices for today do not reflect your regard for them. Then affirm to yourself that you have done the prioritization as best you can, so there will be no guilt or recriminations (although you may at any time choose to redo the prioritization).

Appendix A. We encourage you to record the visualization or order the CD version so that you may turn the guided narrative on and off during the course of the visualization. To begin, learn this visualization on its own; in practice it will be preceded by the Identity Visualization and will segue into the Inspiration Visualization. These visualizations continue to develop and deepen each time you do them, forming an Inner Edge foundation for your daily encounters with your outer world.

Double-Edged Swords: Loyalty, Responsibility, Service, and Duty

Some of the greatest difficulties found with the Integration allocation process stem from the concepts of *obligation to a higher cause*. These concepts are so powerful that it is extremely difficult to "neutralize" them. Therefore they require special mention here. Without doubt, in their *highest form*, such concepts as loyalty, responsibility, service, and duty legitimately belong in the Integration process, subordinating self-interests to a greater good.

However, there are many instances when people subordinate their interests to a "higher cause" inappropriately. It is possible that these people may be misinformed by someone with unprincipled motives. But more often, the problem is a case of self-delusion—when the "higher cause" is not a current reality but Unfinished Business. In other words, the loyalty, responsibility, service, or duty is based on out-of-date behavior patterns no longer appropriate to today's circumstances. For example:

- The parents of a thirty-year-old daughter who continue to intrude into the daughter's life excessively, based on their sense of "parental responsibilities"
- The person who justifies his insensitive and overbearing behavior as "Just doing my duty"
- The people who question your loyalty by saying, "Love it or leave it!"

This phenomenon reemphasizes the importance of neutralizing *all* external demands, especially those that appear to have a "privileged" or "preferential" priority, the legitimacy of which is not readily apparent. Once that is done, your Integration process can proceed on a level playing field.

We'll explore further the issues of loyalty and responsibility and their relationship to the workplace in Chapter 13.

A Final Word on Integration and Balance

We'd like to repeat here the quote from the beginning of this chapter:

If I am not for myself, who will be for me?
If I am only for myself, what am I?
If not now—when?

This essential "spiritual" question raises the issue of how to strike an appropriate balance between looking out for one's self-interests and looking out for the concerns of others.

Finding that balance is elusive. The tendency seems to be to fall on one side or the other. We read of individuals completely driven by self-interests, behaving as though they were not constrained by any of the laws or rules designed to regulate decent human behavior. And then we encounter people who seem to be incapable of looking out for their own interests and are easy prey for exploiters and opportunists. Most likely, the majority would like to strike a balance, if they knew how to do it.

Pragmatic Spirituality offers a simple and straightforward technique for achieving that balance between self-interest and service. But it also offers the potential for rising above our normal limitations and soaring higher. As we will discuss in the next chapter, once we have established the Dimensions of Identity and Integration, we are then ready to transcend our rational means and access the powerful resources of the Inspiration Dimension—one step closer to achieving your Inner Edge!

Chapter 7 Highlights

Integration *deals with external demands (versus* Identity, *which has an internal focus).*

Each day, prioritize your time and energy among your Self-maintenance needs and the external demands you select.

Neutralize your external demands (those with an Unfinished Business "hook").

Setting appropriate boundaries is your responsibility. (Most people have either inadequate *boundaries or* isolating *boundaries.)*

The Integration Visualization segues from the Identity Visualization. Ropes to your external factors are burned, thus freeing you to make appropriate prioritizations.

Integration is achieving a balance between self-interest and service to others.

8

INSPIRATION: THE THIRD DIMENSION

*By learning to contact, listen to, and act on our own intuition,
we can directly connect to the higher power of the universe and
allow it to become our guiding force.*

— SHAKTI GAWAIN

*The struggle to learn to listen, to respect our own intuitive inner
promptings is the greatest challenge of all.*

— HERB GOLDBERG

ONCE THE IDENTITY DIMENSION has put you in contact with your full self, and the Integration Dimension has guided you in allocating your time and energy, you are now in a position to fully benefit from the third Dimension of Pragmatic Spirituality: *Inspiration*. The word *inspiration* comes from the Latin derivation "to be breathed from the place of the divine." This is a similar source as the word *aspire*, wherein one is "breathed with purpose." The clear connotation is that of being invigorated by the winds of spirit. The idea of "being inspired" encompasses both gaining a higher perspective and being motivated toward higher ground.

Inspiration affirms both the Identity and Integration Dimensions and enables you to access resources beyond your normal limits of perception. The combination of all three Dimensions opens the path to the Inner Edge, as exemplified by the concept of a Fully Functioning Adult (which will be discussed in the next chapter). Something unique happens when you truly "occupy" the *whole* of your being: the wholeness is projected into your day-to-day experiences in the world.

The integration of your perceptions and the dimensions that lie within you can open you up to an awakened state of significance never before experienced.

All of the great religions have recognized the evolving stages of human capabilities, with the final stage being one of *spiritual* awareness. In this stage, one not only becomes more aware of the interconnections of mind, body, and spirit within oneself, but also of the interconnection of self with all the dimensions of the outer world.

In our everyday conversations, the word *inspiration* denotes an improved human state brought about by something we hear, see, or experience—a dream, an encounter, a creative idea.

Not "Religious" Versus "Secular"—Rather, "One Path" Versus "Many Paths"

You will recall our statement in Chapter 2 that Pragmatic Spirituality is neutral and complementary with other forms of spiritual practices and doctrine-based religions. This is based on our belief that the perceived source of inspiration may be either religious in nature, intuitive in nature, or a combination of the two. Throughout history, every culture and belief system has acknowledged the potential of the human intellect: the Inspiration Dimension focuses on realizing that potential.

A person's perception of the nature and source of inspiration is understandably influenced by how he was brought up. A person raised in a religious environment will tend to interpret inspiration in terms of a revelation from the divinity of that faith. A person raised in a secular family may be more inclined to attribute inspiration to intuition. And further along in life, some people explore alternative sources of inspiration. What does it matter what label is placed on the source? If each of us is called upon as a human being to achieve our full potential, the important thing is that we strive to accurately receive the message "breathed from the place of the divine" and incorporate it into our lives.

Our perception of ultimate truths is captured by the Buddhist metaphor of heaven as the top of a mountain, with humans at the foot of the mountain: there is not one way to heaven, but many, many paths winding up the sides of the mountain. For each person, it matters not which path one is on. What matters is whether one is *climbing*!

Therefore, inspiration may come from intuition or from a divine source. Since religious/spiritual practice is a very individual thing, we will focus on the

> **WE BELIEVE THAT,** given the complexity of the universe—from the infinitesimal intricacies of DNA and subatomic particles to the vastness of the heavens—it is most unlikely that the human mind is capable of conceiving more than a small fragment of the ultimate truth. The human perception of God seems analogous to a pet goldfish's comprehension of the realities of the room that houses its fish tank—and the complex world beyond. The joke about one tropical fish saying to the other, "If there's no God, who is feeding us?" brings some perspective to theological disputes on the human level.

intuitive source of inspiration. If you have spiritual or religious practices through which you prefer to access inspiration, they can work equally well in the Pragmatic Spirituality process. For others, a combination may be more effective: it need not be either/or.

In fact, differing perceptions on the source of inspiration may very well be irrelevant. From the standpoint of left/right brain theory, *all* inspiration—whether answered prayer, divine guidance, or an intuitive "a-ha"—is received in the same way: through the right/intuitive side of your brain.

Right Brain/Left Brain

Brain function studies over the past several decades indicate that each part of the human brain has certain primary functions. More recent work looking into the complexities of the brain has revealed that the right/left brain concept is vastly oversimplified; however, we use it as a means of illustrating the varied functionality of the mind.

- **The left brain** specializes in rational, sequential thought processes such as solving mathematical problems and stringing words together into effective communication. For decision making, it collects data into systematic arrays for analysis.

- **The right brain** specializes in "holistic" processing such as music, poetry, three-dimensional imagery, and spatial relations. It is the source of "gut feel" decisions, of "out-of-the-blue" ideas, of creative insights and flashes.

In a typical group of businesspeople, the great majority have probably spent most or all of their time at work in the left/rational part of their brain. Some, when they get into a different context—a concert, gardening, daydreaming, sailing, for example—might move into their right/intuitive brain, but most would likely just stay with their left/rational side.

Some managers have learned how to improve their decision making by using both sides of their brain while at work. The left/rational side is used for what it does best: analyzing, assessing, and arranging data and information. However, seldom does the available information lead conclusively to a clear answer, because of missing data or uncertainty about future events and pertinent factors that cannot be quantified. Here is where the right/intuitive part of the brain is helpful, when a "gut feel" is needed. Ask a manager with a superior track record of decision making how she arrived at a particular decision, and you'll likely get the strong impression that the intuitive part of the brain was involved.

One of the primary characteristics of an Inner Edge is a heightened effectiveness in thought processes and decision making resulting from improved collaboration between the left/rational and the right/intuitive parts of the brain. Once your Identity and Integration Dimensions are in place, the Inspiration Dimension is the gateway to your intuitive resources, facilitated by the techniques discussed later in this chapter for working with your intuitive Icons. In Section III, "Pragmatic Spirituality in Your Workplace," we will explore in detail specific techniques for using intuition to enhance the decision-making process, based on Ron's consulting work with managers and organizations.

A TANTALIZING INDICATION of the mind's untapped potential is revealed by what happens when the two brain hemispheres are balanced. As the brain moves from one hemisphere to the other, there is a momentary balance. This balanced state has a brain wave picture that is quite distinct from the picture of either the left- or right-brain state. Interestingly, the balanced brain scan is very similar to a brain scan done on a mystic, deep in trance, wherein he has slowed his heartbeat and other body functions. This example points out the exciting possibilities yet to be discovered as medical research explores the potential of the brain.

The Inspiration Visualization

The purpose of the Inspiration Visualization is twofold:

1. To consolidate your Identity and Integration Visualizations
2. To facilitate access to resources and wisdom beyond the limits of your rational mind

Because of its nature, the Inspiration Visualization is much less structured than the Identity or Integration Visualizations. The Inspiration Visualization's purpose is to get you out of your left/rational brain and reality-grounded perspective and open you to unlimited possibilities. Our suggested visualization on page 90 uses the image of light, but you may develop other images that serve you even better.

You have the option of following the visualization or moving into a "prayer" modality based on your particular religion or faith system. As stated earlier, we feel that both access essentially the same source, but some people will feel more comfortable looking toward a specific deity and using familiar terms and symbolism.

Do not begin with an agenda, but simply be in the presence of a power that is above and beyond your normal experience. (The wonderful results of such an unfocused experience are aptly described by the words with which some people describe their feeling during meditation: "It's like coming home.") If there is a particular need or topic to be focused on, this may be articulated as a prayer, in religious terms, or just "put out there." There should be an expectation that there will be a response, and an acceptance that the response may be different than you might hope. As the old preacher put it, "You'd do much better in your prayers to spend more time listening and less time telling God what to do."

It is most unlikely that you will come away from your Inspiration Visualization with anything concrete or specific: if you do, it should be viewed with suspicion as possibly coming from your desires or intentions. (Later on, as you become more proficient with intuitive decision-making techniques, it is possible to arrive at a specific answer, but that process is a more focused follow-up to this visualization.) Remember that responses from inspiration will come through your right/intuitive brain, which operates in symbols and images. These can be full of meaning but not readily perceived by your left/rational brain.

Don't be impatient to translate these symbols into words and logic, for a too-hasty transition from right to left brain may lose much of the meaning and nuance. Have faith that, in its proper time, the meaning will become clear. It may be an intuitive feeling that becomes increasingly strong. It may occur somewhat later when the pieces fall into place. It may be in the form of an unlikely synchronistic event, such as encountering someone who just happens to be able to give you what you seek. (The final part of this chapter includes more discussion about how the results of the Inspiration Visualization, as well as other communications from your intuitive brain, can be interpreted.)

As with the other visualizations, the following is a summary. The full visualization may be found in Appendix A, and we encourage you to either record it or obtain the CD version so that you may listen to the guidance, turning it on and off to best fit with your needs.

With all three visualizations fresh in your mind, let us move on to find out more about how the intuitive mind works, and how to get the two sides of the mind to work in concert.

YOUR INSPIRATION VISUALIZATION

Normally this will segue from the end of the Integration Visualization. If you are doing this as a stand-alone, be sure to set the stage. Affirm the holographic image of your Identity: well grounded with self-acceptance. Acknowledge the external demands arrayed around you, serene that the Integration prioritization has properly dealt with them.

Then visualize a brilliant and healing light shining down from above, permeating every cell of your being. Invite the healing light to focus on a specific need or challenge related to you or someone close to you; a problem to be dealt with, a decision to be made, a part of someone's being that needs healing. It may be a simple question, such as "How may I best deal with this situation?" Relax and be open to whatever input you may receive, which may be in words but more likely will be in symbols and images of the right brain (*Icons*). Don't be impatient to translate these to your left/rational brain, which might lose the message or its nuances.

After a time, even if you are not aware of a specific message having been received, trust that some part of you has received something that will, in time, become more apparent. Give thanks to all three Dimensions—Identity, Integration, and Inspiration—for their contribution. Bring the wonderful feelings from your visualization with you into all aspects of your day.

How the Intuitive Mind Works

In studying the use of imagery and intuitive information, Ron discovered that the intuitive mechanism works through all five senses. Intuition isn't so much an independent sensory apparatus as an inherent mechanism associated with the physical senses. Along with this observation, he established the following:

- Images operate more like Icons, which have embedded levels of meaning. People who use *rational* imagery to search for the symbolic meaning often miss many of the multidimensional levels of meaning inherent in the images.
- Intuition operates *at all times*. It isn't a matter of a person being intuitive or nonintuitive. It is more a matter of being able to *pay attention* to one's intuition.
- Intuitive awareness often transcends the normal function of our senses, as well as of space and time.
- The intuitive function is the key to understanding oneself more deeply and experiencing an interconnection with the elements in the world around you.

THE **INTUITIVE FUNCTION** operates so commonly in our interactions that we often take it for granted. Some examples include

- A mother's ability to read the meaning behind her baby's cry
- The ability to sense when you are in a dangerous or unsupportive environment
- The many documented instances when someone suddenly "knew" that a loved one was ill or in danger
- Instances of "synchronistic" events: that is, very unlikely "coincidences" that answer an unspoken need

Two Modes of Intuition

Intuition can be expressed in two different modes. One is a *direct intuitive expression* whereby one knows or feels something without any intermediate processes. Direct intuition may be spontaneous, such as an idea coming "out of the blue," or it can be ongoing. An example of ongoing direct intuition is a feeling of needing to be vigilant because of a sense of long-term danger in an environment.

The other mode of intuition requires a *dialogue* between the rational (left) mind and the intuitive (right) mind. The two don't speak the same language— literally! The rational mind works in a linear manner; the intuitive mind works holistically and metaphorically. So, for any kind of a dialogue to occur, the rational mind must learn the language of the intuitive mind.

Your Intuitive "Internet" — Search Engines and Icons

Rapidly evolving computer and Internet technologies provide a useful metaphor for understanding how to access one's intuitive resources—by treating the intuitive mind as an internal Internet system. As with the Internet, the most efficient way to find information is to create "search engines." When working with the intuitive mind, these search engines take the form of putting forth a question and then quieting the mind to create receptivity. In time, a response in the form of Icons will arise from one's deeper consciousness. These Icons are loaded with complex meaning, so it is necessary to learn how to "open" them and to decipher their compressed information.

Anyone can learn to "surf" the intuitive mind and obtain a wealth of personal and professional knowledge. The person seeking increased self-awareness can find much to assist in the personal growth process, such as a greater awareness of the roots of one's fears, the strength of one's resources, the potential of one's relationships, or insights into questions about one's mission in life. For the businessperson, there are countless applications for intuitive sources: hiring decisions, market trends, creative solutions to business situations, product development, customer needs, increasing sales and productivity, new market opportunities, and so on.

Whatever your need, in any facet of your life or activity, your intuitive mind is full of untapped resources. It is up to you to learn how to take advantage of them.

Guidelines for Processing Intuitive Icons

Just as an icon on your computer screen can be "clicked on" to reveal prodigious amounts of multilayered information, so the *intuitive Icons* of your mind represent boundless resources for all aspects of your life. However, it is necessary to have a proficiency in working with these Icons.

One of the pitfalls is that your rational mind will want to step in immediately and begin analyzing the information that comes through. Therefore, we offer the following guidelines to help you have a more profitable experience.

Guidelines for Maximizing the Intuitive Process

- Allow adequate time for centering yourself and entering into your internal framework and imagery process.
  - A powerful visualization for centering yourself is to create a personal "place of peace" based on a remembered place (a pleasant grove or a mountain retreat, for example), or an imagined place that evokes a supportive, tranquil feeling. Close your eyes and take time to be in that place. Once there, go systematically through your five senses and ground each in the experience. (*See* the textures and colors, *hear* the sounds, *smell* the fragrances, *taste* the environment, and *feel* on your skin the ambience around you [the sun, wind, and other elements of nature].) Finally, "become" the place of peace.

- When an Icon (any kind of image) emerges, encounter it in whatever way it chooses. Don't rush to raise it into conscious focus or try to assess the meaning analytically or try to put it into words. Instead, retain the metaphorical sense of the Icon.
  - An eagle can be a metaphor for strength, acuity, straightforwardness, vision, or swiftness.
  - An Icon can be an amalgam of physical elements: for example, a cat woman can be a metaphor for the relationship of femininity with strength and prowess.
  - A marshmallow with a steel ball inside in answer to a question regarding a person's character can communicate a sense that he is soft on the outside, but strong and hard on the inside.

- Focus on the *qualitative*—not quantitative—aspects of the Icon that emerges. Hold off calling on your rational mind to analyze, interpret, weigh, or measure. Respect the Icon as a *metaphor* with many shades and levels of meaning.

- Honor your initial responses by not judging them in any way.

- To better understand the Icon as a metaphor, role-play that you are the Icon.
  - "I am an old WWI airplane, and even though I was built to fly, I don't feel adequately prepared to handle the challenges of the world around me, which sometimes wants to machine-gun me down."
  - "I am a sunflower whose face changes with the movement of the sun. Within me are many potential sources of energy."
  - "I am a butterfly. I may appear small and fragile, but I have a great capacity to travel immense distances by using the environmental resources around me."

- Focus on the *dynamics* of the Icon and its movement. Its specific content is not as important. Attend to the pattern, script, metaphoric, or thematic aspects. Note key words that may highlight a theme.
  - "I am a flower that is unfolding with deep roots that reach into the earth and tap into many resources. I may appear fragile on the outside, but I have a great deal of character and strength on the inside."
  - "I am a violin that has been left on a shelf. Because people have neglected me I don't play to my potential. I am just waiting for someone to come along and draw out my potential."
  - "I am a worm digging through the earth. Even though I appear nondescript, I am a tremendous worker and have the strength to move the earth and to take advantage of the resources that lie hidden."

- Be flexible in your interpretation of the Icon, including humor and plays on meaning. The intuitive mind often uses visual puns, such as seeing a tin can to communicate a person being fired (canned).

Guidelines for Unzipping the Many Levels of Meaning in the Icon

- To explore the many levels of meaning in an Icon, be the voice of the Icon and describe it in first person, present tense. As you become more adept at the metaphoric reading of Icons, you will develop a growing selection of words and phrases to characterize the meanings of each one. Examples include

— "I feel heavy."
— "I taste the bitterness of the situation."
— "I hear the sound of agony."
— "I see beauty."
— "I feel a lightness of being."

- To more fully understand an Icon, share it with another person. Don't attempt to "characterize" it but describe what you experienced as a flow of images, phrased in the present tense, such as in the examples previously given.

- If you are working with a partner to decipher meaning from Icons that involve that person, request feedback from her to gain perspective and real-life context for the metaphor presented. For example, two people work as partners on intuitive insights, each focusing on the other with this question in mind: "Where does this person stand in her own world?" The responses might be
  — **One person's intuitive "reading" of the partner:** "I see a Punch and Judy puppet show, and Punch is hitting Judy repeatedly over the head. My sense is that there is a great deal of stress and abuse."
  — **The partner's reaction:** "Your metaphor of the Punch and Judy puppet show is very revealing about my work situation, where I feel like a puppet to my supervisor and battered by the demands being made on me."

- Focus on the feelings connected to the multiple meanings that you experienced when you "became" the Icon in order to better understand the metaphorical meaning.

- Note details of your Icon, which may give it a special meaning.
  — "I see a manure pile alongside your beautiful garden. The pile is being neglected and smells."
  Special meaning: The sense is that even though you have your life in order and have plentiful resources, there is an area that relates to the overall scheme of your life that you are avoiding and it is beginning to bother you.

— "I see a volcano, but it has a big boulder plugging up the opening and there is immense pressure in the interior."
Special meaning: The feeling is that there is a great deal of repressed anger in your life.

- Acknowledge in yourself, and for your partner, areas of resonance (inner impact for the other person) in order to give validity to the experience. Also, a *lack* of resonance should be noted. This is a good way to check out the fit and significance of a metaphor.

- Remember, logic doesn't work with Icons. Meaning evolves from the process of dialoguing and becoming the voice of the Icon.

Pitfalls to Avoid in Processing Icons

- Being impatient and not allowing adequate time to experience the Icon

- Overquestioning and judging the nature of the Icon
  Example: "I don't like seeing a dead dog in the road."

- Bringing in cognitive interpretations that shift internal validity to external validity
  Example: "I think that is a Freudian symbol that says he has a hang-up."

- Selective omission or perception because of one's own fears and prejudices
  Example: "I didn't want to mention it, but this volcano was exploding." (fear of anger)

- Overfocusing on past history to the exclusion of current relevancy of the Icon
  Example: A person who didn't want to acknowledge the relevancy of the intuitive feedback that was presented: "I dealt with that long ago. I no longer have that problem. It doesn't bother me anymore" (denial)

- Making moral judgments regarding the rightness or wrongness of an Icon

Example: "No matter what you say, I think the Icon that came up is lame and offensive."

Be Patient with Yourself

This chapter is an introduction to accessing your intuitive function. Be patient in your first efforts, and don't push too hard for results. Bear in mind that you, and everyone else, had strong intuitive capabilities early in life; however, schooling and societal values and beliefs tend to separate people from their intuitive senses as they grow up. Thus most adults have their intuition pretty much locked away, out of reach. Understandably, it will take you some time to reverse those attitudes and unlock your intuitive talents.

There will be more techniques and examples of using intuition in practical situations in Section III (Chapter 11, "QDM: Quantum Decision Making") and Section IV (Chapter 17, "QDM: The Bottom-Line Power of Intuition in the Organization").

Putting the Three Dimensions to Work

Now that you are familiar with Unfinished Business, Self-resolves, the three Dimensions of Pragmatic Spirituality, and the techniques for accessing your intuitive resources, in the next chapter we'll combine all of these into some specific techniques that you can use daily to achieve and maintain your Inner Edge. And we'll further explore the useful concept of the Fully Functioning Adult.

CHAPTER 8 HIGHLIGHTS

Inspiration both affirms the Identity and Integration Dimensions and enables you to access resources beyond your normal limits of perception, opening the path to your Inner Edge.

Inspiration may draw from intuition and from a divine source: either intuition or a religious practice (or a combination of the two) may be used to access it.

The human brain's functions can be characterized (in an oversimplified manner) as having a left/rational part for logical, sequential functions (such as solv-

ing math problems) and a right/intuitive part for holistic processing (such as music and imagery).

The Inner Edge comes from both sides of the brain working together. For most people, the left/rational side dominates. The Inspiration Dimension allows you to free up the right/intuitive side.

Your Inspiration Visualization is summarized on page 89.

The intuitive mind is like the Internet. It can be accessed with "search engines" (proper techniques). Answers come in the form of Icons *with layers of embedded meaning.*

Learning how to interpret Icons is essential so that the right/intuitive and left/rational parts of the mind can cooperate in maximizing the Icons' benefits.

Guidelines for Maximizing the Intuitive Process are on page 93.

Guidelines for Unzipping the Many Levels of Meaning in Icons are on page 94.

Pitfalls to Avoid in Processing Icons are on page 96.

9

ACHIEVING YOUR INNER EDGE: THE FULLY FUNCTIONING ADULT

He who wishes to teach us a truth should not tell it to us, but simply suggest it with a brief gesture, a gesture which starts an ideal trajectory in the air along which we glide until we find ourselves at the feet of the new truth.

—José Ortega y Gasset

CONGRATULATIONS! IN SECTION II, you have learned what Unfinished Business is and how to deal with it, the three Self-resolves, the three Dimensions of Pragmatic Spirituality (Identity, Integration, and Inspiration), and how to interpret the Icon images from your intuitive resources. Now you'll learn how to put them all together in two techniques that you can use daily and/or whenever needed to establish and maintain your Inner Edge. As you've gone through each of the Pragmatic Spirituality visualizations, we hope you've experienced a new dimension within yourself, one of greater perspective, creativity, and wholeness than you'd imagined possible.

Implementing the Pragmatic Spirituality Process

The goals of Pragmatic Spirituality are enhanced *authenticity* (to your essential self and in your actions) and *appropriateness* (in reacting to each situation you encounter). The outcome is not only an enriched sense of self, in all its ramifications, but also improvement in every aspect of your performance—the Inner Edge.

Having considered the core elements of Pragmatic Spirituality and how they apply to your specific situation, you have an understanding of how powerful—and insidious—Unfinished Business can be in undermining day-to-day effectiveness and the achievement of your long-term potential. You have acknowledged that Unfinished Business has held you back, and begun the Four Rs process to identify and transcend your various items of Unfinished Business. It will be a long process because they are deeply embedded, but the synergy of Pragmatic Spirituality enables you to progress on many levels, with one reinforcing the others.

Figure 9.1 summarizes two simple techniques that encapsulate the elements of Pragmatic Spirituality so as to be readily accessed:

1. The Daily PS Focus
2. The Quick Re-Focus

FIGURE 9.1 DAILY APPLICATION AND IMPLEMENTATION OF PRAGMATIC SPIRITUALITY

Each day at your regular time do a Daily PS Focus (15–20 minutes)

Affirmation

Restatement of Self-resolves

- Self-accountability
- Self-maintenance
- Self-discipline

3D Visualization

- Identity (Compassionate Observer)
- Integration (guilt-free prioritization)
- Inspiration (faith-based or intuitive access)

Start your day with an Inner Edge!

When and if needed during the day do a Quick Re-Focus (30–60 seconds)

3D Review

FFA Cross-Check:

"What would a Fully Functioning Adult do in the current situation?"

(Later) Ask:

"What Unfinished Business was at work?"

Your Daily PS Focus

The Daily PS Focus, on page 102, is a ten- to twenty-minute period you spend with yourself each day, preferably at the start of the day. Finding time may not be easy, but giving your Daily PS Focus top priority reflects your commitment to achieving the benefits of the Inner Edge. This time should be private and uninterrupted.

Quick Re-Focus

Quite often, events of the day do not work out as planned, and you may feel destabilized. This calls for a *Quick Re-Focus*—taking a brief interval (thirty seconds to several minutes) to regain the centering of your Daily PS Focus, to quickly retune your prioritizations, and to call on the relevant Dimensions of Pragmatic Spirituality for support. Of necessity, this usually will have to be done without setting the stage. An example of a Quick Re-Focus is on page 103.

The Fully Functioning Adult

In the instructions for the Quick Re-Focus, after you reaffirm your desire for authenticity and appropriateness you ask, "How would a Fully Functioning Adult handle this?" (Or, in retrospect, you might ask, "How would a Fully Functioning Adult have handled that situation?") As explained in Chapters 3 and 9, the Fully Functioning Adult (FFA) is an idealized concept—a goal to work toward. Or it may be viewed as the exemplification of the full application of Pragmatic Spirituality—the Inner Edge. It is not a realistic goal to achieve, but a valid exemplar for guidance.

REAL-LIFE EXAMPLES

The role of the Fully Functioning Adult is not to point out our shortcomings, but to exemplify what we are working toward. Here are a variety of real-life situations—each followed by a commentary on how a Fully Functioning Adult might have handled the situation, along with the relevant FFA principle. Remember, in this section we're focusing mostly on personal life issues. In Section III, we'll turn our attention to how the Fully Functioning Adult deals with the workplace.

Parents

Situation: Joe's father constantly made him feel guilty by pointing out that Joe wasn't as good as others or that he could have done better. Joe hated

YOUR DAILY PS FOCUS

1. Begin by setting the stage (Appendix A, page 269).
2. Say to yourself the "Affirmation of My Potential."

    I have the potential to . . .

    reach a higher state of consciousness,

    access my full resources,

    achieve an enhanced level of authenticity for myself,

    and respond appropriately in all situations I encounter.

3. Next, briefly reaffirm your Self-resolves:
   — Self-accountability
   — Self-maintenance
   — Self-discipline

   Nothing elaborate. For example:

   "I take full accountability for my situation. I resolve to give myself appropriate priority, and I will honor my commitments to others and myself."

4. The main part of your Daily PS Focus is your 3D Visualization, which merges the visualizations for the three Dimensions as described in the past three chapters and Appendix A. Orient the 3D Visualization to what you expect the day to bring:
   — Use the *Identity* part of the visualization to solidify your self-acceptance and balance your Critical Judge with your Compassionate Observer. ("I Accept Myself Completely Visualization," page 64)
   — In the *Integration* prioritization, include the major items you will face that day, taking into account your Self-maintenance needs and other external demands to end up with a guilt-free allocation of your time and energy for the day.
   — Offer up any particular problems or issues you are wrestling with during the *Inspiration* part of the visualization. Trust that guidance will come during the day, and be alert to handle any intuitive Icon responses appropriately.
5. Sit quietly and feel the healing of the Pragmatic Spirituality process permeate your being, creating your Inner Edge.
6. Begin your day feeling grounded, self-confident, and energized.

YOUR QUICK RE-FOCUS

1. Take several deep breaths. Consciously center yourself (focus on your center of being).
2. Briefly define the problem or change, including your inner response.
3. Go to the relevant part of the 3D Visualization to make adjustments: Identity to recover your sense of self, Integration to reprioritize, Inspiration to call forth intuitive resources.
4. Affirm your desire for authenticity and appropriateness. Ask, "How would a Fully Functioning Adult handle this?"
5. Move back into action.
6. As soon as practical, consider what, if any, Unfinished Business of yours was triggered by those events—and what insights that gives you.

---

it, and it caused him to act out in various ways with his father, which he often regretted afterward.

FFA Principle: You are not the target. Criticism and judgment often reflect the internalized injunctions of the critical person. We tend to criticize in others what we fear in ourselves.

FFA Rework: Joe was very hurt when his father pointed out his shortcomings, but he realized that his father was projecting his own expectations of himself onto his son. Joe confronted his father and said: "I know how important it is for you to do things right, but I would appreciate it if you would let me do things my way."

Situation: Laura was doing the best she could to take care of her newborn child, but was constantly monitored and criticized by her mother about how Laura could do better with her child's care.

FFA Principle: People react from their own insecurities, thus creating insecurities in others.

FFA Rework: Laura took a well-considered position with her mother: acknowledging her mother's experience in child rearing but then firmly requesting that her mother allow her space to rear her child as she feels is best.

Situation: Peter was always under suspicion because of his past behavior with drugs. He had kicked the habit, but his parents continued to invade his room, looking for evidence of transgressions.

FFA Principle: Personal respect involves holding to boundaries that protect one's personal space.

FFA Rework: Peter discussed with his parents the progress he had made and his desire to establish constructive boundaries, asking that if they have concerns they first talk with him rather than invade his private space.

Situation: Seth's father cared a great deal for his son, but he always felt it necessary to give advice, even when it was uncalled for.

FFA Principle: Respect can be asked for.

FFA Rework: Seth acknowledged his father's experience, but asked that his father respect his boundaries by first asking whether advice was desired.

Being Male

Situation: Greg was always known to be a sensitive person, but was teased by his friends and father as a "wuss" when he cried or otherwise showed his feelings.

FFA Principle: Being accommodating to social pressures doesn't mean negating the truth of your own emotions.

FFA Rework: Greg became more attuned to the "rules of appearing male," and more discerning as to when and where his feelings would be expressed.

Situation: Harry, a lawyer, always felt that drinking was a necessary part of being "one of the boys."

FFA Principle: Core values are essential to self-definition.

FFA Rework: Harry realized that living up to the criteria of others could compromise his character. He now thinks twice before following the crowd, and is less concerned about the opinions of others.

Situation: George was told that part of being a man was to "fix" things. So his approach to everything was to try to fix it and make it better. This frustrated his wife, who was mainly looking for a sympathetic ear.

FFA Principle: Being a man involves being flexible and discerning, and choosing the appropriate strategy for each situation. "Being" can often be more supportive than "fixing."

FFA Rework: George began to realize that "fixing" was not the answer for every situation. He expanded his "tool kit" to include being a supportive listener.

Situation: After his first child was born, Mike was torn between the beliefs handed down in his family about what a father should and should not do and his own feeling about sharing the parenting role equally with his wife.

FFA Principle: Becoming aware of the present context begins the process of extricating oneself from the beliefs that are tied with the context of the past.

FFA Rework: While respecting many of his family's traditions, Mike decided he would not be a prisoner to the past. He assumed the father role most comfortable to him, and politely dealt with the criticism of his relatives.

Being Female

Situation: Mary had been told she could have everything—be a mother, wife, and career woman—but the price was that she was stressed to the verge of a nervous breakdown.

FFA Principle: Fulfilling set roles creates rigid expectations. Carrying out the spirit of the roles with flexible boundaries allows an orchestration of energies that gets things done but isn't tied to expectations.

FFA Rework: Mary realized that she could balance her roles by focusing on her priorities, and she became discerning as to what was important and what could be released or delegated.

Situation: Joanne always felt obligated to "go too far" when she went out on a date. This stemmed from a feeling of guilt if she didn't reciprocate "properly."

FFA Principle: One can find joy from detached giving and receiving (and having no ancillary agendas).

FFA Rework: Joanne discovered the value of her feminine energy and its enhancing effect on the men she dated. She discovered a reciprocity of favors and enhancements from this posture, which enabled her to maintain a standard of integrity with which she was comfortable.

Situation: Each morning, Sally set her VCR to record the day's soap operas, which occupied so much of her life that she rarely went out with friends or spent time developing any type of relationship. Every evening she replayed all the day's episodes, and on weekends she would dress as one of her favorite characters and live that character's life for the weekend.
FFA Principle: Addictions reveal a deep hunger for emotional significance that can only be truly satisfied with real people and substantive relationships.
FFA Rework: Sally's next-door neighbor helped her realize that she needed to redirect her life outward. With the help of a counselor and friends, she developed a wide circle of acquaintances and activities.

Situation: Margaret went rapidly up the corporate ladder thanks to her astuteness and ambitious behavior. Unfortunately, in the process she intimidated a great many people and had few friends.
FFA Principle: A "male impersonator" creates a state of disingenuousness in the workplace. Authenticity provides power for support and respect.
FFA Rework: In her next job, Margaret worked hard on being honest, direct, and firm, but didn't suppress or hide her feminine nature. Her ability to assess the moment and relationships, coupled with her engaging professional demeanor, earned her great respect and support from her peers.

Relationships

Situation: Betty was engaged to a young man everyone liked—except herself. He had all the symbols of success, which all her friends admired, and her parents adored him because he presented an image that had high social status.
FFA Principle: When it comes to relationships, the heart holds higher wisdom than the cognitive mind.
FFA Rework: With great difficulty, because of the arguments put up by her friends and parents, Betty listened to her heart and reached the conclusion that the relationship was wrong for her.

Situation: Everett was caught in an emotional quandary. He was not in love, but he was very comfortable in a relationship.

FFA Principle: In life, we tend to repeat situations of comfort, which can lead to an emotional rut. Discernment and courage are needed in order to move into a life of authenticity and fulfillment.

FFA Rework: Everett came to understand that comfort and love are not the same, and he tapered down the relationship. Afterward, he realized that the relationship had been comfortable because it felt so much like his family of origin.

Children

Situation: Trevor was sixty-seven years old and the CEO of a family-owned company. He treated his son, Sean, who was forty-five, as if he were still his little boy and unable to make intelligent decisions.

FFA Principle: Life changes; we need to renew our perceptions of the growth in people around us and to see the newness of life each day.

FFA Rework: After prompting from close associates, Trevor began taking time to listen to Sean rather than constantly projecting on him the judgments of the past.

Situation: Pierre's father had grown up in fear and oppression during the war in Europe. Pierre still acted out those fears in many ways, even though the present circumstances did not warrant those feelings.

FFA Principle: To identify the origins of our feelings is the beginning of the process of letting them go.

FFA Rework: Pierre talked with his father in order to better understand the context of those feelings. He began a process of dissociation, acknowledging that the feelings he embodied were not his.

Health Issues

Situation: Elliot prided himself on being stoic. One day, after collapsing during a golf game, he had an emergency appendectomy. The doctor told him he could have died if he had waited longer.

FFA Principle: Neglecting physical pain is dismissing the feedback mechanism provided by the body that tells you something is wrong and requires attention.

FFA Rework: Elliot learned that when a pain becomes persistent, it means his body is giving him a signal that should not be ignored.

Situation: Grace had headaches every afternoon. Over time, her use of pain-relief drugs increased.
FFA Principle: Pain often communicates a sense of being "out of balance" in terms of the body's state of homeostatic integrity. Ignoring this creates a state of diminished functioning.
FFA Rework: Grace determined to find out the source of her headaches, which turned out to be stress related.

Situation: David frequently had a few drinks to give him a sense of relaxation from the stresses of his job. After a while, alcohol began to affect his health and his relationships.
FFA Principle: Stress is "in the eye of the beholder" (person being stressed). It is a response, not an input. One can learn how to react non-defensively to a stressful situation.
FFA Rework: David turned to another means of stress management. He found ways to look at the demands of his job as challenges and not become a victim of the stress.

Authority Figures

Situation: William was good at accommodating the needs of a demanding superior. Out of loyalty, he said nothing bad about his boss, but he was aware that he did not have respect from his coworkers, who regarded him as obsequious.
FFA Principle: Loyalty must be reciprocated to have value. Loyalty as a prescriptive value doesn't include loyalty to one's own sense of integrity and core values.
FFA Rework: William discussed with his boss his need for respect as a two-way street, and he gradually found ways to be an effective lieutenant without compromising his feeling of integrity.

Situation: Jack worked late hours and overextended himself in expectation of a promotion, but when the time came he didn't get it.

FFA Principle: Working from a place of projected assumptions often leads to disappointment. Determining and negotiating expectations leads to a place of mutual respect.

FFA Rework: Jack decided to work smarter rather than harder. He took time to get a clear perception of what his superiors wanted, and also determine whether his expectations were reasonable.

Situation: Judith was constantly harassed and verbally demeaned by her boss, but didn't take steps to stop it because she had experienced this type of belittlement and dismissal in her family of origin.

FFA Principle: Setting boundaries is the cornerstone for maintaining a sense of integrity.

FFA Rework: Judith realized that to retain her integrity and her sense of respect, she had to set boundaries in the workplace.

Feedback and Flexibility

As the preceding examples illustrate, a Fully Functioning Adult has the ability to be highly perceptive about what is going on in a situation and to adapt with appropriate behavior. In order to assess all types of feedback from the situation and to act on it, you need to be *disengaged* from what's happening. If your identity is "hooked," you cannot react in the most appropriate manner.

You will need to be aware of subtle *external* feedback you might otherwise miss:

- The other person's hesitation before replying to your statement
- Your child's lower level of enthusiasm for a favorite treat
- A slight edge in the voice of the person on the phone
- The sense that the other person is no longer focusing on what you're saying
- The incongruity of a person's body language and words

The other type of feedback often ignored is that which comes from *within yourself*:

- You are becoming increasingly impatient as you listen to a person who can't seem to come to the point.

- There is something about the person you are dealing with that feels untrustworthy.
- Someone seems to be treating you in a very condescending manner, and it is getting your ire up.
- As your child acts up, you become increasingly concerned that this could turn into an embarrassing scene.
- What is resonating inside you is not consistent with what is being presented to you externally.

The more feedback—external and internal—you monitor, the more appropriate your response will be. The more flexible you are, the more successful that adaptation will be.

Resistance to the Concept of Flexibility

There are certain attitudes that perceive flexibility as an unattractive characteristic:

- "I won't do that as a matter of principle."
- "The one who blinks or backs down is the loser."
- "Give 'em an inch, and they'll take a mile."
- "Indecisiveness is a sign of weakness."

Such attitudes are often justifications for a "do it my way" mentality, an unwillingness or inability to be adaptable.

Let's be very clear that we are advocating the desirability of learning a very important skill—that of being *flexible*. We are *not* advocating a weak backbone, or always giving way to another person, or compromising any of your significant moral or ethical principles. If it feels that way to you, then we suggest you look at it in a clear, two-step approach.

1. First, learn how to be flexible.
2. Then, on the merits of each particular situation, you can decide the degree to which you choose to be flexible.

Certainly, at times it is necessary to take a stand. The pertinent considerations are whether each "stand" is appropriate and just how often a taking-a-stand situation occurs. The person who finds it necessary to take a stand or prove a principle *frequently* is most likely someone with some heavy-duty Unfinished Business. We'll get into this more deeply later on when we discuss "political" situations in the workplace.

The Shadow

We briefly discussed the *Shadow* in Chapter 4. The Shadow represents parts of yourself that you have disowned. These parts are not necessarily negative aspects of yourself, but they are parts that, deep down and at an early point in life, you denied because they were associated with very negative feelings or were considered unacceptable somehow—socially, culturally, or spiritually.

As you proceed in the Pragmatic Spirituality process, it is likely that the Shadow part of your personality will begin to project itself in some manner into your environment, forcing you to deal with what you have denied within yourself. It is very healthy to recognize and accept your Shadow characteristics, as illustrated by the adage

What you resist will persist.

Once your Shadow is accepted as a valid part of your life, you will discover its potential for assisting in your self-development, for among those Shadow characteristics long regarded as unacceptable in your life will be found aspects that are necessary for you to have a well-balanced life. The reason that some healthy Shadow elements may have been judged "bad" is because they contradicted certain unhealthy, Unfinished Business injunctions imposed on you to your disadvantage. Here's an example of a Shadow element that was discovered to be beneficial:

> In an imaging exercise, I was asked to visualize an animal coming down the road of life. (Later I was told this visualization was a metaphor for myself.) I saw a horse, whose characteristics I described as "loyal, hardworking." Then I was asked to do the same for a second animal walking behind the first. I saw a hyena, which I described as "opportunistic, living off the efforts of others." (I was physically repulsed by this image.) Next, I was asked to name the reverse characteristics of each animal. The horse had no life of its own and all its work was for others. The hyena had a very strong sense of self-preservation and looking out for itself.

I was then told that the first animal represented how I perceive myself, and the second animal represented my Shadow.

The image was spot on! The horse represented the values of longsuffering service to others that I had grown up with, whereas the hyena symbolized a part of me that I needed to develop—the ability to look out for my own interests.

In such ways your Shadow can become your guide, providing you with additional feedback as you travel the path toward developing your Inner Edge.

Dealing with Anger and Other Strong Negative Emotions

One of the most beneficial skills of a Fully Functioning Adult is handling those emotions that are considered "negative." When strong emotions such as anger arise, you have a feedback situation with a strong potential for self-learning; however, it is essential to understand the forces at work.

Anger is one of the most powerful emotions we have as humans. Although normally associated with negative outcomes, the energy generated by anger can transcend significant obstacles to bring about change: politically, socially, and on a personal level. Consider the following examples:

- The founder of MADD (Mothers Against Drunk Drivers) used her anger to change the drunk-driving laws in this country.
- A father whose son died of cancer used his anger to raise money to develop a research institute so that others would not have to go through the pain his son had suffered.
- A person with a catastrophic illness used her anger to search for alternative solutions for healing herself and created a whole new path of healing for thousands of ailing people.

How you use anger and other strong emotions is dictated not only by your conditioning, but also by your degree of understanding. When you understand the characteristics of anger, you can better control this emotion rather than being controlled by the fear of its power.

Anger is:

- A powerful emotion that you can harness

- Neither inherently bad nor good

- Judged by its function and the way it is expressed

- Often expressed in "hand-me-down" ways you learned, which can be unlearned

- A powerful motivational driver that can be transformational

- A *secondary* emotion, reflecting some unmet expectation or need

- A potential feedback tool that can enhance your understanding of your needs and expectations

- A double-edged sword:
  — When it is focused on a vision, it can create constructive change.
  — When it is focused on guilt, it can create indulgence in self-pity and depression.

Saying that anger is a secondary emotion emphasizes the need to ask yourself, "Why do I have anger?" The reason for the anger is found in another emotion, more deeply buried: fear, outrage against a perceived wrong, or frustration, for example. If other emotions are suppressed, they will express themselves via anger. For some men, anger is the only emotion available, since sadness, fear, and compassion are regarded as unmanly. This illustrates the feedback potential of anger. When you feel angry, look beneath the anger and find out what is *really* going on.

> **REMEMBER,** angry people can't hear one another while in a state of anger, so continuing an angry encounter is futile in terms of constructive communication and potential resolution.

ANGER MANAGEMENT TECHNIQUES

The most difficult forms of anger to deal with are those that are embedded in old Unfinished Business from the past, because you are reacting to those old patterns rather than the current situation. In such cases, the anger is often disproportionate to the circumstances at hand (because an old wound has been opened). In these situations, it is essential to have a technique or script that will take you out of the situation and create a "time-out."

Stage 1: Disengage

When you are angry, say one of the following to the other person:

- "I'm sorry, but I need some time to figure out this situation. I will get back to you then."
- "Please give me some space so I can figure this out."

Be assertive, because the person may not want to disengage. After disengaging, if only slightly, you can then move into stage 2.

Stage 2: Perspective

Ask yourself these introspective questions:

- *What are the unmet needs and expectations in this situation?* These lead to frustrations, which in turn lead to anger. Understanding the unmet needs and expectations and addressing them in the dialogue dismantles the anger.
- *Who is the anger directed at?* Anger is often displaced onto others. An example would be a husband displacing his anger at his boss onto his wife when he comes home from work.

These three origins of anger (unmet needs, unmet expectations, and displaced anger) often come from one's Unfinished Business.

Stage 3: Dialogue

This allows healing. Return to the people involved in the anger situation.

- Use "I" language and focus on the origins of the anger.
- Focus on the dynamics behind the anger.

Dialogue from a place of acknowledgment, insight, and the wish for resolution creates healing that begins to dissipate the oppressive energy accompanying anger. For example, you could say, "I am sorry for the miscommunication. I understand that you had some unmet needs here that created the anger. Here is what I propose for meeting your needs."

The way Unfinished Business works in conjunction with anger is that historical parts of a person—including attitudes, expectations, and needs—are projected into that person's current environment and relationships. When there is dissonance between these internal elements and the external situations the person encounters, frustration occurs, followed by anger. In this way, anger is an *opportunity* for self-examination and movement toward growth. When you don't use anger as a feedback opportunity, then the patterns will repeat themselves, leading to escalating anger and increasing destructiveness.

You now have an understanding and beginning foundation of how the Pragmatic Spirituality process can give you an Inner Edge on an individual level. In the next section, we will move to the workplace, a much more difficult and challenging environment requiring a more sophisticated understanding and proficient practice of Pragmatic Spirituality.

Let's take Pragmatic Spirituality to work!

Chapter 9 Highlights

Pragmatic Spirituality is implemented with a Daily PS Focus *(page 101) and a* Quick Re-Focus *(page 102).*

The Fully Functioning Adult *(FFA) is an idealized concept exemplifying the practice of Pragmatic Spirituality. Asking oneself, "What would a Fully Functioning Adult do (or have done) in this situation?" is a useful tool for assessing situations.*

Two key FFA capabilities are (1) being fully aware of all feedback (external and internal) related to each situation (especially if it is problematic), and (2) being highly flexible so as to be able to respond most appropriately to the situation.

Flexibility does not *mean compromising principles. First, learn to be flexible. Then, on the merits of each particular situation, you can decide the degree to which you choose to be flexible.*

The Shadow *(disowned) parts of yourself may, in fact, have potential for assisting in your self-development.*

Anger often hides other emotions. When anger or other strong emotions arise, you have a feedback situation with a strong potential for self-learning. Take advantage of it!

Anger management techniques are on page 113.

PRAGMATIC SPIRITUALITY IN YOUR WORKPLACE

III

10

APPLYING PRAGMATIC SPIRITUALITY IN YOUR JOB

There are those who work all day, those who dream all day, and those who spend an hour dreaming before setting to work to fulfill those dreams. Go into the third category, because there's virtually no competition.

—STEVEN J. ROSS CEO, Time Warner, Inc.

SECTION II GAVE YOU a working knowledge of Pragmatic Spirituality and its application at the personal level—leading to the development of your Inner Edge. In this section, we'll address how Pragmatic Spirituality can give you that Inner Edge at work. But first, to put things in perspective, it would be useful to quickly review how the work environment has changed dramatically in recent years. One of the most significant changes is in the type of employee best suited to deal with the new type of organizational role: adaptable, quick learner, able to assess and respond appropriately to changing situations, comfortable with the tenuous nature of today's job. In short, these are the attributes of a Fully Functioning Adult as described in Chapter 9.

The Radically Changing Workplace

Over the past several decades a number of radical changes have occurred in the organization and the workplace:

- Jobs don't last as long.
- Skills don't last as long.
- Organizations don't last as long.
- Technologies and products don't last as long.
- Organizations are structured and run in radically new ways.
- "Regular" jobs are being replaced by contingency hires and outsourcing.
- The marketplace is increasingly global in nature.
- Information generation is increasing exponentially.

With all this turnover and turmoil, "job security"—which employees have traditionally desired (although seldom in reality experienced)—is a thing of the past.

The perception of job security was based on the implied contract between employer and employee: "Be loyal and work hard, and the company will take care of you." The long-term job was the goal of most employees, and they willingly bought into the idea of the company as family. This served the interests of employer organizations; however, it must be recognized that the key contributing factor was the typical employee's desire to find his sense of identity at work.

The widespread downsizing in the 1980s and 1990s came as a painful wake-up call, both to employers (the need for new ways of doing business) and employees (the need for a new attitude toward employment). As a silver lining of those troubled times, the stigma of being laid off pretty much disappeared and the need to "manage your career" was reluctantly accepted—amid occasional wishful hopes that the good old days might return and we'd be "taken care of" again.

Congruence Between Employer and Employee Interests

As stated earlier, one of the results of the changes in the modern workplace is that today's organizations require a radically different employee from the traditional organization (see Figure 10.1).

Clearly, the evolving organization needs employees who have the Inner Edge—the authenticity and appropriateness achieved by Pragmatic Spirituality and exemplified in a Fully Functioning Adult. This growing congruency between the needs of organizations and the needs of individuals should result in a reduction of the polarization between the two and a growing recognition of their mutual interdependence. In Section IV we will examine the implications of this on the organization from the employer's standpoint. The remainder of this section will focus on how the principles and practices of Pragmatic Spirituality from Section II can best be put into practice in the workplace. For a more complete discussion of the radically changing workplace, see Appendix B.

FIGURE 10.1 TODAY'S ORGANIZATION NEEDS A NEW TYPE OF EMPLOYEE

YESTERDAY'S EMPLOYEE	TODAY'S EMPLOYEE
Sends information up the organization and acts on instructions received from superiors	External market conditions require him or her to react quickly, taking initiative within established guidelines.
Has been working with the same information base for years	Must be able to assimilate frequently changing information, including quantum changes
Degree of decision-making scope is limited by one's place in the hierarchy.	Is given considerable latitude in decision making
Assumes he or she will be with the company for entire career	Expects to stay as long as one's skills are needed, but not for a long time
"This job is my identity"	"This job is a job"
Termination would be very traumatic; employee would have difficulty finding the next job	Keeps one's network current; accepts it will be necessary to find other jobs
Has limited flexibility, adaptability	Is very adaptable
Good communicator within accustomed context	Able to communicate and deal with varied situations

Applying Pragmatic Spirituality to Your Job—a Challenging Arena for Personal Change

This may sound familiar:

> I start the day off with a meditation, which leaves me with a great sense of well-being and stability. The world seems bright and good. I'm able to transcend the petty irritations of commuting into work. I arrive at work resolved to maintain that feeling of balance and serenity throughout the day. But very soon, that resolve is lost in the harsh realities of deadlines, bickering, and fragmentation. I end the day with that familiar depleted feeling, so different from how I started the day.

Why is it more difficult to apply Pragmatic Spirituality in the workplace than in other parts of life? There are two basic reasons:

1. Work, for most people, is the source of many factors of identity: economic livelihood, social interactions, status with others, pride of accomplishment, and so on.
2. The workplace is a much tougher environment in which to maintain one's identity.

For these reasons, it is clear why a Pragmatic Spirituality practice that has been developed on the personal level may need some bolstering to contend with the harsh realities of the workplace.

Maintaining the three Dimensions of Pragmatic Spirituality—Identity, Integration, and Inspiration—under the pressures of the workplace requires a much higher degree of proficiency in these techniques. Part of this proficiency comes from plain old-fashioned practice, every day. And part comes from a clearer understanding of the destabilizing forces in the workplace.

Pragmatic Spirituality in the Workplace: The Identity Dimension

The discussion in this and the following chapters assumes that you are thoroughly familiar with the material on the personal level of Pragmatic Spirituality in Section II.

The essence of *Identity* is a realistic, well-balanced understanding of who you are, along with a well-developed sense of self-acceptance. Once you have worked on this at the personal level, the next step is to see how your identity stands up under the rigors of the workplace. Don't be surprised when you start regressing into old patterns of "Who am I?" or "How am I doing?" Especially for people who have derived much of their sense of self from their work, arriving at a clear, intrinsic sense of identity will take some time—and the place to do it is at work.

Is Your Identity Intertwined with Your Job?

Work is a very powerful factor in the lives of most people. It provides not only material livelihood, but also a significant social context and a major stage for gaining and demonstrating proficiency. In short, for many people, work is a primary source of identity. The problem arises when one's identity becomes too intertwined with one's work situation—the antidote includes the following:

1. Find the locus of your identity within yourself.
    A retired CEO discovered that his golf buddies for over twenty years stopped seeing him after he retired. He realized that they were playing golf with his "role" rather than with him as a person, and he worked through the initial hurt to find a sense of self not dependent on others.

2. Establish boundaries for your professional role.
    An executive assistant began having panic attacks when her boss began using her to get his laundry, buy his wife gifts, and run numerous personal errands for him. She realized that he had made her his second wife, maid, and personal assistant, which interfered with her job-related duties.

3. Maintaining your sense of identity within all the roles you play.
    An assistant department head turned down a promotion. She was in the process of a divorce, and realized that she would not be able to reconcile the conflicting demands of both roles or maintain her inner balance and the other interests in her life.

Work is a tougher environment for maintaining your identity. Your successes or failures are more obvious and can have profound implications, for the organization and for your livelihood. As you move up the organizational ladder, there are fewer and fewer clear-cut rules and yardsticks for measuring performance, and politics becomes increasingly prevalent.

Let's review some of the aspects of the Identity Dimension discussed in Chapter 6, this time from the perspective of the workplace. The essential aspect of the Identity Dimension is that your sense of self—your identity—must be *yours*, not a hand-me-down version. You must have achieved a genuine acceptance of yourself—faults and all—and weeded out all of the inherited "shoulds" and "oughts" until each holographic strand in your Identity Visualization is authentically *you*. Then your identity will be well grounded and resilient enough to deal with the most challenging situations you may encounter.

Doing/Having Versus Being

In Chapter 6, we discussed the importance of achieving a balance between the *Being* and *Doing/Having* aspects of identity. Since the emphasis of most work environments is strongly on the Doing/Having, it is important to give sufficient attention to your Being in order to keep your identity in order.

The "I Accept Myself Completely" affirmation used in your Daily PS Focus is a good stabilizer with which to begin the workday.

> *Whatever my track record,*
> *whatever my imperfections,*
> *I accept myself completely—*
> *without reservations.*

The beauty of this affirmation is that it works both ways. If your track record has been disappointing, it affirms your self-acceptance in spite of that. If your track record has been above average, it is a reminder to not make your self-worth dependent on rewards and accolades, however pleasant and satisfying they may be.

On-the-Job Advisers: Your Critical Judge and Compassionate Observer

Remember these two inner voices from Chapter 6? We hope that in your inner work from the last section, you've established your Compassionate Observer as a spokesperson to balance out your Critical Judge. But be sure the Compassion-ate Observer accompanies you to work! While you're on the job, monitor your self-talk going just at the level of conscious awareness. You will probably find that the Compassionate Observer can be a great help in dealing more construc-tively with yourself *and* with your fellow workers.

Use Your PS Techniques on the Job

Start out each day with a regular Daily PS Focus, including the 3D Visualization. That forms the basis for a Quick Re-Focus when needed during the workday.

- As you arrive at work, do a Quick Re-Focus, reaffirming your self-acceptance, your Identity hologram, and your feeling of groundedness and value. Make your Quick Re-Focus as much of a habit as checking your appearance in the mirror.

- If at any time you feel your identity becoming ungrounded or your inner balance disturbed, stop, take a breath, and do a Quick Re-Focus. Let it bring you back into proper perspective.

- Following a disturbing incident, take a few minutes to reflect on what hap-pened. What was it that threw you off balance? What were the "button-pushing" words that got to you? Quickly write down the key points so you can consider them later.

- If possible, get an objective perspective from someone who witnessed the incident. Her perspective of what actually transpired may be more objec-tive than your recollection. Write it down! (Pay attention to the degree of discrepancy between the objective account and your perception.)

- Review the incident. Ask, "How would a Fully Functioning Adult have reacted?" What are the lessons for you? What Unfinished Business does it indicate? Do a more in-depth Daily PS Focus or a QDM session (discussed in greater detail in Chapter 11) to get a deeper perspective. Find a key word to weave into your regular Daily PS Focus to reinforce your increased understanding.

In this way, day-to-day events can become useful feedback about additional work needed on your Unfinished Business.

Your Integration Dimension in the Workplace

The Integration Dimension has to do with the allocation of your energies in a manner most appropriate to the present circumstances. As we discussed in Chapter 7, the first allocation is between your Self-maintenance and external demands; the second allocation is among the various external demands. That's difficult enough on the personal level, but the real challenge comes in the work context, where there is never enough time. People and projects compete for your attention, and there is a strong tendency for the job to take precedence over everything—family, friends, and yourself.

The allocation done during the Integration part of the 3D Visualization is very similar to the prioritization commonly done in business—determining how limited assets should be distributed among competing applications. However, there is ample evidence that proficiency in prioritizing business matters does not necessarily impart a proficiency in the Integration Dimension of Pragmatic Spirituality, as the following two examples illustrate.

A top movie producer was deeply enmeshed in his business. The pressures of his work left little time for his wife or children. Unfortunately, he never thought in terms of emotional priorities. Pulled by its stimulation and gratification, he spent more and more of his time in his work. He became aware of the fallacy of his priorities only when he lost his son to drug abuse and his wife to alcoholism. He wasn't the cause; he just hadn't been there when they needed him.

Anne was both a manager and a supermom. She had difficulty in juggling her roles of professional woman, mother, wife, den mother, and housekeeper. Only when she had a nervous breakdown did she realize the absolute necessity of prioritizing her life for her emotional and mental health.

What Are the Criteria for Prioritization?

A valid business prioritization cannot be made without a business plan that defines longer-term strategic goals. This characterizes the environment in which the organization operates (the strengths and weaknesses of the organization vis-à-vis the competition) and arrives at a plan that makes best use of the company's assets with the least downside ramifications to its liabilities.

Likewise, the prioritization done in the Integration part of the Daily PS Focus requires a set of criteria. These criteria start with the Identity part of the Daily PS Focus, which then forms the basis for the Integration determination—which, in turn, is informed and reinforced by the Inspiration Dimension. A more detailed set of criteria could be determined by a QDM session. Thus, Pragmatic Spirituality enables you to establish criteria from a sufficiently broad context, avoiding the all-too-common mistake of the "successful executive" who realizes, too late, that his tunnel-vision prioritization failed to adequately encompass those he loves.

Looking at the full context of one's life does complicate decisions, especially related to work.

> In the classic tale *The Man in the Gray Flannel Suit*, the protagonist had to choose between attending a business meeting very important to his career or his son's ball game. He chose the game. This seems insignificant now, but in the days when executives put their jobs above every other aspect of life, this was a brave—and, from a career standpoint, potentially costly—decision.

Most of your Integration prioritizations will most likely be concerned with less momentous issues, but big or small, make sure they are consistent with all three of your Pragmatic Spirituality Dimensions.

Self-Maintenance and Self-Discipline

These tools, which were described in Chapter 5, need to be well polished and proficiently used in the workplace arena.

- Knowing what is needed for your Self-maintenance and making sure it is done is not easy, particularly in a context of heavy overtime and business travel. If you don't look out for yourself, who will?

- Being able to say "no" and to set limits is vital to your self-interests and your effectiveness on your job.

Once again, the pressures and demands of the workplace make it more difficult to assert these behaviors—and more important that you do assert them.

It might be useful to go back over Chapter 5 periodically to keep the "edge" on your Self-maintenance and Self-discipline. And stay alert for any Unfinished Business that might undermine your effective use of these tools.

Boundaries in the Workplace

Recall that in Chapter 7, we discussed the importance of boundaries and outlined how to establish and maintain them. You will find many opportunities to use boundaries in the context of the workplace—with a strong payoff when you do, as demonstrated in the following example.

> My boss was notorious for unrealistic deadlines. She would come in at 4 P.M. and say "I'd like this finished before you leave today, please"—and it would be a two-hour project. I'd leave work at 7, late for my date or dinner, cursing her. Finally, I realized it wasn't her—it was me! I met with her one morning, explained that I was fully willing to support her and pull my fair share, especially in emergencies, but these routine

HERE ARE SOME SUGGESTIONS to keep in mind:
- Be mindful of your boundaries.
- If your boundaries are violated, discuss your thoughts with a coworker for some objective feedback.
- Consider whether you should discuss it with a supervisor before addressing it with the person at issue.
- For your meeting with the boundary jumper, choose your words carefully. Write a "script" and practice it. Try it on someone.
- Meet with the person with whom you have an issue at a nonstressful time.
- Start with, "This may be something that you're completely unaware of, but it's important to me that I discuss it with you."
- Stress "I" language (explaining your perspective) rather than "you" language (which tends to sound accusatory to the other person).
- Listen carefully to the other person's reaction. If he sounds defensive, stay centered and defuse the situation.
- Be ready with an alternative suggestion that would work for both of you.

last-minute assignments were very intrusive on my time. I said, "I really need to have an assignment on my desk by 3 in the afternoon with some prior notice or I may not be able to complete it that day because of an existing personal commitment." My heart was in my mouth, but she agreed with me and apologized. Things have been much better since then.

"GOOD FENCES MAKE GOOD NEIGHBORS," and "Good boundaries make healthy work relationships."

Most supervisors and managers would probably agree with the concept of boundaries, since they are consistent with the concepts of task allocation, effective interactions, and appropriate behavior in the workplace. However, Pragmatic Spirituality reminds us that the responsibility for establishing *appropriate boundaries* is up to the *individual* involved, not the supervisor.

The Integration portion of a Daily PS Focus can be very useful for shifting gears and dealing with changing work demands. The important thing is that reprioritization is done in a systematic way so that you can trust the outcome, and so that you are able to move on to the new course of action without a lot of second-guessing as to whether you made the right decision. A Quick Re-Focus centering on Integration will give you greater clarity about balancing your Self-maintenance, the demands of your job, prioritizing tasks and needs, and ensuring that you don't hamstring yourself due to any Unfinished Business.

Your Inspiration Dimension in the Workplace

Interestingly, inspiration has always been recognized in the workplace, although in different terms. Few, if any, people in business would disagree that "flashes of insight" or "intuitive awareness" do occur on occasions. No doubt, you can recall when you had an out-of-the-blue inspiration or made an excellent decision based mostly on gut feel.

Pragmatic Spirituality gains greater access to your nonrational intuitive resources in two ways: the 3D Visualization in your Daily PS Focus, and a focused inquiry technique called *Quantum Decision Making* (QDM) described in the next chapter. QDM, which has been proven in both individual and business contexts, is an extension of the Inspiration Dimension. Ron has taught QDM to managers in a variety of organizational situations to enhance the effectiveness of decision making for both individuals and groups. It involves learning how to get your right/intuitive mind and left/rational mind to act in concert.

Be Alert to the Limits of Pragmatic Spirituality in Some Workplaces

Using the Pragmatic Spirituality principles will enable you to perceive situations more clearly and deal with them more appropriately, your actions based on the reality of the circumstances rather than being compromised by old inappropriate behavioral patterns by yourself or others. In a workplace where the overall agenda is to further the organization's well-being by working smarter and more efficiently, Pragmatic Spirituality techniques have the potential to make a big change for the better for both you and your coworkers.

However, there are other kinds of workplaces, where the underlying agenda is less constructive and results oriented, and certain work circumstances are out-

---

PRAGMATIC SPIRITITUALITY may not be possible in every workplace, for example:

- It may be that workplace problems revolve around one individual, and that the person in charge is unaware of the situation or incapable of dealing with it. In that case, you may be able to work with the supervisor or head of human resources as a change agent.
- It's trickier if the cause of the unhealthiness is the person in charge. In a larger organization, it may be possible to appeal to a higher level of supervision, although that route must be done very diplomatically and is fraught with danger for you. It is highly unlikely that the higher-ups are unaware of your boss's behavior; therefore, there is probably some reason that it has been allowed to continue.
- If you're in a smaller organization with a dysfunctional workplace, your chances of ameliorating the situation are very slim. Whoever is the source of the problem, the boss has allowed it to continue and has a need for it in one way or another—as much as she may protest to the contrary.

right pathological, such as covert money laundering or drugs. Most business organizations have reasonably constructive objectives and intentions, but occasionally in pockets within the organization, the work environment can be poisoned by one or more individuals.

In these situations Pragmatic Spirituality will enable you to see clearly what is happening, which is extremely important because highly manipulative people are very skilled at shrugging the blame onto others. With Pragmatic Spirituality you will be able to work more effectively within these circumstances. The question is, how long should you stay there?

Bear in mind that it is extremely difficult to change anything within an organization. It takes a lot of time and energy, and the "change agent" is always on shaky ground. If you persist in trying to make significant changes in the workplace—without having been formally appointed as a change agent and receiving appropriate support and compensation—it may be that your motivation is less idealistic and more connected with some Unfinished Business.

Workplace-Specific Unfinished Business

Career counselors are accustomed to dealing with people trapped for long periods in unhealthy work situations because of a lack of awareness or ability to leave and find another job. This behavior clearly stems from some Unfinished Business related to the need for dysfunctional relationships or for lost causes.

It may be that you missed these Unfinished Business items in your personal Pragmatic Spirituality work because they are specific to the workplace, such as preconceptions with a distorting influence on your attitudes and behavior about work. If you are willing to take a dispassionate look at these, there can be surprising outcomes leading to a deepening sense of yourself and a clearer sense of what you should (and should not) do. Here are some examples of common workplace misconceptions:

- The company is loyal to you.
- Your job will always be there.
- The business is too powerful to be overthrown by the winds of change.
- There is only one vocation in which you fit.
- Your identity is with your job.
- Your job is more important than your personal relationships.
- The value of your job lies in how hard you work.

At this point you can see where Pragmatic Spirituality becomes a turning point in defusing these invalid scripts and moving ahead in greater authenticity and appropriateness to develop your Inner Edge at work.

In the next chapter we'll explore the details of Quantum Decision Making (QDM) as a practical application of intuition in the workplace. Then the subsequent chapters will examine specific pitfalls in the application of Pragmatic Spirituality in the workplace.

CHAPTER 10 HIGHLIGHTS

Sweeping paradigm shifts are changing workplace circumstances radically, creating a potential congruence between the interests of the individual and the organization.

The evolving organization needs employees who have the Inner Edge—the authenticity and appropriateness achieved by Pragmatic Spirituality and exemplified in a Fully Functioning Adult.

Maintaining the three Dimensions of Pragmatic Spirituality—Identity, Integration, and Inspiration—in the workplace requires a much higher degree of proficiency than on the personal level.

The Identity Dimension in the workplace is complicated by the powerful influence work exerts on identity and livelihood, the single-minded emphasis on results, competitive environments that create worker friction, dysfunctional and/or incompetent supervisors, and politics. Counter these with awareness of Identity Dimension factors, Being versus Doing/Having balance, your Compassionate Observer, and the Daily PS techniques.

The Integration Dimension: prioritization of one's interests can be extremely difficult because of workplace pressures and one's desire to be a productive team member. Counter these with Self-maintenance and Self-discipline, boundaries, and by using the 3D Visualization to determine criteria for prioritizations.

The Inspiration Dimension supports the other two Dimensions and can be applied to the workplace by the 3D Visualization and the QDM technique.

The potential of Pragmatic Spirituality is constrained in some workplace environments where either the organization is dysfunctional or pockets are poisoned by particular managers.

Pragmatic Spirituality can be of great value in helping you perceive the source of a workplace problem, but resist the tendency to try to solve it unless that is your specific assignment.

Resist the temptation to change an organization unless you have been given the role and full authority to act as change agent by someone who will back you. Otherwise you are better off leaving to find a more salubrious situation elsewhere.

Be alert to Unfinished Business that is work related and that you may have missed in your personal inner work.

11

QDM: QUANTUM
DECISION MAKING

For whereas the mind works in possibilities,
the intuitions work in actualities, and what you
intuitively desire, that is possible to you.

—D. H. LAWRENCE

Focusing on Specifics

In Chapter 8, we discussed Inspiration: the idea that you can open yourself to an awakened state of significance never before experienced by integrating your perceptions and the dimensions that lie within you. In that chapter, you also began developing your ability to access information and creative inspiration from a more *authentic* source—one that is congruent with universal principles interconnecting all of life—and learning to surf your internal Internet. It is in this chapter that the *Quantum Decision Making* (QDM) process launches you into enhancing your intuitional proficiency—initially prompted through your Inspiration Visualization—by giving you a technique to more fully interpret your intuitive Icons and to focus on *specific issues.*

On a day-to-day basis, the Daily PS Focus establishes an underlying level of Pragmatic Spirituality in all its aspects: centeredness, self-worth, prioritization of time and energy, and reconnection with intuitive resources. QDM, on the other hand, is brought to bear when you have a need for intuitive input on a *specific* question or problem. Thus, it is one of the highly operative components of an Inner Edge, and of a Fully Functioning Adult. Going beyond your initial inter-

INTUITIVE PROFICIENCY: The person seeking increased self-awareness will find many ways intuitive proficiency can assist in the personal growth process, such as a greater awareness of the roots of one's fears, the strength of one's resources, and the potential of one's relationships; or insights into questions about one's mission in life. For the businessperson, there are countless applications for intuitive inputs: hiring decisions, market trends, creative solutions to business situations, product development, customer needs, increasing sales and productivity, and new market opportunities.

nal Icons, QDM uses a series of specific questions to unlock the deeper meaning behind the Icons. Ron has used the QDM process in many situations, both with individuals and in the workplace, to help people draw on their intuitive resources to address complex questions and scenarios that are beyond rational and logical analysis.

What Is QDM?

QDM is a problem-solving, decision-making process that involves a dialogue between the intuitive and rational sides of your nature. By including processes of both sides of your brain, QDM achieves an extension of knowledge and awareness that goes beyond what can be accomplished by using only one side of the brain. With QDM, you learn to be *ambidextrous* with your mind, thus expanding the possibilities of gathering data, exercising options, awareness, gaining wisdom, and being more fully creative. The outcome: the ability to bring both sides of your brain into a balance of mutual respect of capabilities, along with an equal level of proficiency on each side—achieving your Inner Edge.

ACCESSING BOTH SIDES of the brain leads to true *wisdom*, which is beyond the external and physical. Wisdom is awareness of "what is," characterized by clarity, nuance, meaning. It is to know the value of balance in all facets of existence—an attempt to be present in each moment of life.

A key element of the QDM process is that it operates in a Socratic fashion—questions are asked in order to assess a situation or a field of facts that have bearing on the problem or issue being addressed. For example, here are five questions that might be addressed when a company is considering the possibility of a co-venture:

1. Which company should we proceed with on this co-venture?
2. Which relationship would best serve the interests of the company?
3. What are the short- and long-term consequences of such a relationship?
4. What are the most critical variables in the relationship agreement?
5. What are the trade-offs between the various candidates?

Use of QDM would *not* be indicated for discerning the answers to a *straightforward* question *where all the relevant data is already at hand,* since this kind of decision is readily made using only the rational side of the brain. QDM, on the other hand, is best suited to bring the resources of both sides of the brain to bear on *complex questions* with *incomplete information.* Most of the more difficult and momentous decisions in life fit into the latter category.

Here's an example of how QDM actually works.

The Publisher

After a seminar on QDM, one of the participants—the head of a publishing company—approached Ron with a question. One of the key success factors for his company was hiring the right people, both employees and subcontractors; however, interviewing and screening people consumed large amounts of his time.

Ron suggested that the publisher create an intuitive "software program" that would act as a screening assessment. The publisher explained that he looked for people who could write well, had good graphic sense, worked well in a team environment, were creative, and had a good repertoire of people skills.

Ron got the publisher into a relaxed state, and then asked his intuitive mind to bring forth an Icon that would communicate the qualities he was screening for. The Icon that emerged was a Swiss army knife. As the publisher looked more closely at the knife, he saw that each tool communicated one of his screening criteria. This resulted in a very effective technique for assessing someone during an interview. He would focus on the person energetically, and then briefly close his eyes. He would immediately see the Swiss army knife. If the knife had less than five of the blades open (each blade representing one of his screening criteria), the interview would not last very long. If five or more blades were open, he would take the time to take the inter-view deeper.

Initially, he kept notes to verify that what was communicated by the "knife blades" was consistent with his rational conclusions and observations. He found that this intuitive mind was very much on the mark.

This example is typical of the QDM process, which has been used and proved effective by managers at all levels, including some who came to the pro-cess very skeptically but went away convinced. (Both the prior and following examples have been condensed for brevity.) In the following example, a group of doubting businesspeople used QDM to coordinate the highly intuitive/creative side of the brain with the rational/analytical side to arrive at an *integrated* solution.

The Computer Company

One of Ron's consulting clients needed to devise a new corporate logo. An outside firm had made several submissions, based on a stylized rendering of the company's name, but there was a sense among upper management that these were off the mark. Ron challenged the management committee, which represented every division in the company, to design a logo. The initial reaction was, "We're businesspeople, not artists." But several of them had worked with the QDM process, and they encour-aged the others to give it a try.

The managers gathered and, after some quieting and relaxing imaging, Ron asked them to use their analytical minds to recall the course of development the com-pany had taken as it evolved into its current significant position in the world market. The managers began to come up with "felt" attributes that they saw as parts of their vision of the company. Though they were initially somewhat hesitant, soon their input came more rapidly, one comment building on another. Each response was listed on a whiteboard. After the momentum slowed somewhat, the group clustered together related inputs and came up with six primary attributes: world leadership, vision, quick response to market needs, having a large share of the market, positively influencing related industries, and strong innovation.

These were discussed further and listed on the board, and Ron began the QDM process by asking the question, "What logo would best reflect these felt qualities of the company?" The majority of the managers had a very fast response, which they shared without any attempt at explanation or interpretation. Several saw dif-ferent kinds of a world globe, and as they shared their thoughts, the image evolved.

Others saw variations on this theme, and suddenly images of an eagle were being mentioned, in different positions: in flight, at rest, soaring, majestically perched on a ledge, and so on. As each person came up with an Icon, the group's perceived image shifted.

The end result was a logo consolidating all the images that, all agreed, captured the essence of the company as they knew it. Everyone was astonished how QDM had achieved such a dynamic outcome in such a short period of time.

QDM can have a profound influence on one's self-knowledge and self-navigation through life. When you have developed clarity about your own essential identity and abilities, then the intuitive mind can in nanoseconds give you feedback as to whether your considered action is in alignment with your true purpose. In whatever context, the answers you receive in the QDM process may very well surprise you.

> **QDM IS A TOOL** for broadening your baseline of information so that timely and incisive decisions and interactions can be made. It enhances your ability to deal with issues related to Unfinished Business, projections, assumptions, hidden agendas, and unconscious dynamics that are intertwined with each situation and interaction.

Three Levels of Perception

An important aspect of the question-and-answer portion of the QDM process is the ability to recognize the full implications and ramifications of a course of action being considered or a solution being sought. QDM does this by examining the *intuitive* response on *each* of three levels of perception.

We are conditioned to see the world through our five senses of physical perception. QDM's three levels of perception involve input not only from your physical senses but also from your emotions and your *intuition*. Therefore, the objects that you are familiar with in the physical world may very well show up as Icons in your intuitive process but—and this is an important distinction—they will have a deeper level of emotional significance and meaning for you beyond the way you normally perceive them.

Level 1: The realm of what is *observed intuitively* about the physical world in conjunction with the perceptions of our five physical senses

Level 2: The realm of *metaphor*, where, beyond the obvious physical properties of our external reality, there are underlying symbols with a sense of *emotional* significance requiring interpretation.

Level 3: The realm of *transcendent significance* applied to one's life in a broader context, fully integrating the intuitive input from your Icons.

The three levels of perception are integral to QDM, as they provide the framework with which to reveal the hidden depths of your Icons. Here are two examples showing how the three levels of perception are used.

Here is an example on the personal level:

Level 1—Observation: A man has a wonderful sailboat (the intuited Icon) that he takes out each weekend and finds pleasure in sailing.

Level 2—Interpretation: The sailboat is a metaphor for his feelings of freedom associated with sailing and being in full navigational control.

Level 3—Transcendent significance: The sailboat represents his life—he wishes to be in control of it in order to find a higher level of meaning within his own ocean of consciousness.

Here is an example in the workplace:

Level 1—Observation: A CEO with an English surname saw an impressive but empty medieval English tower (intuited Icon).

Level 2—Interpretation: The CEO was able to master the outside world of work, but his internal world of feelings and relationships was empty and void of meaning. The tower was a bastion of strength and protection but the inside was cold and devoid of any human presence and connectivity.

Level 3—Transcendent significance: His financial/business empire was highly successful but his personal life lacked warmth and connection with loved ones. Until the outer and inner worlds are integrated, his life will be fragmented and incomplete.

The QDM process employs all three levels of perception to help one fully understand responses received from one's intuitive resources. Again, QDM is used to find answers and solutions to specific problems or issues extending to all aspects of one's life (personal and work)—it is a very focused process with clear objectives of greater and deeper clarity.

The Quantum Decision Making Process

There are three parts to the QDM process, at times looping back and reinforcing one another.

PART I: FORMULATE YOUR QUESTIONS

Working with the intuitive mind, the rational mind needs to create questions that are focused, clear, and concise. Simple and clear questions garner simple and clear answers. It may seem more efficient to put all the elements into one complex question; however, that muddies the water because the intuitive response will then be more complex and therefore more difficult to interpret.

A clear focus coupled with a clear context increases the likelihood of getting a clear answer.

THE QDM PROCESS consists of an ever-evolving series of questions (who, what, when, where, why, and how) geared toward gaining a complete picture. Each question is simple, focused, and within a context. Interpretation of the answers to the questions should take into consideration the three levels of perception: the five senses, emotions, and intuition.

The following are important questions that address personal, interpersonal, social, and professional arenas. Note that each request is made in terms of *one* focus, such as a need, fear, resource, or action, and the focus of each request is placed within a *context*. This can be a time context (within a day or weeks), an environmental context (home, work, school), or a relationship context (interpersonal, you and a company, you and an opportunity).

- What does [my relationship, the company, my family, my department . . .] need in order to [solve, heal, rectify, uncover, have closure, move forward, conquer inertia, function well, realize a profit . . .]?

- What is missing in my [life, relationship, job, family . . .]?
- What is my [shortcoming, blind spot, weakness, fear, denial, obstacle . . .] in [my job, my marriage, my relationships, getting closure on this deal, moving forward in my life . . .]?
- What is my [mission, opportunity, lesson, best resource . . .]?
- What could I do differently to ensure [success, completion, closure, a win-win situation . . .] in the area of my [job, relationship, sales, investments, health, associates . . .]?
- What do I have that is required or needed by my [company, spouse, children, market, competitors . . .]?
- What attributes do I have that are rejected by [the market, my spouse, my children, my work, my associates . . .]?
- What are the consequences of this [action, choice, decision, focus, direction . . .]?

These questions are extremely powerful and concise. You need not ask all of them, and you need not ask them in a particular order. But you must ask only one question and keep only one focus at a time. What determines the direction you take in dialoguing with the intuitive mind depends on what type of information is needed to make a decision or to just understand the nature of an occurrence. The QDM process is iterative in that you continue asking questions until you feel you've attained a level of clarity that has meaning for you.

INTUITIVE ANSWERS MAY COME directly to you in an instant "inner knowing" without QDM or other processes. The advantage of the QDM method is that it provides you with a systematic process for putting questions to your intuitive mind and techniques for interpreting the Icons that come in response. Four important things to bear in mind:

1. If an intuitive answer is not clear, ask again.
2. In order to obtain clear answers, be centered, calm, and present in your body. If these conditions are elusive, find another time and place.
3. To discover their meaning, you must treat intuitive Icons *metaphorically*.
4. Analyzing Icons with the rational mind will not lead to clarity.

Part 2: Process the Icon Responses

Reviewing the "Guidelines for Processing Intuitive Icons" in Chapter 8 (page 92), you will see that the intuitive mind can be accessed readily after you have learned the discipline of being in a state of receptivity. The QDM process takes this to a higher level, making an *empathetic connection* with the intuitive mind's answers to your questions via the Icons you've received.

No matter how simple or trivial the Icon may appear to be, it may contain a great deal of meaning. The more you can be "one with the Icon"—the empathetic connection—by means of your senses, the greater amount of information will come to you, moving you from the perceptions of Level 1 (observation) into those of Level 2 (interpretation) and Level 3 (transcendent significance).

At first it will seem awkward to work with these Icons because it is unlike anything you normally do. It is also frustrating, because there is no way to know whether you're doing it correctly. Bear in mind that this is a *Being* (rather than a *Doing*) experience in which none of the rules of the left/rational brain apply.

Once you give yourself permission to unlock the intuitive dimensions, your mind will respond by giving series of Icons that, when brought together, provide deeper and broader levels of meaning for the issues and questions you put to it. Consider the following example.

Mrs. Hendrickson

Mrs. Hendrickson, who had recently lost her husband, was seeking new avenues for dealing with her current life conditions and tenuous financial state. She wanted to explore options that went beyond the advice she was receiving from friends. Her question was, "What do I need to consider that would bring back meaning in my life and a source of financial support?" The Icons that emerged were

- An old dust-covered sewing machine that had been used by her mother
- A piece of cloth with frayed and unraveled edges lying on the machine
- An attic in which the machine was being stored

In role-playing the different Icons that came through, Mrs. Hendrickson received these responses (through the three levels of perception—observation, interpretation, and transcendent significance—for each Icon).

- **The sewing machine:** "I am a machine capable of making garments, mending tears, and creating designs on clothes. My function is to make meaningful garments for the loved ones of this household, but I have been put to rest because I'm no longer valued for my capabilities and potential."

- **The frayed piece of cloth:** "I once had a function and was part of a larger gar-ment. Because my threads are now separated and worn, I am a piece of scrap with no value."
- **The attic:** "I am a storage place for items that no longer have value in the house-hold. I hold a great deal of stored potential and await the time when someone can discover the value of the things stored in my space."

After understanding the metaphorical aspects of this scene (Level 2), she remembered how excited she had been when her mother taught her how to sew and to appreciate textiles and the different creative ways in which to create garments that reflected her personality. In her experience of the Icons, she became aware of a lost passion she'd had when she was a young woman. She also became aware that in the marketplace there was a very high interest in specialty cloths and textiles (Level 3).

Eventually, she developed an Internet website for selling a specialty couture line of textiles, a business that also allowed her to explore her love of travel. In Europe she found sources of unusual woven materials, which became the basis for establish-ing a new business of selling limited-edition textiles to individuals who loved design-ing and sewing their own garments.

Through the use of the QDM process, Mrs. Hendrickson was able to exam-ine how an old passion could be revived in a meaningful way, which would meet her present needs not only financially, but in an emotionally significant manner.

Part 3: Implement Your Intuitive Input

Once you have determined the full meaning of the Icons and, if needed, repeated the process (back to Part 1, page 141) with additional questions and interpreta-tion of the Icons, then the ramifications and implementation begin. This leads to additional questions, prompting additional Icons.

As you move toward implementation, your questions can be increasingly detailed and even analytical. The answers you receive will translate readily into rational terms. You may be surprised by what the intuitive mind will provide that complements rational information and planning. In this manner, the *unfolding* of answers and questions continues until you have achieved the greatest under-standing you need to uncover solutions or resolutions. As we suggested earlier in the book, you may want to keep a journal or notes of your Icons, interpretations, and meanings—or even record your QDM sessions to aid you in further under-standing your intuitive responses.

JOURNALING IS ANOTHER WAY of seeing within yourself—a way of creating an emotional/historical map that shows you a larger perspective of your life's terrain, reveals insights about who you are, and helps you understand more clearly what your needs and aspirations are. It is a window into your inner being.

Whole-brain functioning allows intuitive wisdom to be put into practice. The visionary remains a dreamer without taking into consideration physical realities. An architect may envision a wondrous building, but until her concepts are translated into proper engineering specifications, the building cannot be realized. This is analogous to the way in which QDM puts into operation the contributions of both sides of the brain, an integrated mind approach.

As you begin to increase your trust in your intuitive abilities, you will find that they will play a greater part in your life. Not only will you become comfortable in using your intuition in problem solving, you will find that your intuition will speak to you in a variety of ways that are connected with inner needs or interests. The following are examples:

One CEO had a war injury he could feel during certain periods of his life. He found that whenever he encountered a situation that would in time jeopardize his space or psychological well-being, his shoulder would provide pain to signal that some situation was not right for him.

A woman executive developed a feedback mechanism when it came to moving in the right direction by getting goose bumps on her arm when something "rang true" for her.

These are examples of how a person can attain feedback from his body. When you have a deep sense of your own mission, you will find that your intuitive mind will align with your body to provide valuable feedback—your body will automatically act like a compass in giving you intuitive feedback as to the correct action and direction to take in your life.

You now have an understanding of how to go from the Inspiration Dimension of the Pragmatic Spirituality process, which achieves and maintains your

Inner Edge, to the techniques of the QDM process, which is focused on obtaining intuitive input through Socratic questions related to a specific need. (Additional examples of using QDM in the business context are found in Chapter 17.) In this chapter we have covered the QDM process, delving more deeply into your vast ocean of intuitive insights through the use of Icons and your interpretive abilities. As you learn to trust the "inspired" information that comes through for you, as well as your interpretive abilities, you'll discover just how important a part intuition can play in your life.

In the coming three chapters, we'll examine a number of factors that complicate the application of Pragmatic Spirituality in the workplace: *adaptability* and *politics*, *loyalty* and *responsibility*, and *accountability*.

CHAPTER 11 HIGHLIGHTS

QDM is a problem-solving, decision-making process that involves a dialogue between the intuitive and rational sides of your nature. With QDM, you learn to be ambidextrous *with your mind, thus expanding the possibilities of gathering data, exercising options, awareness, gaining wisdom, and being more fully creative.*

QDM is used when you have a need for intuitive input on a specific question or problem, whereas your Daily PS Focus is used regularly to maintain an underlying level of Pragmatic Spirituality in all its aspects: centeredness, self-worth, prioritization of time and energy, and reconnection with intuitive resources.

The QDM process operates in a Socratic fashion—questions are asked in order to understand a situation or a field of facts that have bearing on the problem or issue being addressed.

QDM's three levels of perception involve input from not only your physical senses but also your emotions and your intuition. The Icons with which your intuition communicates may be familiar objects, but they will have a deeper level of emotional significance and meaning well beyond the way you normally perceive them.

Part 1 of QDM consists of formulating your questions. *The QDM process consists of an ever-evolving series of questions (who, what, when, where, why, and how). Each question is submitted, and the responding Icons are processed, as described in Part 2. The back-and-forth exchange continues, with subsequent questions building on the previous intuitive Icon response. The outcome is an increasingly complete understanding of what your intuitive wisdom is telling you.*

Part 2 of QDM involves processing the Icon responses, *following the guidelines for processing intuitive Icons (Chapter 8, page 92) and making an empathetic connection on as many levels of perception as possible. The more you can be "one with the Icon," the greater amount of information will come to you.*

Part 3 of QDM is the implementation of your intuitive input *in your life and work. During this phase you may choose to loop back to Parts 1 and 2 to further refine your understanding of the intuitive message or to get further input on courses of action you are considering. As you move toward implementation, your questions can be increasingly detailed and even analytical. The answers you receive will translate readily into rational terms.*

You may want to keep a journal or notes of your Icons, interpretations, and meanings—or even record your QDM sessions to aid you in further understanding your intuitive responses.

12

ADAPTABILITY, RAPPORT, AND POLITICS

Progress is impossible without change; and those who cannot change their minds cannot change anything.

—George Bernard Shaw

Now that you have learned how QDM can increase your access to intuitive resources in life and on the job, the remainder of this section will shift the focus back to applying other Pragmatic Spirituality principles in your work. As before, we're taking what you learned in the previous section and fine-tuning it for the rigors of the workplace. We'll begin with an attribute that is key to success: *adaptability*.

Adaptability

As discussed in Section I, our shorthand definition for Pragmatic Spirituality and its goal, the Inner Edge, is *authenticity* (to self) and *appropriateness* (to the situation). One means of enacting this at work is *adaptability*: the ability to perceive when a new kind of behavior is called for and to respond appropriately (with action or nonaction) while remaining true to oneself.

This ability to sense and respond differently applies equally to all situations you encounter, from the subtle to the more significant situations. For example:

- The demeanor of a coworker changes. You note this and step out of your usual interaction routine to sensitively determine what is going on.

- The new department head seems to want to know much more detail about the work process, as opposed to just the end results. Some of your coworkers resent the new boss's "micromanaging," but you readily shift into the new behavior of keeping her posted on a regular basis.

In yesterday's workplace, greater emphasis was placed on following procedures and going by the rules. Today's fast-moving work environment places a premium on the ability of all members of the organization to respond more rapidly and effectively.

It might seem that the importance of adaptability would be self-evident. However, therapists and career counselors know there is a wide gap between a person recognizing the importance of adaptability as a concept and actually *being* adaptable in a real-life situation. There are several contributing factors for this:

- The normal human tendency is to get into a familiar routine and stick to it.

- The "shoulder to the wheel," "nose to the grindstone" type of conscientious employee often is too focused on his work to note the subtle, early signs of change.

- Old patterns and Unfinished Business tend to blind one's perceptions and hobble one's adaptability.

Remember, we're not talking about situations where two people have differing points of view, but rather where both feel they are behaving appropriately.

It would seem somewhat obvious that if a person *were* aware of not adapting well to a situation at hand, she would do something else. An exception is the cantankerous person being intentionally uncooperative just out of perversity, but there's little place for this kind of attitude in situations with a common goal of getting the job done. We're referring to circumstances where cooperation is expected of everyone, but someone's lack of adaptability is a hindrance.

Very likely that person's lack of flexibility is due to an internal script that either (a) clouds awareness of what's going on or (b) enables him to justify not adapting to this situation—or to rationalize being inflexible in general. If you listen carefully, you can hear the Unfinished Business that is limiting the person's adaptability, and in some cases causing him to see it as a virtue:

- "I am consistent."
- "Those others are compromising their principles."
- "There is a right way and a wrong way."
- "I can't stand indecisiveness!"

In a certain context, each of these statements might be completely valid and the lack of flexibility justified, but in most instances of this sort it is Unfinished Business crippling the individual's ability to see the whole situation clearly.

In the workplace, a contributing factor is traditional high regard for incisive decision making as a management trait. The person who is perceived to hesitate or frequently waffle might not be considered "management material." In fact, truly competent managers don't rush ahead for the sake of expediency, but try to gather as much relevant information as possible before making a decision— and are not averse to deferring or reversing a decision if circumstances change or the initial results are not as expected.

The QDM process discussed in the previous chapter is very helpful in finding the correct balance between incisiveness and adaptability when assessing data and making decisions. QDM enables the consideration of six main components of adaptability:

1. To fully perceive a situation within a particular field of interaction, and then to go beyond this field to be able to see the other less obvious dimensions and ramifications
2. To recognize the three forms of intelligence (intellectual, emotional, and spiritual) and to use all three to fully comprehend a problem or situation
3. To be able to reprioritize and reconceptualize based on new data received
4. To understand when the decision database needs to be expanded
5. To comprehend that fear and other emotions can be projected onto data and to recognize when these are hidden drivers behind a proposed course of action
6. To be able to include your essential principles or values among the criteria used to make a decision—in spite of its complexity

Work and business are competitive, and in certain circumstances the willingness to be flexible, to reverse a decision, to admit to being wrong, could be perceived as being vulnerable. In some situations, vulnerability may be interpreted as weakness—and "a company needs strong managers" (yet another kind of rationalization for lack of adaptability). But this does not have to be the case if vulnerability is seen as a transitional state that leads to a better decision than would have been made with more precipitous action and to a better avenue or solution to a problem.

Vulnerability

Analogies to war or sports are often drawn in business—especially contact sports. In those activities, to be vulnerable is to invite defeat, if not serious injury or even death. In the traditional business paradigm, a tough exterior was expected, along with the gumption to make hard decisions when necessary. "The company must have a firm hand at the tiller." "When the going gets tough, the tough get going." "Bite the bullet."

With other changes in organizational paradigms, this "tough equals rigid and insensitive" mentality is being reexamined. This shift in attitude has been caused by both the changing needs of the organization and the increased presence and influence of women. Women managers at all levels of responsibility are demonstrating that openness and sensitivity are not incompatible with effective decision making and inspired leadership, provided all is done in a manner appropriate to the situation. Vulnerability can be a part of more appropriate decision making and implementation.

The tough-versus-appropriate issue can be illustrated in how two managers handle the termination of an employee.

The *tough* manager dislikes firing people, so he gets it over with as quickly as possible. Little time is spent on preparation, and once the meeting begins, it is clear the manager is impatient to finish. Even if it is a "no-fault" termination—a downsizing caused by external factors—in order to justify the action, the manager may say or imply that the employee is at fault. Rather than create an atmosphere during the meeting that is respectful of the impact on the employee, the manager may allow telephone calls or other interruptions. There may be little or no comment on the employee's positive contributions, or encouragement about his prospects. The manager won't permit his emotions to enter into the transaction, so the whole discussion is done in a very impersonal manner, probably accompanied by banal comments like, "These things happen" or "Can't win them all." The employee leaves shell-shocked, with many questions unformulated and unanswered.

The *compassionate* manager does not relish the firing process any more than the tough manager, but she vows to carry it out in the most constructive way possible. She prepares what she will say with care and sets aside sufficient time, assuring there will be no interruptions. The manager warns the employee that this will be a tough discussion for both of them, announces the decision, and stresses that it is irrevocable. Then she directs the discussion toward validating the employee as a person, either referring to good performance (if it is not a "for-cause" termination) or otherwise affirming wherever possible. She goes over the details of the termination, including the timing, confidentiality issues, forms to be signed, severance pay, benefits, outplacement counseling, and so on. Depending on the situation, she might give brief encouragement about future employment prospects and make it clear that the employee's feelings are understood and respected. Since the employee may be in partial shock, the manager puts important information in writing and makes it clear what the employee is to do after the close of the meeting. The interview is not overly long, but the entire focus is on maintaining the self-respect of the employee.

The examples illustrate the application of several underlying concepts of Pragmatic Spirituality in the workplace: combining the rapport gained from a certain degree of vulnerability, while using Self-discipline to remain focused to deal effectively with a tough situation. The actions of the compassionate manager certainly reflect both *authenticity* and *appropriateness*.

Adaptability is particularly important as the work environment evolves to deal with challenges of the new marketplace. In traditional hierarchical structures, supervisors had the clear authority to say "Do it!" and expect obedience. In today's flatter, more flexible organizational situations, many person-to-person transactions take place where there is little or no clear "who reports to whom" relationship. These interactions depend on management and communication by persuasion, consensus, or other nonauthoritative techniques. Here, an important aspect of adaptability is the ability to establish and maintain *rapport*.

Rapport

Consider a person-to-person work interaction: *A* needs *B* to do something—the *task*. As the interaction begins, in person or by phone, the tendency is for *A* to immediately focus on the task. But this fails to take into account the principle of rapport and task:

Every interaction has two elements: the task and rapport.
First establish rapport,
Then the task *can be achieved more effectively.*

Building rapport is particularly important where *A* does not have well-defined authority to get *B* to agree to a task. In yesterday's organization, it was more likely that *A* could make *B* agree to the task, but today's workplace is characterized by interactions between managers and employees who are essentially on a peer basis. It is here that the ability to establish rapport gets the job done faster and more efficiently.

Most people understand the value of building rapport, but they are selective in applying it. Without a doubt, *A*, as a salesperson, would take time to schmooze *B*, if *B* was a prospective customer. However, if *B* is instead a coworker, *A* may be tempted to skip the small talk and get down to the task needed from *B*. This may be done in the interests of "saving the company's time"; however, it's much more in the company's interest for *A* to establish rapport so that *B* is more receptive to the task.

Even if one employee has spoken to another recently, it is worthwhile to reestablish or reaffirm the rapport at the beginning of each interaction that involves a task. An "old-time" manager might consider this a waste of time. In the new workplace, it is the effective way to communicate and motivate.

How Adaptability Is Inhibited by Unfinished Business

In Chapter 4, we examined how Unfinished Business from earlier life experiences can create behavior patterns that work against a person's best interests. It should not come as a surprise that one of the primary reasons for lack of adaptability is Unfinished Business—early messages such as "grow up," "don't be a baby," and "be strong," as well as examples of behavior given by adults trapped in yesterday's patterns of behavior.

> In my first ten years of work, I was all business. I held my staff to high standards and set the bar even higher for myself. "I can't" was not an acceptable answer. Then I got into a really complex situation that was completely beyond my control. I'll never forget that day when I said to some coworkers, "I can't do this alone; I need help." It was as if the wall between us suddenly came down. They pitched in, and we got the project done. And I was very careful not to let that wall go up again, because the new way felt much better.

From as early in life as I can remember, I never let anyone get close to me. I worked hard in my job, never realizing the impact of distancing myself from others. One day at work, I suddenly had this image of myself—in a suit of armor, like a knight in a childhood book. I had worn the armor for many years (it was all dented and cracked). I was sure that if I took off that armor, or even loosened up one of the joints, someone would stick a knife in me. I finally was able to shuck the armor—and the improvement in my life and relationships was dramatic.

TYPES OF UNFINISHED BUSINESS THAT INHIBIT ADAPTABILITY

There are several types of Unfinished Business that can inhibit adaptability:

- Old personal behavioral models of the "correct" pattern to follow in a situation or a role. Until these are overcome, no alternative behavior is possible.
- Highly critical or judgmental messages about other's behavior that are perceived as "incorrect." These must be transcended in order to deal with situations in the context of *now* rather than with preprogrammed behavior.
- Low self-esteem. This requires continuous attention to inner issues, thus reducing the amount of energy available to focus on the situation at hand and to grasp the subtleties of what is actually happening.
- Rigid role expectations where the person defines her role according to certain behaviors—for example, "I don't do cleanup—that isn't part of my job."

As discussed in Chapter 4, the first step to overcoming Unfinished Business is to acknowledge the existence of inappropriate patterns, and then to take the necessary steps to identify and transcend the specific patterns that are inhibiting your ability to be adaptable.

Toxic Attractions in the Workplace

There is an extreme example of not only a lack of adaptability, but an actual *attraction* to unhealthy workplace situations—a toxic attraction to certain types of people and situations that one cannot deal with effectively. It is the result of powerful Unfinished Business, probably connected with family issues. Career counselors encounter this in going over a client's work history consisting of one unsuccessful job after the other, each with a similar unhappy ending.

Upon further inquiry, a pattern emerges. Each of the client's supervisors was very similar in personality and management style. It becomes apparent that the employee is drawn to this type of boss and situation, resulting in a two- to three-year scenario of abusive behavior by the supervisor, passivity by the employee, and finally an act of inappropriate assertiveness and the employee's dismissal. The following is an example of how this might be resolved.

Jonathan's father belittled him from childhood until he left home at age eighteen. Throughout his career, Jon found himself drawn to work situations with denigrating bosses, resulting in a string of painful jobs that ended badly. Finally, as he worked on his Unfinished Business, he began to see clearly that he had been searching for healing by proving himself adequate to a boss with the same traits as his father.

Most people are attracted to certain types of unhealthy work situations to some degree. Being aware of this pattern will enable you to make sure it does not control you.

The *ultimate* test of a person's adaptability is the ability to deal with "political" situations in the workplace.

"Office Politics" in the Workplace

In the Harvard Business School Club of New York Career Seminars, Dick's favorite session was the one dealing with "politics." It started out with participants listing their best-case/worst-case boss, coworker, and work-environment situations. (See Appendix C for a summary of the exercises used in the seminar.) The first objective of this session was for each participant to scrutinize his or her best-case examples in terms of "Why do I want this?" and "How realistic is it as an expectation?" The second objective was to construct a personalized "Must have/Must avoid" list to use as a yardstick in assessing job opportunities.

The discussion about worst-case workplace situations inevitably gravitated to the subject of office politics, about which most of the people in the seminar had a very negative opinion. However, when examples were solicited from the participants, it quickly became clear that "politics" was not the same for each person. Even though each seminar participant found the particular political situation he recounted to be intolerable, it was clear that other coworkers in the same situation had been able to deal with it. Also, there was disagreement among the seminar participants about whether a described situation was or was not "political." Some had not only tolerated similar situations, but *flourished* in them. The discussion ended with a new practical definition: "Politics for me is something that *I* cannot deal with (but others can)."

In fact, politics in the workplace can be extremely useful in diagnosing your Unfinished Business and dysfunctional patterns, a kind of do-it-yourself Rorschach test.

- One person gave this example: "I sat down and made a list of the political situations at work I had difficulty dealing with. They all had the same basic elements: one of my coworkers—in my perception—was getting away with something (such as not following the company's rules), and his supervisor wasn't doing anything about it. So I did or said something to address the impropriety, and I always ended up in more trouble than the person breaking the rules." (Unfinished Business: need to be in control)

- Isabell was never able to confront people who became adversarial. She dealt with this by spreading gossip about them. (Unfinished Business: fear of rejection)

- Dean was the "good guy" who spent a lot of time rescuing coworkers, whom he allowed to take advantage of his generosity with time and money. This gave him a feeling of importance, although in reality he was allowing those people to maintain their inadequacy and state of codependency. (Unfinished Business: low self-esteem from being an enabler)

These kinds of realizations can lead to very useful insights into patterns and attitudes that need to be updated. The results may be an increased ability to deal with a broader range of heretofore highly political situations—or at least to become aware of the type of situation to *avoid* in the future.

Being Judgmental Hamstrings Adaptability

Our discussion of office politics raises an interesting question: if *A* is having difficulty dealing with the political situation, while *B* is taking it in stride (or even benefiting from it), *why doesn't A try to learn some tips from B?* That seldom happens; instead A may be very critical and judgmental of B, associating B with the politics.

A can't deal with the political situation because it triggers some Unfinished Business injunctions. A assumes that since B is dealing quite readily with the situation, B is also violating those same injunctions. This may or may not be true, but the point is that A is in no frame of mind to *learn* anything from B about how to handle this kind of situation—a lost opportunity. Quite likely, A perceives B as an opportunist, a "brown-noser."

Every highly conscientious person can look back and recall many examples of people like this who didn't seem to play by the rules. But in the work context, the reality is that these people are also skilled *situationalists*, and the employee who is seeking greater adaptability *can learn something* from them. Situationalists are always in touch with what's happening *now*. They understand the hot buttons of the people they work with. They are able to adapt their behavior to suit their best interests, and they know how to look after themselves. These are useful traits, and you'd be smart to pay attention and pick up some pointers.

A frequent reaction by seminar participants to this idea was, "Are you suggesting I compromise my principles?" The answer is, "Definitely not!" We're advocating the desirability of developing a broader skill set to better deal with the realities you face in the workplace. Once you have greater adaptability, you will then be in the position to choose when to adapt or not. Each person will encounter situations in which he chooses to draw the line on an ethical or moral basis—but it's better to have the choice.

How Adaptable Are Loyalty and Responsibility?

Loyalty and responsibility are two deep-seated values that are often a part of value systems and behavior patterns related to the workplace. In the changing circumstances of the workplace, the old definitions no longer serve. In the next chapter we will examine loyalty and responsibility in a context more appropriate to Pragmatic Spirituality in the workplace.

CHAPTER 12 HIGHLIGHTS

Adaptability *is defined as the ability to perceive when a new kind of behavior is called for—and to respond appropriately.*

Today's workplace calls for a higher degree of adaptability by all employees, since there are fewer defined authority relationships.

Resistance to adaptability is often disguised as a virtue—of consistency, decisiveness, and so on.

A reexamination of the old "tough equals rigid and insensitive" mentality is leading to greater appreciation for how vulnerability can improve the quality of decisions and their implementation.

Every interaction has two elements: the task *and* rapport. *First establish rapport; then the task can be achieved more effectively. This is particularly important in today's less structured workplaces.*

Adaptability can be inhibited by Unfinished Business, which in extreme cases can even cause people to be repeatedly attracted to people and situations that are highly toxic for them.

"Political" situations in the workplace are those a particular person cannot deal with effectively, thus offering an opportunity for the person to diagnose her Unfinished Business.

Being judgmental can interfere with your ability to observe and learn from people who are expert "situationalists," skilled at figuring out and dealing with situations.

Compromising your principles is not necessary. First become highly adaptable—then you can choose whether to take a particular course of action.

13

LOYALTY AND RESPONSIBILITY REDEFINED

The one with the primary responsibility to the individual's future is that individual.

—DORCAS HARDY

HAVING RECOGNIZED THAT ADAPTABILITY IS VITAL to overcoming Unfinished Business and achieving your Inner Edge, let's examine two concepts, *loyalty* and *responsibility*, which can be significant impediments to adaptability. You need to have a clear understanding and working definition of these terms—appropriate for today's workplace situations—to ensure that Unfinished Business is not compromising your Inner Edge. Let's consider Norman.

Norman

Loyalty and responsibility and a sense of "duty" were always very important to Norman. He did his best to exemplify these values in his life, and this behavior certainly was one of the factors for his success in work and other activities. These values were highly motivating in the first part of his career, driving him to high standards of performance. They also caused him to be very demanding of himself. When he did not perform up to his expectations, Norman would beat himself up verbally and psychologically. Over time he came to realize that his sense of duty and his high self-expectations were taking a heavy toll on his family and himself.

When Ron suggested that he reassess these values of loyalty, responsibility, and duty, Norman's first reaction was resentment: "So what do I do instead—learn to be irresponsible?" The answer, of course, lay not in the "black or white" but in the gray area that characterizes so much of real life. Norman worked to develop new interpretations of duty, responsibility, and loyalty. By becoming aware of old patterns and reconceptualizing them, Norman was able to "finish up" this aspect of Unfinished Business and work on balancing his dutifulness to include the full spectrum of his life—including himself.

Loyalty and Responsibility as Core Life Values

Loyalty is defined as "faithfulness to any person, government, country, or other cause to whom fidelity is owed." The essence of loyalty is setting aside one's self-interests in favor of a larger cause. Each nation's heritage reveres its history replete with heroes—known and unknown—whose sacrifices established and preserved their homeland. Every group effort depends on the commitment of each of its members to the common goal. Consider your personal reaction to the words *disloyalty*, *betrayal*, and *traitor* as a reminder of the strong emotional and moral connotations of loyalty and the stigma attached to its being compromised.

The words *responsible* and *responsibility* cover a wide range of meanings: "in control of and answerable for," "fit to be placed in control," "capable of acting rationally," and "causing a particular result." In this chapter we're dealing with the common usage, "to take responsibility for," as meaning "to consider oneself answerable for."

The root of both words is the Latin *respondere*, which means "to pledge in trust," so here again we have a word with deep-seated moral and cultural implications. Any group, from a primitive tribe to a large business entity, owes its continued existence to its members being answerable for their actions with a mutual trust between the individual and the whole.

These are two very powerful word symbols capable of evoking strong emotions in the speaker and listener—two concepts that are universally agreed to be essential parts of our social and organizational fabric.

Loyalty and Responsibility—Potential for Abuse

Let us recognize, however, that it is the unquestioned validity and necessity of loyalty and responsibility that impart their strong motivational power. In the military context, loyalty and responsibility can motivate members of a fighting unit to risk death as they follow orders to achieve a stated objective. In sports, loyalty and responsibility motivate players and fans to transcend other facets of their lives. And organizations have long used these concepts to motivate and control their employees. Loyalty and responsibility are capable of bringing out the very best in individuals and groups.

On the other hand, these admirable values can also lead to exploitation when they are defined inappropriately. For example, the *majority* of a group may interpret loyalty and responsibility as follows:

- **Reciprocity:** All parties share a commitment to goals and values.
- **Allegiance to principles:** These include freedom, team spirit, and shared power.

Whereas another part of that group may be working under a *different* set of interpretations:

- **Pseudo-reciprocity:** Mutual loyalty is spoken, but other agendas are at work.
- **Blind allegiance:** Individuals are asked for loyalty to leaders or the company without reference to ethics, accountability, or moral considerations.

It is reasonable and appropriate for followers to expect the *same* level of loyalty and responsibility from their leaders as their leaders ask of them. Failure to be aware of this can lead to exploitation of the dedicated by the cynical.

With regard to the workplace, it is useful to visualize a continuum: on one end, the constructive actions of the supervisors and managers of an employer organization directing employees to achieve a mutually beneficial goal; on the other end, exploitation of employees by employers preoccupied with their own self-interests. Most situations fall somewhere in the middle of this spectrum; however, each employee needs to *balance* his "dutifulness" between duty to outside demands and duty to self. Self-maintenance and Pragmatic Spirituality techniques are a means of remaining vigilant.

The Traditional Organization

In the traditional organizational context, loyalty and responsibility were very influential factors in the employer-employee relationship. The implicit contract was "Work hard and be loyal, and the company will take care of you." In most instances, this was more of an employee perception (and desire) than a commitment on the employer's part, but it was a strongly shared value. The relatively slow pace of change made it possible for long-term loyalties and relationships to exist. Work units were relatively stable. People tended to start at the bottom and evolve upward in the group, placing a high emphasis on "team" loyalty and responsibility.

Loyalty and responsibility brought many positive benefits. The organization could count on the long-term commitment of its employees. Employees derived great satisfaction from working in a team. There was a sense of mutual loyalty— up to a point.

Negative Implications in the Work Context

The work context of the traditional organization had strong components of paternalism on the part of the employer and childlike trust on the part of the employee. The company became "family," supervisors "parents," and coworkers "siblings." In such a climate of employee trust, it was not unusual for loyalty and responsibility to be misused, as the following examples illustrate.

The illicit relationship between the department head and his secretary was no secret to upper management, but nothing was done—in spite of a company policy against "fraternization." In time, the woman became pregnant, and the company terminated her employment. She was given a financial incentive to "go away and not make trouble." In spite of urgings by her friends to talk to a lawyer, she took no action against the company for which she had worked more than fifteen years.

A truck driver had worked for a manufacturing company for twenty years. Periodically, he would be directed to take a load of 55-gallon drums out to a remote area and dump them. After many years of this, he asked his supervisor why the company didn't use an outside disposal service. His supervisor said that was not necessary, and that he was depending on the driver's loyalty to the company to keep this confidential.

One small-town company had a close-knit management team that had come up through the ranks together. One of them had a serious drinking problem, which the company not only tolerated but covered up. Then one night, that manager was driving while intoxicated and was involved in an accident in which several people were killed. The company tried to hush it up, but the details were eventually uncovered by a reporter. The reputation of the company and its top management was badly damaged.

These are reminders of the strong hold that loyalty and responsibility can have on employees. As one person recalls, even looking out for one's own interests might have been considered "disloyal."

> I remember my first boss talking about the type of employee "who keeps his updated résumé in his desk, ready for use." Nowadays, that is commonplace, but back then, it was not done by "good company men."

Many employers *were* motivated by a high degree of concern for their employees' well-being, considering staff as a resource to be developed rather than as an expense to be shaved. The esprit de corps in companies like IBM and Xerox helped them attract and keep good people, and provided a powerful competitive advantage. Unfortunately, that could not be maintained against the tides of change.

The latter 1980s and the 1990s were turbulent times for business organizations. Their marketplaces became global. Time frames accelerated: technologies evolved at an accelerating pace, diminishing product life cycles. The traditional hierarchical organizational structure lacked the responsiveness and flexibility to maneuver in these new waters. The result was widespread downsizing of facilities and staff, which radically changed the realities of loyalty and responsibility.

Loyalty and Responsibility in the Evolving Organization

Clearly, the concepts of loyalty and responsibility need to be reinterpreted in order to have relevance in the new workplace. Two factors will tend to impede this reinterpretation:

1. Employers will be slow to change. This is because of the inertia of organizations, and because the old concepts of loyalty and responsibility work mostly in the company's favor. Those managers who enjoy having authority and power over others will not be eager to move into a more cooperative, consultative style of relationship with their subordinates.

2. There will continue to be employees who are unconsciously seeking a work situation in which they will be taken care of (the company as family) or where they can reenact Unfinished Business patterns. They will not be interested in redefined concepts of loyalty and responsibility.

Loyalty Redefined

In the new work context, loyalty remains an essential element. However, because the duration of the employer-employee relationship is, or is likely to be, shorter, then loyalty must of necessity be of a more *conditional* nature. And because of the diminution of formal procedures and the higher turnover within the organization, loyalty is better defined in terms of *parameters* and *duration*.

Here's a practical example of a new perception of loyalty that is more appropriate to the realities of the evolving workplace.

The Independent Contractor Model

Consider a consultant or technical specialist doing a project for an organization as an independent contractor. The consultant wants to do a good job in order to receive the project fee plus incentives, as well as to increase the likelihood of future projects—and to be able to add another satisfied client to his list of references. On the other hand, if the contractor devotes all of his time and energy to this project, then the marketing effort to find the next project—essential to his interests—will be neglected. In a real sense, the independent contractor must be loyal to two masters. Success requires balancing the interests of both. How does a competent independent contractor balance these loyalties and take *responsibility* for his own Self-maintenance?

- Clearly define the scope of the project.
- If there is ambiguity, agree on appropriate contingency measures (for example, renegotiation of a time line).
- Create and stick to a realistic time line.
- Write out the project's parameters, including a protocol for all parties concerned.
- Define collaborative responsibilities so that no one misunderstands who is to do what and when.
- Schedule periodic progress review sessions so that necessary redirection or reprioritizations can be done in a timely manner.
- If what is done does not reflect what was agreed to, determine whether other agendas are at work and deal with them.

The objective is that the client's perception regarding the amount of loyalty to be expected from the consultant is consistent with the consultant's planned allocation of loyalty to the project. Clearly, every possible eventuality cannot be anticipated, but the discipline of calibrating expectations will go a long way toward establishing the basis for an effective relationship.

This model offers a perspective for loyalty between employer and employee in the new work context, based on a conditional quid pro quo: "I will undertake to accomplish thus-and-so in my work assignment in return for the employer providing me with thus-and-so." This quid pro quo needs to be updated periodically or when circumstances change. Loyalty, then, consists of making good on what has been agreed to.

Granted, this is more time-consuming than the old, "Welcome to the department—Harry will show you your desk" introduction to an assignment. And, in most cases, it will be the responsibility of the employee to initiate this interchange, since the supervisor is likely busy and might prefer to leave the definitions somewhat blurry.

In practice, the good intentions of an employee to balance out her interests may be sabotaged by her Unfinished Business about *responsibility*, so we need to take a fresh look at that other very powerful value.

Responsibility Redefined

In the old subconscious patterns of many people, responsibility is mostly directed *externally*: responsibility to one's job, parents, family, religious institution, and so on. The social antecedents of this external responsibility are clear. However, as we discussed in Chapter 5, one of a person's primary responsibilities is toward *oneself*—an *inner* responsibility. Failure to pay proper attention to Self-maintenance will result in deteriorating effectiveness and possible inability to function.

Consistent practice of the Daily PS Focus technique enables you to better maintain that balance between the external and the internal. The *Identity* part of the 3D Visualization reaffirms your self-worth and your determination to work within the context of today's realities rather than respond to old patterns. The *Integration* part of the 3D Visualization focuses on achieving a balance between your external responsibilities and your responsibility to yourself.

This leads to a redefinition of responsibility:

Responding appropriately *to each specific situation.*

Within the context of Pragmatic Spirituality, this appropriate response is based on all the elements of your Daily PS Focus—your Identity and Integration, enhanced by the input from your Inspiration resources.

This redefinition of responsibility as "appropriate responsiveness" is the antithesis of a responsibility based on old patterns and fixed allegiances. The new concept of responsibility calls for constant awareness of the current situation in order to respond appropriately.

The New Collaboration

Loyalty and responsibility for the evolving workplace paradigm are characterized by flexibility and appropriateness to the situation. Rather than being prescribed and rigid, as in the traditional organization, they are tied to the process of reaching a specific goal. The organization's tasks and goals are increasingly set within the context of fast-changing events and circumstances. Success requires both clear definition of the task and expectations by the employer, and flexibility and responsiveness by the employees. Likewise, clarity by both sides will also increase the likelihood that expectations on the employees' end will be realized.

When loyalty and responsibility are focused on a goal with flexibility, the relationship between employer and employee becomes more like a collaboration between the two. There is a well-informed mutual commitment to the process of achieving agreed-upon goals.

Putting It into Practice

In this chapter we've reexamined the concepts of loyalty and responsibility with an eye to dislodging old traditional patterns in favor of new interpretations more appropriate in today's workplace. The day-to-day implementation of this new concept depends on the tool of *accountability*, which we'll examine in the next chapter.

CHAPTER 13 HIGHLIGHTS

Both loyalty and responsibility have pervasive moral and cultural implications, as well as strong motivational power—bringing out the best in individuals and groups. They can lead to exploitation when they are not defined appropriately. It is reasonable and appropriate for followers to expect the same *level of loyalty and responsibility from their leaders as their leaders ask of them. Failure to be aware of this can lead to exploitation of the dedicated by the cynical.*

Each employee needs to balance *his "dutifulness" between duty to outside demands and duty to self. Self-maintenance and Pragmatic Spirituality techniques are a means of remaining vigilant.*

In the traditional organizational context, loyalty and responsibility were very influential factors in the employer-employee relationship. In such a climate of trust on the part of the employee, it was not unusual for loyalty and responsibility to be misused.

Even employers who were motivated by a high degree of concern for their employees' well-being were forced to downsize facilities and staff, radically changing the realities of loyalty and responsibility.

The new definition of loyalty *is the* Independent Contractor Model, *which requires assertiveness and thoroughness by the employee to clearly define all relevant aspects of the position.*

Unfinished Business about responsibility may sabotage an employee's best intentions.

The new definition of responsibility *is "responding appropriately to each specific situation." This is based on all the elements of the Daily PS Focus and calls for constant awareness of the current situation in order to respond appropriately.*

14

ACCOUNTABILITY

We cannot hope to scale great moral heights by ignoring petty obligations.

—AGNES REPPLIER

THE PREVIOUS TWO CHAPTERS addressed several ways in which you can overcome difficulties in applying Pragmatic Spirituality to the workplace, which is much more challenging than doing it in your personal life. However, the payoffs for becoming proficient with your Inner Edge at work make the effort worthwhile, both in terms of your satisfaction and your demonstrated effectiveness. Now we'll address one more concept, *accountability*. This is a commonly used term—especially in business, where it is essential to have a clear interpretation and an effective working knowledge in order to keep your Inner Edge keen.

One-Way Accountability

In the old organizational workplace, most accountability was in one direction—*up*. Each layer of employees was accountable to their supervisors, who in turn were accountable to their supervisors—on up the organizational hierarchy. "I'm holding you accountable" had a negative, confrontational connotation.

Two-Way Accountability

In the evolving organizational context, a new kind of accountability is needed because job descriptions and reporting relationships are increasingly fluid and undefined. This calls for an accountability that is *two-way* and *current*.

Understanding the ramifications of accountability in both traditional and evolving workplace situations is important to avoid ambiguities and inefficiencies as you deal with people in all aspects of your job, inside the company and out.

Effective accountability is the mechanism for clarifying what each person can expect from all the other parties within a work relationship:

- Between two coworkers
- Among the people of a department
- On an interdepartmental project team
- With customers
- With vendors

This mechanism can be a dynamic and flexible alternative to the hierarchical reporting relationships and prescribed roles and procedures of yesterday's workplace.

The Integration Dimension of Pragmatic Spirituality is about how you can best deal effectively with a myriad of relationships and maintain a healthy balance between your self-interests and your commitments to others. In the job context, it is useful to think of accountability as the *scorekeeper* for the Integration Dimension, on two levels:

1. *Intra*personal accountability: holding *yourself* accountable to yourself
2. *Inter*personal accountability: holding *others* accountable in a transaction

Work, with its many psychic and economic ramifications, is likely one of the most influential external factors competing for your time and energy. Keeping a balance between intrapersonal accountability and interpersonal accountability is a good way to maintain your Inner Edge as you do your job.

Intrapersonal Accountability

Intrapersonal accountability involves making good on your day-to-day commitments to yourself in spite of distractions. Constructively looking after yourself was discussed in Chapter 5 with your Self-resolves; however, healthy Self-maintenance is much more difficult to achieve in the workplace. At the beginning of each day, do your Daily PS Focus and identify what you need to do for yourself that day. During the day, be accountable to yourself:

- Create boundaries so that you can do the work you are committed to.
- Organize your work so that the items with greater priority will get your attention.
- Use your own time prudently and hand off jobs that can be done by others, so that you give full value to your work and creativity.
- Focus on being present with each person you meet and each assignment you take on, so there is no time wasted backtracking because you weren't listening or focusing in the moment the first time around.
- Create the pauses that refresh you—avoid burnout. Have breaks and meals that allow you to step back from work.

INTERPERSONAL ACCOUNTABILITY

Interpersonal accountability involves making contracts with each of the people you interact with in the workplace. It involves an explicit mutual understanding as to *what*, *who*, and *when*:

- What is to be done?
- Who is responsible for each component?
- When will each component be completed?

This is straightforward, but few people do it—resulting in incalculable friction and decreased efficiency in the workplace.

Use this idea of a contract as one of the ways you implement Pragmatic Spirituality in your job. It should result in an enhancement of authenticity and appropriateness in each facet of the workplace you touch. Here are some suggestions to increase the effectiveness of your interpersonal accountability contracts:

- Reach agreement about who will take the lead for each part of the task, and how the other person should respond.
- Establish the protocol for a feedback loop that keeps all parties up to date, with provisions for red flags if needed.
- Walk each person through each step to ensure there is a mutual understanding. For example, you might say, "Let me tell you what I want, then you respond with your understanding. Once we reach agreement, I expect you to fulfill it by the agreed-upon deadline within the context of your resources. If at any time you become aware that you will not be able to

perform as agreed, you must immediately make me aware of that so we can come up with an alternative course of action." After agreement is reached, state: "Do you have the time and everything you need to complete this project by the deadline?"

THE MECHANICS OF INTERPERSONAL ACCOUNTABILITY

It is up to you, and each individual in the workplace, to take the initiative in holding others accountable; however, this need not be done in a heavy-handed fashion. The following are simple suggestions for implementing the contracts.

- Contract making is most effective when it is done in a collaborative tone: "Let me make sure I understand who's doing what," rather than, "I'm holding you accountable for this."
- It is best done in small rather than large chunks. Break up the primary task into subtasks, and do a mini-contract on each.
- *Record* the contract. In some cases it will suffice to have the other person see you writing it in your calendar. In other cases, you might choose to send the other person an informal note confirming the commitment, so long as it doesn't look like you're giving orders or trying to "set up" the other person.

Deadlines and Follow-Up

The key to effective interpersonal accountability is *follow-up*. In too many workplaces, deadlines are set, the date comes and goes, and the lack of timely action isn't noted until later, if ever. These are *not* potent deadlines, nor are they effective accountability.

It is vital that coworkers know you *will* keep track of deadlines and hold them to their commitments. A useful technique is the *interim reminder*: a combination of "The date's almost here" and "I'm not going to forget." Here are some examples:

- "I was going over my notes from our meeting last week. Is there anything more you need from me to have the results by next Wednesday at 10 A.M., when we agreed to go over your first draft?"

- "Is 3 P.M. still good for you to go over your rework of the data as we agreed last week?"

Some supervisors seem to have the attitude that once they assign a task, they are no longer accountable for ensuring it is done on time. If the deadline passes with the task unfinished, the supervisor may be unaware of this for some time. Eventually, it comes to mind, and there ensues a critical confrontation between the supervisor and the subordinate—a "gotcha" type of situation that does little good. (If this happens frequently, it is a good indication of some Unfinished Business on the supervisor's part.) When this happens, *both* parties are in the wrong: the subordinate for having missed the deadline, and the supervisor for dodging her ultimate responsibility of ensuring the task was accomplished.

Once your coworkers understand that you are consistent in following up on the accountability process, people will tend to be more realistic in what they commit to—and more conscientious in meeting their commitments.

Accountability Works in Every Direction

As the modern work context is changing from a hierarchical/vertical structure to a collaborative/horizontal structure, the nature of interactions is becoming more complex. You will find that accountability is an effective technique for the two main levels of interaction.

Peer-to-Peer Interactions
This is explicit, organizationally defined accountability in which both parties have equal power. Use of proper accountability techniques in each interaction will clarify roles and responsibilities in a manner most appropriate to the situation.

Supervisor-Subordinate Interactions
Two-way accountability can make each interaction more constructive—in whichever role you find yourself.

When you are the person in authority, the accountability process will enable you to do the following:

- Ensure that the subordinate has an accurate understanding of what is to be done and the ability to do it
  - "Could you review for me the key points of this task to make sure we're on the same page?"

  — "Take some time to evaluate the support you need to do this task in a
    timely manner. Whether or not you need support, get back to me
    regarding your resources or need for further resources."
- Create a sense of involvement and "buy-in" on the part of the subordinate
  — "What are your thoughts and feelings about accomplishing this task?"
  — "Please read this over and see what considerations you would add to
    this project."
- Allow the subordinate to have input into the timing so that the deadline is
  perceived as reasonable
  — "Give me a reasonable time that you can have this completed so that I
    can work with the materials."
  — "Tell me how you can rearrange your priorities so that you can get
    this to me by the deadline I mentioned."

When you are the subordinate, it may take some diplomacy to get a mini-contract with your boss, but when properly done it makes a very positive impression.

- Keep the focus on accuracy and efficiency.
  — "I understand that this is important, but I need your help to under-
    stand how this priority fits in with the other things on my plate. That
    way we can both be clear as to when each of them is due."
  — "Just to make sure we're on the same page, in order to get this done
    by the deadline you indicated, there are some things I need in order to
    make it happen."
  — "I need to review with you what's already on my plate—my commit-
    ments to you and some other people. After we can get the priorities
    clear, maybe we could advise the others of how their projects will be
    affected."
- Use good Self-maintenance as you demonstrate receptivity to taking on the
  new task.

The Teflon Employee

You know the type. He or she talks a good game, makes promises, but usually
manages to avoid delivering—and no one calls him on it. If you look at that type
of person, you'll probably find that this is one of those highly adaptive "situa-

tionalists" we discussed back in Chapter 12—preoccupied with self-interests and skilled at getting his or her own way.

This person represents a real test of your ability to implement effective accountability. Once you've recognized this slippery type, it's time to ratchet up the accountability discipline—in a nonconfrontational manner. Repeat the commitment several times at the close of your "contract" interaction. Record it in a note, with a copy to someone influential. Mark some interim reminder dates in your calendar, and act on them.

If, in spite of all your efforts, the Teflon employee still fails to honor commitments, it's time for a constructive one-on-one confrontation:

> This is not the first time you've made a commitment and then failed to make good on it. I need you to help me understand what's going on here. We're all dependent on each other to get the work done, and when one person drops the ball, it's bad for everyone—and for the company. The job you committed to do still needs doing. This time I'd like you to tell me what is needed so that you will meet the next deadline we set.

Listen to the response. Most likely, you will get some insights into the Unfinished Business patterns that are causing this behavior. Your job is not to "cure" this person, but you may be able to force him or her to better deal with reality—at least for your interactions.

Clearly, if someone's lack of accountability is impairing your ability to do your job, that information is relevant to the person to whom *you* are accountable. And, if it comes to recounting the problem to that person, notes from your "contract discussions" will enable you to present a strong, well-documented case.

Accountability as a "Litmus Test" for an Organization

In Chapter 12, we discussed politics in the workplace. One yardstick of the degree of politicization in an organization is the consistency between the stated rules and the type of behavior actually rewarded in practice. The larger the gap between stated policy and reality, the greater the politicization—or lack of integrity.

Another yardstick of an organization's integrity is the degree of accountability—to employees, to customers, to vendors, to the community, to shareholders. Generally, if there is a high degree of accountability in employee interactions, especially between supervisors and subordinates, that integrity will be reflected in the organization's other interactions with customers, vendors, shareholders, and the community in which it operates. We'll explore this further in Section IV.

One more specialized aspect of Pragmatic Spirituality remains to be discussed: when you are no longer in a job and looking for the next. Chapter 15 discusses how having a strong Inner Edge really pays off in the market assessment and self-marketing for the job acquisition phase of your Career Management Cycle.

CHAPTER 14 HIGHLIGHTS

In the old organizational workplace, most accountability was in one direction—up. "I'm holding you accountable" had a negative, confrontational connotation.

The evolving organizational context needs accountability that is two-way *and* current, *in order to deal with reporting relationships that are increasingly fluid and undefined.*

In the job context, it is useful to think of accountability as the scorekeeper *for the Integration Dimension on two levels: (1)* Intrapersonal accountability: *holding* yourself *accountable to yourself, and (2)* Interpersonal accountability: *holding* others *accountable in transactions.*

Interpersonal accountability involves making contracts with each of the people you interact with in the workplace regarding who, what, *and* when.

It is vital that coworkers know you will *keep track of deadlines and hold them to their commitments.*

Interpersonal accountability is effective for every kind of interaction: peer-to-peer, supervisor-subordinate (where you are the supervisor), and subordinate-supervisor (where you are the subordinate).

Dealing with the "Teflon employee" is a real test of your ability to implement effective accountability.

Generally, if there is a high degree of accountability in employee interactions, especially between supervisors and subordinates, that integrity will be reflected in the organization's other interactions with customers, vendors, shareholders, and the community in which it operates.

PRAGMATIC SPIRITUALITY AND YOUR CAREER MANAGEMENT CYCLE

If you don't know where you're going, any road will lead there.
I'm lost—but I'm making good time!
We have met the enemy, and he is us.

—Dick's "Career Management Bumper Stickers"

THE REALITY IN TODAY'S WORKPLACE is that you, and every other employee, will probably be changing jobs—possibly sooner than you expect. Most people don't have many positive recollections of or associations with being "between jobs," but, in fact, career transitions can be times of growth that result in major life enhancements. Pragmatic Spirituality can make all the difference between feeling like a helpless victim of circumstances and using your Inner Edge to take charge of each career transition.

Taking charge means managing your career *proactively* and *proficiently*. Yet it is amazing how many people have not fully accepted that reality. Why? One reason is inertia. Another is that they are encumbered by old Unfinished Business patterns of "looking for a family" at work or lack of self-dependency.

Pragmatic Spirituality is the foundation of effective career management. It calls every individual to clear self-understanding, ardent self-acceptance, and dependency on oneself. In this chapter, we will focus on the specific applicability of Pragmatic Spirituality to effectively managing your career.

Of necessity, we can only skim the surface in this chapter. For additional information about effective career management we refer you to *In Transition*, a book based on eighteen years of career management seminars conducted for the Harvard Business School (HBS) Club of New York. (For more information, see Recommended Reading, page 293.)

Three Principles of Effective Career Management

It used to be possible to get by without much, if any, attention to career management. But that is no longer the case because of recent radical changes in the workplace and the global markets in which employers operate. Nothing lasts as long as it used to—companies, technologies and products, skills—and therefore jobs. Suffice it to say that these widespread and irreversible changes necessitate a complete shift in previous ways of thinking about life and career, as evidenced in the following three principles of career management:

1. The first principle is to accept that *you*, and only you, are responsible for managing your career. Many people have not yet fully made that commitment, nor have they made the accompanying shift from depending on the company or the boss to complete self-direction and self-accountability.
2. The second principle is to recognize that career management is an *ongoing* process. Career transitions are no longer relatively short periods of turbulence between long periods of stability. In the new work realities, each person is in transition throughout his entire career.
3. The third principle of effective career management is to develop a high degree of *competency* in all the skills and techniques related to career management—especially self-marketing and networking.

One way of putting these principles into practice, transcending old patterns of thinking about jobs and work, is to embrace a new model for managing your career: the Career Management Cycle.

The Career Management Cycle

The name says it all: *cycle* emphasizes the difference from the old linear career concept of a job-for-life. It is based on the assumption of ongoing change, and accepts that each career will have many cycles, each consisting of three phases (see Figure 15.1):

FIGURE 15.1 THE CAREER MANAGEMENT CYCLE: PHASE 1

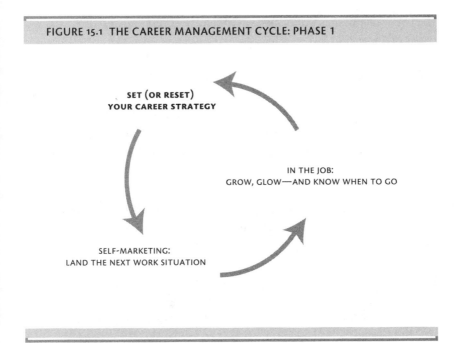

SET (OR RESET)
YOUR CAREER STRATEGY

IN THE JOB:
GROW, GLOW—AND KNOW WHEN TO GO

SELF-MARKETING:
LAND THE NEXT WORK SITUATION

1. Set (or reset) your career strategy
2. Self-marketing: Land the next work situation
3. In the job: Grow, glow—and know when to go

Phase 1 of the Career Management Cycle: Set Your Career Strategy

Just as there are many ways to formulate a business strategy, there is no single right way to formulate a career strategy. But there are several important criteria:

- It should be written (writing encourages objectivity).
- It should be *yours* (many people are still working on goals set for them by others).
- It should involve risks appropriate to your stage in life and your financial reserves (you can risk more at some times in life than at other times).
- It should start with broad horizons (outside-the-box, push-the-envelope thinking) and then gradually sharpen its focus.

Let's examine the two components of the career strategy: *self-awareness* and *market assessment*.

SELF-AWARENESS: THE FIRST COMPONENT OF A CAREER STRATEGY

When you go into the job-hunt phase of the Career Management Cycle, you will be in a *marketing* modality. And the first rule of marketing is: *Know the product*.

But—as every career counselor knows—few people have a clear understanding of themselves at the outset. They are hindered by their lack of self-awareness in two ways:

1. They are unaware of *attitudes* and *behaviors* that are self-limiting and self-sabotaging, which continue to work against them.
2. They are unaware of their strong *potentials*, which remain unrealized.

They are very much like a salesperson who hasn't taken the time to become knowledgeable—and enthusiastic—about the product.

You need to be an effective salesperson who knows the product—*you*—thoroughly. How do you get to "know the product"? One way is through exercises or instruments with which you can look at yourself with a new perspective. Appendix C lists a number of self-assessment exercises used by Dick in the HBS career seminars as an indication of the varied types of instruments and their focus.

If you choose to work with a career coach, beware of one who promises to "take the work off your shoulders." Managers accustomed to delegating detail work to staff helpers may find such an offer tempting, but the self-awareness process can't be handed off. As to fee arrangements, we strongly prefer a by-the-hour fee arrangement rather than a package fee (all or part paid in advance). There are at least two disadvantages of the package fee:

1. If you require more or less time than assumed in the package price, either you or the coach suffers—and it's seldom the coach.
2. Good chemistry with the coach is important, and you can't be sure that exists until you've done some work together.

Doing introspective exercises, with or without a career coach, is not the only way to increase your self-awareness. In your day-to-day activities, you get a lot of self-awareness input.

- You do something: it goes well or it goes poorly.
- An experience is satisfying or it is not.
- You get feedback from people: some formal (like a job performance review), most of it informal.

The key aspect of being able to increase your self-awareness from life situations you encounter is *objectivity*. However, being objective in assessing results and hearing feedback about yourself is not easy. The most potentially useful self-awareness feedback comes when things *don't* go as you intended, and that is when it is most difficult to accurately hear input and learn from the experience. The natural tendency is to go on the defensive, to justify what you did—and the opportunity to increase your self-awareness is lost.

It should be apparent that people who have addressed their Unfinished Business and developed a proficiency in Pragmatic Spirituality have a much easier time developing the self-awareness component of their career strategy. Once the process of identifying old patterns has been started, it is much easier to do the exercises and come up with the insights. And someone grounded in Pragmatic Spirituality will be more likely to hear day-to-day feedback and observations to enhance her self-awareness.

Whatever way you do your self-awareness process, the outcome should be some kind of *written* description of your career criteria—including

- Your current definition of success
- Your near-term priorities and trade-offs
- Your underlying values and motivations
- Your areas of strong competitive advantage
- Your short suits and low tolerances
- Your key must-have and must-avoid factors related to work

Market Assessment: The Second Component of a Career Strategy

Market assessment focuses on *where* and *how* your career criteria, developed in your self-awareness process, might be best satisfied—your best-fit work situation.

Market assessment focuses on the realities of *what's out there*, as opposed to self-awareness, which focuses on acceptance of *what's in here*. Part of market assessment is based on systematic research: at the library, on the Internet, and so on; but the majority of market assessment involves input from other people, some of whom you know but most of whom you *don't* know when you start the process. That involves networking, which we'll discuss later.

The amount of market assessment needed during any career cycle depends on the degree to which you're changing markets. If you're doing a *significant* career course change, you should do a lot of market assessment.

Think of market assessment as a well-organized program of marketing research, with the goal of identifying prospective "buyers" of "you" (the "product")—in terms of two criteria: *fit* and *probability*.

- Fit includes two components:
  — Whether what you offer fits the buyer's needs
  — Whether the situation satisfies *your* career criteria

- Probability has to do with *market* factors (pricing, supply and demand).

Too many people shortcut the market assessment process. They finish their self-assessment process saying, "That's what I want," and then expect to find it. But a sound career strategy must take into account the realities of the marketplace.

FORMULATING YOUR CAREER STRATEGY

The results of your self-awareness and market assessment processes combine to formulate your career strategy. This will be your compass, your Pole Star, to direct your day-to-day career management. The process should culminate in some sort of *written* career strategy document—a work in progress that you will revise again and again over time. It need not be long. We suggest that it include

- Your career criteria (from your self-assessment)
- Market factors: *fit* and *probability*
- Your strategic goals
- Which criteria you will use to monitor progress
- A time line with checkpoint dates when you will take stock and check your progress

Bear in mind, your career strategy document is not set in stone. It is very much like a business plan, which initiates actions toward a goal—and then is periodically reviewed and modified.

Phase 2 of the Career Management Cycle: Self-Marketing

Visiting your local bookstore or surfing the Internet will confirm the large number of books and resources available on the details of self-marketing: résumés, interviewing, using the Internet, negotiating, and so on. Some are excellent. Others, especially those recommending "get a job quick" shortcuts, are unrealistic, bordering on irresponsible. Unfortunately, even the best of these resources are usually poorly utilized.

The sad truth is that most people jump into self-marketing prematurely— *before* they know what they are selling or what market they are targeting. They rush out, like a novice salesperson, enthusiastic but unprepared. Such behavior is understandable in action-oriented manager types, but the "ready-fire-aim" technique wouldn't be tolerated in a business context—and it does not lend itself to effective self-marketing.

That's why setting or resetting your career strategy *precedes* self-marketing in the Career Management Cycle, because you can't market yourself effectively without the preparatory work of self-awareness and market assessment. Once these are firmly in place, you will be in a position to use the many techniques of self-marketing to best effect.

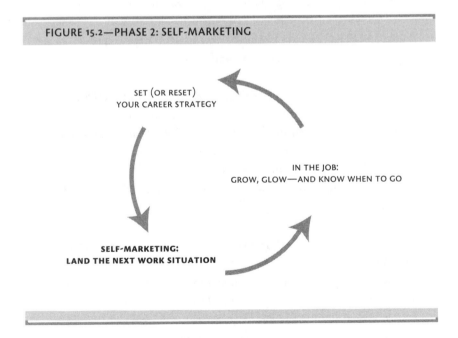

FIGURE 15.2—PHASE 2: SELF-MARKETING

SET (OR RESET)
YOUR CAREER STRATEGY

IN THE JOB:
GROW, GLOW—AND KNOW WHEN TO GO

SELF-MARKETING:
LAND THE NEXT WORK SITUATION

Clarity about your goal is a giant step toward achievement of that goal. Advocates of proactive visualization believe that developing a detailed inner picture of what you seek will increase your likelihood of finding it. In terms of Pragmatic Spirituality, that's where the Inspiration Dimension comes in, working in unexpected ways—through your Daily PS Focus and QDM sessions—to further your goals.

NETWORKING

Earlier, we referred to the single most important self-marketing technique—*networking*. The great majority of jobs and work opportunities come about not as a result of ads, Internet listings, or recruiters, but through a word-of-mouth, someone-knows-someone process. Networking is closely related to the Inspiration Dimension of Pragmatic Spirituality, if properly done.

Unfortunately, what most people do in the name of networking is a pale approximation of the real thing. The underlying premise of networking is simple:

- Once you have defined your goal, there are people who can lead you to that goal.
- Few (if any) of these people will be people you already know.
- Networking is a systematic process in which you start with the people you know and build a *network chain* of new contacts until you reach the person(s) who can put you in contact with your goal.

When Dick and Mary invited successful alums back to the HBS career seminar to recount their successful marketing campaigns, one theme was consistent among their varied experiences: they networked skillfully and aggressively, making hundreds and hundreds of contacts to eventually reach their goal.

As an indication of the importance of networking, an entire chapter of *In Transition* was devoted to this subject. Here, we'll summarize the most important steps of effective networking:

1. You need a well-organized database to encompass all your prospective contacts. Make a list of all the people you have ever known from work, family, social life, religious and community activities, neighbors, and so on. When you have a need, skim over the list. For example:
   — You need an introduction to XYZ Company located in Milwaukee. Skimming over your database, you recall that a person you used to

sing with in a choir has a brother in Milwaukee. You organize a network contact with your old choir mate to gain an introduction to the brother, who might lead you to a firsthand contact with an XYZ manager.

2. For each network contact, you need to prepare a script that clearly states
   — What you are seeking (as specific and succinct as possible)
   — Your reason for contacting this person
   — Examples of how she can help you establish another link in the chain
   — Your willingness to get back to her after some time
   Also have ready contingency scripts in case you encounter a voice mail or an intermediary, so that the message you leave is well crafted and compelling.

3. Decide whether the contact requires a face-to-face meeting. Much networking is more efficiently done by phone.

4. Make the call. Persevere appropriately as necessary.

5. Facilitate the networking conversation in the following ways:
   — Be considerate. If you're well prepared, you can focus on how the other person is reacting and respond appropriately. Don't corner him. Offer to call back if the time is inconvenient.
   — Be concise. If you are well organized, the other person will be impressed by the process and more likely to want to try to help.
   — Customize each network contact for the specific circumstances.

Every networking interaction is unique. Its success will depend on *how well you help the other person help you.*

Before each network contact, it's very useful to do a Quick Re-Focus. This will center and ground you, so that you can focus all your attention on responding appropriately during each part of the contact—and accepting whatever the results happen to be.

Phase 3 of the Career Management Cycle: In the Job

Congratulations! You found a wonderful application for your talents that you so carefully defined. Now for the third phase: *grow, glow—and know when to go!*

As we've discussed, rely on Pragmatic Spirituality to assist you in perceiving clearly what the actual circumstances are and how you can best relate to them. This will enable you to respond to others empathetically, to adapt as appropriate, and—most important—to look out for yourself.

Your relationship with your boss is the first order of business. Focus your attention on figuring out her expectations and preferences. (Use the checklist in Appendix D as a guide.) As soon as practicable, schedule a one-on-one orientation meeting. Accept your boss as she is, without focusing on what you might regard as shortcomings. Understand that your role is to make your boss look good in a work context. Be alert to any old Unfinished Business patterns that may be stirred up in you by your boss and sort through them. Remind yourself that this person is your boss—not your parent, adversary, or any other positive or negative old pattern or model.

Adapt the same attitude with your fellow workers. Assess them, but don't pass judgment. Focus on skills. Look for people who know the ropes, and learn from them. Note those who seem to have agendas other than getting the job done. Use the techniques from this section, such as the interpersonal accountability contracts, to keep your interactions constructive. Take time to build rapport. Watch

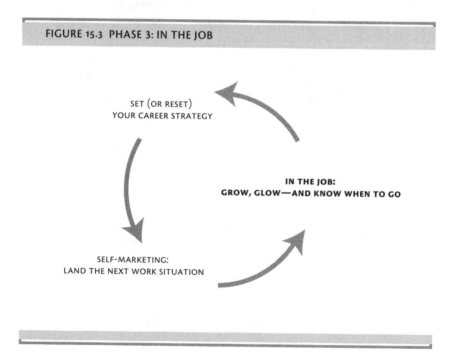

FIGURE 15.3 PHASE 3: IN THE JOB

SET (OR RESET)
YOUR CAREER STRATEGY

IN THE JOB:
GROW, GLOW—AND KNOW WHEN TO GO

SELF-MARKETING:
LAND THE NEXT WORK SITUATION

out for old constructs of loyalty and responsibility that might trip you up. When you encounter political situations, walk carefully and see what you can learn about others and yourself.

Do your Daily PS Focus at the beginning of each day, and a Quick Re-Focus as you come into the workplace and any time during the day that you seem to be losing your centeredness or need a self-esteem boost. And if you find yourself having difficulties dealing with certain people or situations, skim back over the earlier chapters on adaptability (Chapter 12), loyalty and responsibility (Chapter 13), and accountability (Chapter 14) to get a better perspective on what's going on.

And when your Intuitive input from your Daily PS Focus and your QDM work indicates that it's time for you to move on, pay attention! Crank up your Career Management Cycle: Reset your career strategy and update your network contacts. In most cases, this preparatory work can be done while you're still in the job, but once you move into the self-marketing phase of the Career Management Cycle, it is usually best done as a full-time endeavor. Leave your old position in good order and on good terms, so that you have yet another set of positive references as you move on to the next stage of your career.

That's effective career management, through one career cycle and on to the next—each time adding to your store of self-awareness and market assessment as you move toward your evolving life goals—toward success, however you choose to define it!

CEO of Your Career

The part of *In Transition* that generated the most positive feedback from readers was the advice to

appoint yourself CEO of your career.

Doing so offers three benefits:

1. It reminds you that managing your career is your primary responsibility.

2. It addresses the question of "I can't control external factors," which some people use as an excuse not to plan their lives. A CEO of an organization has *limited control* over the environment in which the company operates. However, the CEO's role is to

— Analyze the marketplace

— Assess the strengths and weaknesses of the organization

— Determine the courses of action that will result in the greatest return on assets with the least downside risk from liabilities

And, of course, that is exactly what is involved in managing your career

3. When you appoint yourself CEO of your career, you'll be aware that you need what every effective CEO needs—a *board of directors* (people to back you in your career management). A good board supports the CEO in three ways:

— Helps the CEO maintain objectivity

— Provides access to a broader range of outside information and resources

— Gives the CEO support and encouragement

So, by all means, appoint yourself CEO of your career, and make sure you have a strong board of directors. Managing your career is *not* something you can do on your own.

Common Obstacles to Effective Career Management

"We have met the enemy, and he is us." This wonderful quote from Walt Kelly's comic strip *Pogo* is all too relevant, unfortunately, to career management. Career counselors are quite familiar with the pattern: a person with a succession of jobs, having sabotaged himself in similar fashion at each position. And the most difficult part of the counselor's work is to get the person to understand what has been occurring and change his behavior.

This is a vivid reminder of the degree to which people can be unaware of major Unfinished Business issues that are at the core of their career problems— something obvious to everyone but them. The problem is compounded when the person has gone through the trauma of losing a job that provided a significant part of her identity. Career counselors are very aware that offering the right advice is the simple part. The difficult part is getting the struggling person to *hear* it.

Here's where Pragmatic Spirituality really pays off, since the obstacles people encounter invariably stem from Unfinished Business. Rereading Chapter 4 reminds us of the many ways in which people sabotage themselves at work and in other facets of their lives. The management of your career won't be hampered

TYPICAL CAREER MANAGEMENT IMPEDIMENTS

Not listening	Poor self-image
Inability to face reality (acceptance)	Inefficient work habits
Inaction	Perfectionism
Inappropriate reactions	Poor self-maintenance
Poor interpersonal skills	Depression
Problems with authority	

by such impediments if you have developed a proficiency in the Pragmatic Spirituality process and you do your Daily PS Focus regularly.

CHAPTER 15 HIGHLIGHTS

Because of the shifting workplace paradigm, it is likely that every employee will change jobs fairly often. In spite of their negative associations, career transitions can be times of growth and major life enhancements.

Pragmatic Spirituality is the foundation of effective career management. It calls every individual to clear self-understanding, ardent self-acceptance, and self-dependence.

The three principles of career management are
- Accept that you, and only you, are responsible for managing your career
- Recognize that career management is an *ongoing* process
- Develop a high degree of competency in all phases of the Career Management Cycle

The Career Management Cycle, in contrast to the old linear concept of long-term employment, is based on the assumption of ongoing change and accepts that each career will have many cycles, each consisting of three phases:
- Setting your career strategy
- Self-marketing: Land the next work situation
- In the job: Grow, glow—and know when to go

Career Management Cycle Phase 1: The two components of a career strategy are

- Self-awareness: understanding and accepting *what's in here* (closely related to the Pragmatic Spirituality process)
- Market assessment: researching the realities of *what's out there* (in terms of *fit* and *probability*)

Career Management Cycle Phase 2: Self-marketing must be preceded by the preparatory work of self-awareness and market assessment. Then you will be in a position to best choose among the many available resources to market yourself most effectively.

- Networking can be a very effective adjunct to self-marketing, but few people do it well.

Career Management Cycle Phase 3: Pragmatic Spirituality, augmented by the workplace pointers in Section III, will enable you to perceive accurately, respond appropriately, and work most effectively. Do your Daily PS Focus and Quick Re-Focus, and pay attention when your intuitive input says it's time to go.

Appoint yourself CEO of your career, and make sure you have a strong board of directors to support you. Managing your career is not something you can do on your own.

Obstacles to effective career management are common. Here's where Pragmatic Spirituality really pays off in transcending Unfinished Business, building a solid Identity/Integration/Inspiration foundation, and drawing on intuitive resources for greater authenticity to self and appropriateness in responses.

THE POTENTIAL FOR PRAGMATIC SPIRITUALITY IN THE ORGANIZATION

IV

16

FROM THE TRADITIONAL
TO THE EVOLVING
ORGANIZATION

*Men grind and grind in the mill of a truism, and nothing comes
out but what was put in. But the moment they desert the
tradition for a spontaneous thought, then poetry, wit, hope,
virtue, learning, anecdote, all flock to their aid.*

—Ralph Waldo Emerson

In this final section, we examine the application of Pragmatic Spirituality
at the organizational level, a logical progression from its applicability at the personal level and on the job. We believe the concepts and principles apply equally
well to a large, multifaceted corporation or a small firm, in the private or public
sector, with a goal of profit or charitable purposes. The objective of this section
is to discuss the extent to which and in which forms the principles of Pragmatic
Spirituality can be applied within any group of people working toward a common cause involving interdependency and interaction among its members.

Of necessity, this section is a premise for what might be, and hopefully will
be, accomplished by executives who wish to bring spirituality into their own
organizations—with beneficial effects on each business for its members, its effectiveness, and its bottom line. The approach we offer is vastly different from a
"quick-fix" program injected by an outside consultant. Pragmatic Spirituality in
the organization can only follow achievement of Pragmatic Spirituality at the
personal level and on the job. It must evolve from *within* rather than being
imposed externally, with buy-in needed at all levels, starting from the top. Until

recently, the intrinsic nature of an organization has been highly resistant to such change, but the radically changing environment buffeting today's businesses may not only make the principles of Pragmatic Spirituality possible, but even essential to a company's ability to thrive.

The Organizational World Turned Upside Down

In Chapter 10, we examined changes in the workplace and the organization. Life spans of organizations, technologies, products, skills, and jobs are decreasing. Marketplaces are increasingly global in nature. More data is produced than can be sorted and interpreted. In short, the entire world in which the organization functions is being turned upside down—and the old traditional organizational practices and underlying assumptions are no longer effective. Significantly, these radical changes are opening up new opportunities.

OVER THE DECADES, corporations expanded through growth and acquisition. Bigger did seem to be better. The discipline of Organizational Development came into being with resultant interest in theories of proper organizational practices. Few of these theories equipped organizations for dealing with current and evolving changes.

The late 1980s into the 1990s were turbulent times for business. The marketplace became global. Time frames accelerated: technologies evolved at an accelerating pace, diminishing product life cycles. The traditional hierarchical organizational structure lacked the responsiveness and flexibility to maneuver in these new waters. The result was widespread downsizing of conventional facilities and staff.

Convergence of Organizational and Individual Employee Interests

The following four figures examine the varied ramifications as the *traditional organization* adapts into the *evolving organization* on its management, its workplace, and the people who work for it—both as employees and as individuals.

Let's look at each one of the four in turn.

ORGANIZATIONAL MANAGEMENT

The *traditional organization* evolved in a market environment characterized by limited competition within well-defined geographic or regulatory boundaries. Any profound changes tended to occur gradually over time. The organizational form was largely hierarchical, with established policies directing the actions of employees at lower levels, and top-down decision making. Relatively little of management's attention was directed to long-term strategic matters; the majority of management time was spent supervising, making decisions on matters from below, and passing information up the organizational ladder for decision making at higher levels.

The *evolving organization* faces an environment of vastly more intense competition on an increasingly global basis, with profound changes in markets and technologies occurring virtually overnight. Just as the Rangers, SEALS, and other fast-reaction military units rapidly transcended old hierarchical leadership structures, so must today's managers make their organizations more maneuverable and responsive to market conditions. Keeping strategic plans up to date and ensuring their appropriate implementation has top priority, leaving managers less

---

FIGURE 16.1 THE ORGANIZATION: MARKETPLACE AND MANAGEMENT

THE TRADITIONAL ORGANIZATION	THE EVOLVING ORGANIZATION
MARKETPLACE	
Limited competition	Intense global competition
Changes occur slowly	Changes occur rapidly
MANAGEMENT ALLOCATION OF TIME	
Limited need for strategic oversight	Strategic planning and implementation paramount
Much time spent on supervision	Limited time and staff for supervision

time for day-to-day supervision and operational decisions. "Staying on top of the situation" in a time of increasingly intense information flow has become critical.

THE ORGANIZATIONAL WORKPLACE

In the hierarchical structure of the *traditional* organization, movement within the structure was incremental. Lateral moves from one department to another were infrequent. Vertical movement up the ladder was largely based on time spent in a position and developing expertise. Learning by formal training or on-the-job experience was an ongoing process. Procedures were highly codified. Decision making was "top-down," based on information passed up the ladder by intermediate managers and supervisors. The presumption was that an employee who worked hard and was loyal would be there for the long haul.

To survive and compete effectively in the fast-moving, turbulent marketplace, the *evolving* organization must be flexible and responsive, as different from the

---

FIGURE 16.2 THE ORGANIZATION: WORKPLACE AND VALUES

THE TRADITIONAL ORGANIZATION	THE EVOLVING ORGANIZATION
Hierarchical structure	Flatter, more flexible "structure"
Low employee movement and turnover	Frequent moves in, out, and within the organization
Ongoing training	Little time/staff for training
Information reported up; Decisions come down	Need fast decision by best-informed person

VALUES/ASSUMPTIONS

Work hard + obey = Long-term job	Average stay in company is short (3-5 years)
Loyalty to company	Loyalty to position
Managers/Employees = Long-term "Team"	"Independent Contractor" modality

traditional organization as a highly maneuverable modern patrol craft is from a WWII battleship. Internal boundaries are blurred because the capabilities and interactions of the various functional units must be adaptable to changing requirements. The need for quick reaction requires that the decision-making function be pushed closer and closer to the person "on the spot with the most information." The intermediary manager role so prevalent in traditional organizations is virtually eliminated, making the evolving organization much "flatter." With higher staff turnover (both in and out, and from one department to another) there is little time for training, so employees must be quick studies and very adaptable.

The Employee as a Worker

The "job-for-life" implied contract of the *traditional* organization created a value system in which the organization came first. Of course, in reality jobs often didn't last for life, and terminations were as traumatic for supervisors and surviving coworkers as for the dismayed employee who felt cast out of the corporate family, betrayed and abandoned.

FIGURE 16.3 THE EMPLOYEE AS A WORKER

THE TRADITIONAL ORGANIZATION	THE EVOLVING ORGANIZATION
VALUES/ASSUMPTIONS	
Company = Family	Highest Value = Constructive work relationships
	Multiple supervisors; more informal relationships
Boss = Parent	Finite/Limited-term jobs
Job-for-life	"Grow, Glow—and Know When to Go"
LIFE PRIORITIES	
Job is overriding priority	Desire to balance work with other aspects of life

The *evolving* organization requires employees who are not only quick stud-ies and highly adaptable, but who are also comfortable in situations that lack clear role definition and/or certainty about how long the job will last. These employees need to be conscientious and responsible, but not encumbered with feelings about "belonging" to the organization that would interfere with a clean and professional separation when that comes to pass. Instead, their motivation is to best use each employment situation to add to their knowledge portfolio and their list of satis-fied clients—very similar to an independent contractor. Their work is only one of a number of important factors in their lives, and if one job does not balance well with their other life factors, they will move on to find work that does.

THE EMPLOYEE AS AN INDIVIDUAL

The identity (sense of self) of the typical *traditional* organization employee was largely or wholly based on external doing/having factors, with his employer/title/job content as the primary focus, without much consideration of self-identity or balancing one's life and work. Heavy-duty Unfinished Business behaviors and belief patterns dictated roles in all areas of one's life, minimizing authenticity of relationships and perpetuating stereotypes and prejudices.

The *evolving* organization needs individuals who are striving to integrate all the facets of a Fully Functioning Adult. Such employees are an ideal fit for the

---

FIGURE 16.4 THE EMPLOYEE AS AN INDIVIDUAL

THE TRADITIONAL ORGANIZATION	THE EVOLVING ORGANIZATION
IDENTITY	
Derived from the job, external factors	Internally derived; less dependent on work
VALUES/PRIORITIES	
Subordinate family/self to company's needs	Strive for a balance between job/ family/self-interests

needs of the evolving organization, and—because they function with a free-agent mentality—they will tend to gravitate toward organizations with the most challenging work and constructive work environments.

A Paradigm Shift in the Employer-Employee Relationship

A close examination of the contrasts between the traditional organization and the evolving organization reveals that the fundamental difference between the two is in the nature of the relationship between the organization and its employees. In the traditional relationship, the advantage was definitely with the employer organization, both from the standpoint of calling the shots and "terminating at will," but—more important—because psychically, the employee was in a dependent modality without a strong sense of identity apart from the job.

If, as we hope, more and more people become proficient in Pragmatic Spirituality, they will create a growing "sellers' market" wherein employer organizations increasingly seek out this type of employee to fill their needs. And, because of the mobility and Self-maintenance awareness of these employees, the only way organizations can attract and retain them is to create and maintain an organizational environment that is stimulating and consistent with the principles of Pragmatic Spirituality.

In this way, Pragmatic Spirituality can gradually be a transforming factor in both individual lives and in the fabric and actions of organizations—opening up a more exciting potential for ameliorating the community of the world. The most likely force for achieving significant constructive change on the local or global scale is not governments or religions or "causes," but effectively functioning business organizations. To date, the profit motive has too often been at cross purposes with the general good; however, if Pragmatic Spirituality becomes a technique for improving the bottom line, that would create a force for constructive change of inconceivable potency.

The concluding years of the twentieth century and the start of the twenty-first have overturned many old concepts and institutions. There is also a growing awareness that continued exploitation of our planet is jeopardizing our very existence in this fragile ecosystem. Perhaps the evolving spiritual hunger, evidenced in so many facets of our existence—including business—will weave together these disparate elements into a groundswell for change that will assure the human race a continued existence on this planet entrusted to our care.

WE CAN DO BUSINESS FROM OUR MOST PROFOUND inner consciousness, from which there can be a sense of connection with others in our business. This statement is predicated on each of us acknowledging that we all have an inner wisdom and intelligence that allows us to work with others in extraordinary ways, "anticipating the possible" with fellow workers and bringing the qualities of connection, creativity, compassion, and intuition into every phase of our work environment.

As one indication of the impact of the new paradigm and its openness to new approaches, the next chapter recounts actual instances of Quantum Decision Making (QDM) being used by managers in business organizations to deal with complex issues where insufficient data complicates the normal rational decision-making process. Following that, we will explore other ways in which Pragmatic Spirituality can assist a traditional organization in becoming an evolving organization.

CHAPTER 16 HIGHLIGHTS

Until recently, the intrinsic nature of the organization has been highly resistant to spirituality, but the changes buffeting today's organizations may make the principles of Pragmatic Spirituality not only possible but even essential for an organization's ability to thrive.

The converging interests of the organization and the individual employee are evidenced in Figures 16.1–4. The evolving organization needs employees who require less training and supervision, are able to make better decisions on their own, and are sufficiently self-directed to deal with the realities of indefinite-term employment situations—these employees are very much akin to Fully Functioning Adults.

In the traditional organization, the advantage was with the employer, both because of the workplace ethos and the dependent modality of the typical employee. The evolving organization will need to create and maintain an envi-

ronment that attracts Fully Functioning Adult employees—one consistent with the principles of Pragmatic Spirituality.

Pragmatic Spirituality can gradually be a transforming factor in both individual lives and in the fabric and actions of organizations—opening up a more exciting potential for ameliorating the community of the world.

17

QDM: THE BOTTOM-LINE POWER OF INTUITION IN THE ORGANIZATION

Essentially, the role of a President/CEO is to make decisions . . . hundreds or thousands of them every month. Since business is clearly more of an art than science, intuition should play a critical role in making good decisions. I highly recommend Dr. Jue's QDM process to improve intuition.

—DONALD R. COTTLE, Group Chairman, TEC Worldwide, Inc.

JUST AS PRAGMATIC SPIRITUALITY can bring enhancement to an individual's life at both the personal and workplace levels, we believe that the Pragmatic Spirituality process, with its three Dimensions of *Identity*, *Integration*, and *Inspiration*, can enhance the bottom line of an organization, enabling it to continually evolve and adapt as needed to changing market environments.

The basis for this belief is the ample evidence provided by the effectiveness of Quantum Decision Making, which was described in Chapter 11. Both QDM and Pragmatic Spirituality achieve enhancement through the use of intuitive capabilities; the difference between the two is that QDM tends to focus on one specific situation, while Pragmatic Spirituality deals with the totality of an organism (individual or organization): its antecedents, the integrity of its component parts, its functionality within its environment, and achievement of its potential.

The Varied Applications of QDM

This chapter presents actual scenarios of how QDM can enable a quick, constructive response to organizational needs. These examples, in turn, form the basis for a subsequent discussion in the next chapter of the further potential contribution of Pragmatic Spirituality in an organization.

QDM SCENARIO 1: REDESIGNING A KEY PRODUCT LINE

Ron had introduced QDM to the top executive team of a large corporation. They were intrigued, but somewhat skeptical. Ron challenged them to apply QDM to a difficult decision they were facing at the time. After a brief discussion with the team, the technical head agreed to have Ron work with a group in the research and product development department who had been wrestling with a complex assignment for six months.

The "PDQ" product line had been a mainstay for nearly ten years. When initially introduced to the market, the first PDQ model had represented a major technological advance. Over the years, two additional models were introduced and did well. Recently, however, sales of the PDQ product line had declined. Different departments had diverse recommendations on what should be done. These boiled down to three options:

1. Design and build a new model that would replace all three current models.
2. Make significant changes to one of the models and discontinue the others.
3. Redesign all three models to broaden their applicability into a wider range of market sectors.

The implications to the company's bottom line and industry reputation were profound. Each option had its own set of ramifications. The price tag and time line for each of the three options differed radically, as did opinions about the relative payoffs.

Ron met with the working committee, consisting of representatives from each department affected by the decision. They reviewed the three alternative routes. Their complexities made any rational comparison virtually impossible, and the decision-making discussions had become circular—coming back to the same point of indecisiveness no matter which route was considered.

The sixteen people in the meeting had no experience with the QDM process, but they were aware that Ron was there at the request of top management.

They were also motivated by six frustrating months of indecision, which created a sense of receptivity even if they didn't understand or believe in the process. Ron asked the group to put aside their analytical way of thinking and to focus on the question, "What is the best course of action to achieve a successful product for our marketplace?"

Ron led the group through a visualization, going to a place of peace where each of them could be relaxed, with no expectations of results or outcomes. He explained to them that their intuitive minds would respond to the question with some kind of Icon and encouraged them to resist the tendency to analyze. Instead, they were to simply persevere and experience each Icon, sharing as much as possible of the experience with the group: feelings, sensory input, kinetics, speaking with the Icon's voice, and so on.

They followed the guidelines of relaxation, and soon their intuitive minds began to come up with Icons. Ron had cautioned them that there would be no one correct Icon and that it would be an integrative process. Each shared an Icon as it appeared, one Icon generating others in an evolving process that gathered momentum.

At first, the Icons seemed to deal with ways of adjusting and remodeling the existing machines, but gradually the flow of Icons pointed them in a new direction—and to the final solution. Someone came up with an Icon of a box with many holes, permitting a prospective user to peer in and see the many ways the machine could function, but the Icon also revealed that the surface of the box lacked any indication of which hole showed which function. When this person became the voice of the box (Icon) he said, "I need instructions placed on me so that others can see that I have more potential than most people currently realize." When he said this, the others understood that what was needed was not major redesign but rather a new vision and more effective communication of the potential of the existing machines.

In a sudden "aha" experience, the group realized that they needed a new set of technical literature and marketing materials that would enable customers to use the machines in new ways. The intuitive image captured their imagination, and they quickly came to agreement that the exterior could be redesigned to make it more user friendly, with only minor modifications to the inner mechanisms. The group ended the QDM session in great excitement. The new direction could be accomplished quickly enough for a new marketing campaign to be in place in time for a major trade show, and the budget was far lower than that of any of the options previously considered.

In a subsequent QDM session, the group came up with a new name for the updated machine, which would differentiate it from the previous models. The new name succeeded in combining the reputation of the prior models with the advances of the new model. The new model created great enthusiasm with the company's sales force and the marketplace. Sales exceeded expectations and boosted interest in the company's entire range of products.

QDM Scenario 2: Attracting Key Talent

The top management of one of Ron's European corporate clients asked for his help with a recruitment problem. They had been trying for some time to recruit a very talented engineer from a competitor in Texas. The engineer had said he felt it would be very satisfying to work in the company's research and development department, which was one of the best in the world. The engineer's background meshed perfectly with the company's requirements, and the chemistry with other chief executives seemed to be very good.

The company had made the engineer a very attractive offer: his own laboratory space, staff, housing, and a generous compensation package. Yet the engineer couldn't seem to make up his mind. In telephone discussions with top management in Europe, the engineer seemed to be pleased with the package, but he kept putting them off. Frustration levels were rising. Some were recommending that the offer be withdrawn and a search begun for other candidates.

Ron met with a number of people involved in recruitment to address the problem using QDM. The human resources people were very familiar with QDM, using it frequently in day-to-day matters. Some from other departments had not used QDM, but were aware of its reputation. Ron went through the preliminaries and then formulated the question for the group: "What is needed to have this engineer come to work here?" The participants began to generate Icons, all of which involved not the engineer but various aspects concerning *children*. Ron asked whether the engineer had children. He did, two teenagers. As the Icons evolved and were processed, their theme and character expressed some kind of educational engagement. Ron shared his sense that what was being communicated by the Icons was that the obstacle was the engineer's children and their schooling. The group was surprised, because that had been discussed with the engineer and had not appeared to be a problem.

The managers used their logical minds to develop a list of items that might address the concerns reflected in the QDM process. This included private tutors, bilingual education, involvement in year-round sports, and side trips to different parts of Europe. With this list of possibilities before them, they did another QDM process to create a package, which was then presented to the engineer. In six months, the engineer and his family were established in their new home in Switzerland.

QDM Scenario 3: Dealing with Key Independent Consultants

A company had a number of outside consultants who were key to the company's success. Over time, there had been minor frictions and misunderstandings about work relationships, creating an awareness of the need to set up a format for a revised protocol that allowed the consultants autonomy but facilitated their work on projects involving each other and company employees. Management had made several unsuccessful efforts at coming up with a mutually agreeable solution to this situation, which was complicated by large egos and disparate agendas.

Ron conducted a QDM session with the consultants, whose attitudes ranged from curiosity to skepticism. Soon, however, Icons began to emerge, and the creative and intuitive capabilities of the consultants was evidenced by the rapid and sophisticated manner in which one Icon followed another, each embodying a new component of creativity. The initial Icon was of an airport, with each consultant represented by an airline. This then evolved into the docking facilities, which represented the interface between the company and the consultants, with each consultant needing a different type of docking facility.

In that one afternoon, the QDM process led to a practical business model that was agreed upon by each consultant and covered all aspects of the relationships. The proposal was presented to heads of the business units involved with the consultants, who agreed to the new protocol—some with reservations. The new procedure was put into practice and worked flawlessly. In time, some of the internal organizational procedures were modified to take advantage of lessons learned from the consultants' model.

QDM Scenario 4: Transcending Disparate Cultures

Stan, the vice president of an international company, faced a challenging situation. He had recently been appointed to head up a management team called the Southeast Asia Group that included members from China, India, Indonesia, and Australia. Up until now it had been a group in name only; most of the members had never met each other, and its only communications had been interoffice memos and a few dispirited conference calls. Stan had received permission to hold a team-building meeting in Hong Kong for all the regional company heads in the group.

Stan was acutely aware of the range of racial and cultural differences in perceptions, attitudes, and values that would be represented around the conference room table. He was also mindful of the fact that a number of the participants were new to the company, and that this was the first time the Southeast Asia Group would be asked to do something as a cohesive group. Among the agenda items was the creation of a mission statement for the group. All participants were reasonably fluent in English, but Stan knew the obstacles to cooperation would be far more complex than just language.

Stan had used QDM in his past position, and early in the meeting he introduced the participants to the process. The group members were first led through a process of relaxation, and then asked to focus on the energetic field that had been created by bringing this particular group of people together. They were then presented with several guiding questions and asked to bring forth Icons that represented the working potential of the team. Slowly and then more readily the participants came up with Icons, fifteen in all, which were listed on the whiteboard. During the eliciting of the Icons, a very positive energy was generated among the group, which dissipated the initial reserve with which the meeting had started.

During the animated discussion, the Icons were considered and grouped according to theme. They included, among others, a tall skyscraper with many floors and access elevators, an elaborate heliport, and an oriental farm that had different barns as resource buildings for the farm. The predominant themes were coordinated efforts, fast access to resources and markets, and seeing the group as interdependent resources rather than as competing entities within the company.

Everyone was excited to see the commonality of vision that emerged from this process. They entered enthusiastically into the preparation of a mission statement, which embraced the richness of their diversity, the strength of their resources, and the complementary nature of their ways of thinking and problem solving. During the remainder of the meeting, the variety of Icons on the whiteboard reminded each participant that their differences and similarities symbolized the many talents and resources available to achieve their mutual objectives as a well-coordinated team.

The conference was an unqualified success, thanks to Stan's effective use of QDM.

QDM Can Take a Variety of Forms

These examples of problem solving with QDM involve groups of managers with varying degrees of QDM experience generating and interpreting intuitive Icons under a moderator who explains the process, sets the stage, encourages the group's responses, and facilitates interpretations of Icons. As evidenced by the following real-life examples, QDM is adaptable to a wide variety of circumstances, the essential aspects are

- Trust in the process
- The Socratic process of question and response
- Empathetic interpretation of Icons
- Implementation balanced between left/rational and right/intuitive thinking, always ready for another round of questions and responses when needed

The use of directed intuition in decision making is not limited to large organizations. The following is an example of its use in a modified QDM context by Howard, the owner of a small family-owned firm.

QDM Scenario 5: A Small Family-Owned Business
Howard had proposals from three banks for a new credit relationship, and he needed to come to a decision by Friday. All three proposals were workable; each had pros and cons. He had spent several days doing detailed analysis, but his logical process had hit a wall.

Fortunately, Howard had a close friend, Walt, who was familiar with QDM. They met the next evening, and Walt led Howard through a QDM-like process. After asking the question, "Which bank relationship would be best for the company?" Walt led Howard through a visualization. Beginning in a place of calm, Howard then walked along a path and arrived at the shore of a lake, in the middle of which was an island. Using a causeway to reach the island, Howard became aware of three buildings representing the three banks.

Howard described the first building to Walt, then entered it, giving a running commentary on what he saw, his impressions, and his feelings. Walt asked clarifying questions and recorded what Howard said. This was repeated, in turn, for the other two buildings. Walt then asked Howard which building represented which bank. Howard readily identified the connections.

Walt then said to Howard, "On the count of three, you will know which of these is best suited for you and your company. One . . . two . . . three." And Howard had a strong sense that the best choice was Bank C. Later on, he explained:

Each structure was quite different, and quite vivid. The Bank A structure was very impressive—a tall, commanding building with lots of glass, chrome, and structural steel. As I walked around, though, I couldn't make contact with any of the people I saw.

The Bank B structure had a solid, old-fashioned elegance to it—it inspired trust. As I walked around inside, the quality was impressive, but then I opened a door and found myself in a very austere room that had the feeling of a courtroom, including a "dock" where the defendant stands and a long table for the judge and jury.

The Bank C structure was pretty unimposing from the outside. I went inside, and it felt very comfortable—nothing fancy, but clean and functional. The people were very friendly, and I could feel a strong sense of rapport. One of them offered me coffee, but somehow I spilled it on the nice carpet. He laughed it off and said not to worry.

After I came to the intuitive decision, I realized that there was an important factor I had not considered. Now each of the banks was vying for my business, but if my company got into trouble what would happen? The "courtroom" of Bank B was vivid to me—if I did not comply with their requirements I would be up there on the dock facing the long table of people passing judgment. Bank A was impressive, but if I needed some special attention, could I get it? My strong feeling was that I would get the most cooperation and consideration at Bank C.

Confident of his decision based on this experience, Howard signed the agreement with Bank C. Interestingly enough, some months later, Howard's company did get into difficulties due to a nonperforming vendor, which rendered the firm unable to comply with its covenants with the bank. As foreshadowed in the visualization, the Bank C people worked with him nonjudgmentally and, in time, his company regained a solid footing. Howard's interpretation:

When I did that visualization, I had no conscious awareness that there was trouble down the path for my company. On a deeper level, however, I must have had an intuitive sense of it, because that became the key factor in my decision—thank heavens!

QDM Scenario 6: Intervention with a Difficult Manager

An HR manager had been asked to investigate numerous reports of friction and conflicts between a recently assigned department head and the people under his supervision. The company valued the manager's technical expertise, but the disruption could not be allowed to continue.

It was difficult to get input without compromising the situation, so the HR manager used the QDM process, asking what the nature of the problem was. The intuitive Icon that came up was of a helpless dog barking: When interpreted empathetically, this communicated that—in spite of his considerable track record at other companies—the manager was insecure and lacked confidence, which he covered up by "barking" and being critical of his workers. Further observations by the HR manager and an interview with the department head confirmed the intuitive input. The manager was counseled and was sent to a training course that focused on self-awareness and interpersonal interactions. The manager worked hard to change his old behaviors, and the situation rapidly improved.

QDM Scenario 7: You Can't Judge a Book by Its Cover

Warren, the personnel director for a bank, was nearing the end of a recruitment process for an important position—head of the bank's loan department. A number of promising potential candidates had been interviewed, resulting in a short list of three finalists, each of whom seemed to be very well qualified. In particular, one of the finalists, Ken, had made a very strong impression with everyone who had met him. Ken's education and experience were excellent, and he had an attractive appearance and confident demeanor, which had especially impressed the senior vice president to whom he would be reporting. It was Warren's sense that Ken was highly favored to win the job, but first he had to do a final round of reference checks and interviews with the finalists to make sure all points had been covered.

For some time Warren had been conducting interviews using what he had learned in a QDM course. While going through the particulars of the interview, Warren would focus his intuitive mind on the field of energy of the person being interviewed and ask himself the question, "Is this applicant an appropriate choice for this position?" After the interview, his intuitive input would augment the factual information and his rational observations. He had developed this technique into a very effective interviewing strategy, which was to be demonstrated during his final meeting with Ken.

As he met with Ken, Warren activated his intuitive mind with the question, "Is Ken the appropriate person for this job?" Almost immediately, Warren received a strong negative visceral response: his stomach knotted. As the discussion with Ken proceeded, the image of a dark cloud appeared in Warren's mind, and he abruptly asked Ken, "What did you do wrong?" The question was completely out of context with the rest of the interview, and Ken was taken aback. After a long silence, Ken's demeanor changed and he haltingly revealed that he had been fined and jailed for committing fraud. His résumé had been altered to conceal this, and he had made arrangements with a friend to give specious information when Warren's department checked references. Ken was informed that the interview was concluded, and he left the building quickly.

"I should know by now that you can't judge a book by its cover, but he sure had me fooled," said the senior vice president to Warren after praising him for an excellent job of recruitment due diligence. "The bank could have been seriously embarrassed if we had hired Ken and the truth eventually came out."

QDM Scenario 8: Resolving Conflicting Internal Demands

A very talented person was to become available from another department within the company, and several department heads were vying to get him. The division head did not want to be involved in the decision, so he tossed the decision to the HR manager. The HR manager did a QDM process with several close associates. It yielded the Icon of a key, which reflected the character and skills of the individual. The QDM process continued with images of a number of doors, each representing one of the departments interested in the employee. The intuitive input clearly indicated the key fitting into one of the doors. The HR manager made his decision accordingly, and the use of the QDM process made the results more palatable to the unsuccessful department heads. The fit of the employee in the chosen department was excellent in every way.

QDM Scenario 9: The Bored Receptionist

It is not always necessary to carry out the full QDM process to access intuitive insights, as shown by this example.

An office manager had received numerous complaints about the mechanical and flat tone of voice with which one of the receptionists typically answered the phone. This employee had an excellent record of reliability and dedication, so the office manager tried various ways of addressing the situation. In spite of suggestions and coaching, there was little change. Finally, the office manager met with the employee and asked this simple question: "Who would you have to be in order to make the client on the other end of the phone feel cared for?"

The receptionist thought for a while and then came back with the answer: "I would have to feel that everyone who called was an important client, and I would have to be in a place that enabled me to make the client feel that way." As soon as she was able to visualize this, she found it possible to shift to a place of Being empowered to make a difference with the clients. From that point on, her voice, and the client feedback, changed completely.

The question "Who would you have to be in order to . . ." is very powerful. It tends to bypass Unfinished Business obstacles and calls on the intuitive and visualization powers of the person to come up with not only the answer but with imagery that empowers a change in patterns.

The examples in this chapter offer a strong argument that, just as it is possible to enhance the ability of an individual to better access her intuitive resources, the Inspiration Dimension of Pragmatic Spirituality can be brought to bear on an organization, with a highly beneficial impact on the bottom line.

QDM—a Harbinger of the Benefits of Pragmatic Spirituality

QDM can enhance the effectiveness and creativity of an organization. In that regard, the QDM process foreshadows the further organizational benefits that could be achieved with Pragmatic Spirituality.

We refer back to the concept of spirituality as *enhancement*, and of the Inner Edge that comes from greater authenticity and appropriateness. If these can be realized by an individual, why not an organization?

In the next chapter, we explore the potential of Pragmatic Spirituality in the organization.

CHAPTER 17 HIGHLIGHTS

Just as Pragmatic Spirituality can bring enhancement to an individual's life at both the personal and workplace levels, we believe that its principles can enhance the bottom line of an organization, enabling it to continually evolve, adapting as needed to changing market environments.

Quantum Decision Making, described in Chapter 11, has demonstrated the ability of directed intuition to enhance decision making and creativity in both large and small business organizations.

QDM is adaptable to a wide variety of circumstances. Its essential aspects include the following:

- Trust in the process
- The Socratic process of question and response
- Empathetic interpretation of Icons
- Implementation balanced between left/rational and right/intuitive thinking, always ready for another round of question and response when needed

The QDM process foreshadows the further organizational benefits that could be achieved with Pragmatic Spirituality.

18

THE POTENTIAL FOR
PRAGMATIC SPIRITUALITY
IN THE ORGANIZATION

*All great questions of politics and economics come down in the
last analysis to the decisions and actions of individual men and
women. They are questions of human relations, and we ought
always to think about them in terms of men and women—the
individual human beings who are involved in them. If we can get
human relations on a proper basis, the statistics, finance, and all
other complicated technical aspects of these questions will be
easier to solve.*

—Thomas J. Watson

The demonstrated effectiveness of QDM in calling on participants' intuitive resources to address complex business issues forms the basis for our belief in the applicability of the principles of Pragmatic Spirituality to organizational enhancement on a broader basis—to achieve a workable form of spirituality in business. Our original definition of Pragmatic Spirituality—authenticity and appropriateness, along with the resultant enhancement in self-acceptance and effectiveness—is applicable for one individual or many individuals working with a common identity and goal.

Enhancing Each Synapse in the Organization

Ample proof exists that intuitive and spiritual techniques can increase an individual's mental acuity and enhance the body's use of energy—physical, emotional,

and psychic. These enhancements are achieved (a) by reducing internal dissonance and energy needed for internal maintenance, and (b) through a *centeredness* that focuses all parts of an individual on the project at hand.

Widespread examples are all around us: a heart patient using meditation to
lower her blood pressure, a person achieving greater self-acceptance through visualization exercises, a parent awaking in the middle of the night at the same
moment his first grandchild is being born. Such experiences will become more
commonplace as the validity of human intuitive powers becomes more widely
accepted, overcoming the invested skepticism and suspicion of the rational mind
and many religious and social traditions.

Why should these benefits not also accrue on the organizational level? QDM
has proven the catalytic capabilities of intuition even among hardheaded, skeptical managers. Extrapolating further benefits of intuition from the human experience into the organizational paradigm foreshadows extraordinary possibilities:

- Everyone in the organization with a clearer understanding of their jobs
- All decisions throughout the entire organization accomplished more rap-
  idly and accurately
- Every one of the countless interactions that make up the fabric of the
  organization's transactional efficiency performed more effectively
- Friction, rivalries, and misunderstandings between people and units
  diminished
- "New ways of doing things"—from new products to faster work flow in
  the mailroom—an ongoing occurrence
- Customers responding to increased empathy and rapport from every level
  of the organization
- Relations with all the factors in the organization's "outside world" flowing
  more smoothly because all elements are working in harmony
- The organization's enhanced responsiveness to marketplace demands and
  opportunities achieving significant competitive advantages

Speculation? Yes, but not so far-fetched in light of what has actually been accomplished in varied circumstances through the use of intuition.

Take a moment to visualize *your* organization with its countless "synapses"
—people-to-people interactions through which information flows and action
takes place. Clearly, if each of these could be enhanced by only a small degree,
the bottom-line impact would be enormous!

Keeping the Bottom Line in Spirituality

Note that the justification for Pragmatic Spirituality in the organization focuses squarely on the bottom-line benefits, rather than on doing good or doing the right thing. It is our firm belief that the outcome *will* benefit all stakeholders of the organization, because one outcome of Pragmatic Spirituality is a greater degree of overall authenticity and appropriateness. This is distinct from the well-intentioned introduction of spiritual practices into an organization solely on their own "do-good" merits.

Consider this example:

> The owner of a company had a personal religious experience. He contacted Ron to discuss bringing a higher spiritual tone to his own company. After some discussion Ron strongly advised against a number of the owner's ideas, which did not seem to fit with the company's realities.
>
> In spite of this advice, the owner proceeded on his own to put into effect his interpretation of spiritual practices, including elimination of time clocks, increase in paid vacation and personal days, elimination of drug testing, interest-free loans for employees, and other concessions.
>
> The results were disastrous: a small percentage of employees took advantage of the situation, supervisors felt their authority had been compromised, employee loans went unpaid, a serious warehouse accident was traced to drug use, and there was strong resentment among the conscientious employees who continued to try to do their jobs properly.
>
> The offending employees were fired, and the angry owner reverted back to a highly regimented system, to the dismay of the employees who had not abused the system. Overall, the company was hurt quite badly. The owner returned to Ron, puzzled as to why his good intentions had come out so badly. Ron replied, "Because they were not realistic."

Examples such as this are not that uncommon, both at a personal and an organizational level. People who move to a "spiritual" or "religious" modality can leave their common sense and good judgment behind.

Another example of how spirituality can distort good judgment is the attitude of some spiritual advocates that private corporations "have a responsibility to do good works." That, indeed, seems like a good solution, but it overlooks reality on several levels. As we have commented before, the underlying responsibility of a private corporation is to *survive*. In today's marketplace, unless "doing good" is compatible with the competitive viability of a private corporation, it is not realistic—or responsible.

The core concept of Pragmatic Spirituality at the organizational level is that it should enhance the effectiveness of the organization and thus be evident at the bottom line—in terms of quantitative profits and qualitative results.

For the remainder of Section IV, we will focus our remarks on *for-profit* corporations, both publicly held and privately owned. The principles of Pragmatic Spirituality apply equally to other organizations, but if they work in the profit sector, they should work anywhere.

Applying Pragmatic Spirituality Principles to Organizations

Conceptually, an organization is an organism similar to an individual, with a history, identity, outdated behavior patterns and practices (Unfinished Business), and a number of stakeholders (external demands) competing for its time and energies. Just as with an individual, if Pragmatic Spirituality can enhance organizational authenticity and appropriateness, the interactions between the components of an organization will function more effectively and with less wasted energy.

The Identity Dimension in an Organization

There are many parallels between the discussion in Chapter 6 on Identity at the personal level and the "identity" of an organization. The latter is not located in the mind, body, and soul as with an individual; however, each organization does have equivalent components that combine to give it a sense of self-identity as an entity. There are historical antecedents, times of prosperity and pain, successes and embarrassments. The history of an organization is populated with individuals, some having made a powerful impression—good or bad. A corporation's internal values, beliefs, actions, and conscience figure heavily in how it is perceived by the outside world.

Unfinished Business

Just as the first step in the Pragmatic Spirituality process for an individual is to uncover and address his Unfinished Business, an important step in the process for an organization is to clarify its own identity and scrutinize all of its traditional values and behavioral patterns—some of which are quite possibly no longer useful or appropriate to current situations.

One of the most striking examples of the value of examining old belief systems and behavioral patterns is the necessary strategy of periodically reassessing how a company fits into the marketplace. The annals of business history are full of companies that floundered because habitual patterns doomed them to obsolescence or irrelevance, and of companies who stayed alert to changing market trends by frequently asking questions such as

- "What business are we in now?"
- "How does the market view our company?"
- "What needs must the company address in order to align its purpose with its appropriate market?"

Intuition and QDM are useful tools with which to ensure that the identity of a business remains relevant to its marketplace.

Doing/Having Versus Being

The world in which most for-profit corporations operate is highly results-oriented—particularly true for publicly traded companies whose stock price can fluctuate wildly based on the most recent good or bad news. Although responsible corporate leadership ought to be based on the longer-term perspective, there are strong pressures on CEOs to manage the bottom line quarter-by-quarter.

To a certain extent, this situation stems from the hunger of investors for updates, as well as competition among the news media for the latest information; however, much of it is influenced by the organization's concept of whether its identity is based on Doing/Having or Being.

The organizational identity based on Doing/Having publishes frequent press releases about accomplishments, cultivates contacts with investment analysts and media representatives, and watches its stock price carefully. On the other hand, the organization whose identity has a higher *Being* content operates with an attitude that says, "We've got a strategic goal and we're doing our best to achieve it. Some of our investments and decisions will take some time to bear fruit, but we're not going to manage the company based on quarterly results or the price of our stock."

Each type of organization will attract a different type of following—both media and investors. It may be that the organization whose identity is more balanced between Being and Doing/Having will end up with a more stable investor group, even though its "press" will be less dramatic.

THE INTEGRATION DIMENSION IN AN ORGANIZATION

On the personal level, Integration deals with the allocation of energies and attention between the inner aspects of responsible self-management and the demands of many external factors. Organizations represent a clear parallel with this because the essence of managing any company is the allocation of its resources to maximize the return on assets and to minimize the downside of its liabilities.

This balancing or prioritization process is much more complex for an organization than for an individual for two reasons:

1. An organization's external demands represent an unforgiving competitive environment, where failure can mean the organization's demise.

2. The internal factors that make up an organization, namely its many employees and their myriad interactions, are vastly more heterogeneous and in flux than an individual's. In an organization, there are constant intrinsic stresses: groups of people are prone to interpersonal friction, communications frequently break down, competition is common (either constructive or otherwise), and in addition to the organizational factors, there are distractions and disruptions of events in members' personal lives.

With this perspective, it is clear that the Integration aspects of an organization have a strong influence on how efficiently it functions and whether it survives.

The Integration Dimension also relates directly to the previously mentioned issue of a corporation's responsibility to "do good." The following example is a good illustration of this.

> Assume there are two private corporations, equal in size and resources and competing in the same market. Corporation A heeds the injunctions to "be a good corporate citizen" and diverts a significant amount of resources from its competitive activities into good works that are beneficial to society but give it no marketplace advantage. Corporation B, on the other hand, "sticks to its last" and applies all of its resources single-mindedly to advancing its position in the marketplace. The result? Corporation A loses ground to Corporation B, and unless A reconsiders its strategic priorities it may be forced to lay off personnel and take other painful steps to remain viable.

Which company acted most responsibly?

The concept of Integration recognizes the importance of appropriate prioritization of resources among many competing factors. This is complicated enough for an individual, but for an organization it is infinitely more complex because of the large number of diverse stakeholders who look to corporations for accountability:

- Shareholders (long-term investors versus short-term, individual investors versus institutional)
- Employees (unions; different nonunionized employee groups, including top management)
- Customers and vendors (many of whom compete with one another)
- Communities in which the corporation operates
- Government (local, state, federal; regulatory oversight; laws and regulations—some straightforward, others highly subjective)
- The news media
- Lawyers and the courts
- Wall Street
- Industry associations

THE INTERRELATIONSHIP BETWEEN IDENTITY AND INTEGRATION can offer management a basis for making trade-off decisions related to stakeholders. Integration prioritizations are based on a thorough consideration of one's identity. From an Identity standpoint, an organization might be regarded as having three "personas."

- Persona 1: An organization with a task (profits or other goals)
- Persona 2: An environment in which employees interact
- Persona 3: A potential force for social change

Contrary to popular perception, a great deal of money is spent by for-profit organizations on Persona 3—some of which benefits Personas 1 and 2, and some of which does not. Likewise, many organizations spend much more on Persona 2 than would be dictated by the basic necessities of Persona 1. The overriding principle, as mentioned earlier, is that in the long run Persona 1 must be attended to first, Persona 2 second, and then Persona 3.

BOUNDARIES IN THE ORGANIZATION

The concept of *boundaries* is applicable on multiple levels for an organization. If individual employees had constructive boundaries, interpersonal problems would drop dramatically and workplace efficiency would soar. Each organizational unit, be it a temporary project team or major department, can improve its effectiveness with a working awareness of boundary issues. Managers and supervisors can be much more effective in directing and motivating by taking into account boundary issues when dealing with individuals and groups. And boundaries certainly come to bear in the organization's dealings with its many external demands, including customers, vendors, competitors, regulators, news media, and the community.

THE INSPIRATION DIMENSION IN THE ORGANIZATION

The third Pragmatic Spirituality Dimension, Inspiration, affirms the two prior Dimensions of Identity and Integration and provides greater access to one's potential via intuitive resources. As exemplified in Chapter 17, the power of intuition can bring about dramatic changes within an organization, especially when facilitated by the techniques of QDM. The examples in that chapter show that the beneficial effects of intuition can occur in every part of an organization, enhancing not only creativity and efficiency but also the levels of satisfaction with self and work.

A separate but related aspect is that of Inspiration as applied to leadership. In fact, without using those specific terms, the principles of Identity, Integration, and Inspiration have been used throughout history by effective leaders and managers who intuitively grasp their significance and power. Because of the underlying hunger in the human condition for greater authenticity and appropriateness, it is understandable that people respond more constructively to leadership and management techniques that resonate with these core characteristics.

QDM Addresses Strategic Organizational Issues

The previous chapter described a number of situations wherein QDM was used by groups of managers to deal with complex issues where adequate information was lacking. These examples all dealt with a particular transaction or decision; however, the QDM process is fully capable of addressing questions of a broader perspective related to an organization's Identity and Integrity issues. Such questions include the following:

- "What aspects of the organization's identity might be compromised by the decision we are considering?"
- "What might be the unintended results of this decision?"
- "In what way does this decision affect the organization's values, beliefs, or other important qualitative aspects?"
- "How does this decision affect our relationships with each category of the company's stakeholders?"

Ethics

However they may be depicted in movies, books, or the news media, most business decisions don't involve clear-cut "right or wrong" alternatives. Many decisions in organizations must be made without all the relevant facts, and they frequently involve trade-offs—allocating limited resources among competing demands, determining the least-bad alternative, or assessing the impact on various groups. Many business decisions have some kind of ethical dimension, based on the interests of one or more stakeholders, and it is here that Pragmatic Spirituality can serve a valuable role.

Ethical decisions are among the most difficult encountered in business, because there are no clear-cut guidelines. Typically, a number of parties are involved, each affected differently by the decision. So the decision has three parts:

1. "Who are the affected parties?"
2. "What is the projected impact on each?"
3. "How should the interests of the parties be prioritized?"

The first two parts are relatively straightforward, involving the gathering and quantitative analysis of data. But the third part, deciding the order of interests of the various parties, is seldom a rational, quantitative process; it involves many *qualitative* aspects.

The three Dimensions of Pragmatic Spirituality bring a new perspective and discipline to deal with the complexities of "ethics in business."

- **Identity** helps to clear up Unfinished Business that might interfere with objectively dealing with the issue, and it focuses on the criteria—derived from the organization's values and principles—upon which the prioritization decisions are based.

- **Integration** is concerned with identifying the parties involved and sorting out the priorities of each as related to the decision at hand. Once this is accomplished, the Identity criteria can be applied and a conclusion reached.

- **Inspiration** aids in validating the process of the first two Dimensions and calls upon the resources of both the rational and intuitive minds to assist those individuals called upon to make the complex determinations.

Most complex decisions are of necessity imperfect, and ethical decisions are often among the most complex. Use of the Pragmatic Spirituality Dimensions as described here ensures that all relevant factors have been considered and weighed as carefully as possible, and that the decision is based on principles of authenticity and appropriateness. The record of such deliberations attests to the decision having been made with conscientious due process, giving participants the assurance that they have discharged their duty properly.

Enhanced Authenticity and Appropriateness

We will conclude this chapter with a real-life example of a situation that illustrates how the principles of Pragmatic Spirituality may be put to good use without using that particular "label." It evidences how even a small enhancement in authenticity and appropriateness can make a big bottom-line difference.

Case Study

A major retail firm with hundreds of outlets was concerned about statistics showing declining sales per clerk and increasing levels of customer complaints. Various types of motivation and training had produced only short-term improvements.

One day, the managing director was discussing this with another top executive who told him of a somewhat unconventional training company that had produced dramatic results at his organization. After several meetings with the head of the training company, the managing director gave the go-ahead for a trial at some of the worst-performing stores.

Each store received a one-day session conducted by the training company's consultants. The curriculum consisted of three parts:

- One hour spent on the rudiments of self-esteem, with a number of simple techniques for boosting the participants' feelings of self-worth—both individually and in support of each other. The focal point was, "The better you feel about yourself, the more attention you can focus on the customer."

- The second and central part of the session focused on establishing rapport with the customer: "The customer doesn't care what you know until she knows that you care." The primary technique involved "mirroring" the customer in terms of pacing, energy, and appropriately repeating back the customer's phrasing of the problem or what was needed. Participants paired off for practical exercises to develop an initial understanding and to experience what it felt like when the other person really focused on them.

- The third part dealt with accountability—among employees and between the salesperson and the customer. This was particularly important because a typical customer transaction might involve a number of company personnel, so coordination and proper "handing off" from one to another was key to customer satisfaction and achieving the sale.

The firm's inside training department initially resisted this as being "overly simplistic." However, they were impressed at the receptivity of participants and the very positive initial results. The improvements from this new training continued to increase in the months after the training. Moreover, all employees commented on the change in the atmosphere of the workplace, and supervisors reported that things went more smoothly with less of their attention being required.

Based on the success of the trial, the training was expanded company-wide. At the end of the next fiscal year, the managing director attributed a significant increase in profits directly to the impact of the training.

An unexpected benefit was the result of the training on the personal lives of employees. The training company received many letters from individuals in varied parts of the organization expressing thanks for the positive effect of the concepts and practices on their relationships with their spouses, children, and others close to them. Some of the organization's trainers described the training as a life-changing experience.

Why was this relatively straightforward training so effective?

- It addressed the identity issue simply but effectively.
- The rapport "mirroring techniques" promoted empathy and focus, bringing greater authenticity and appropriateness to each interaction between a sales clerk and a customer.
- The accountability techniques established a standard of behavior for the individual and between coworkers.

Again—this is a strong indication of the powerful potential of the *simple* principles of Pragmatic Spirituality. No doubt looking back in your career you can bring to mind similar situations that, in retrospect, validated the elements of Pragmatic Spirituality—although not carried out under that "label."

Unlimited Potential—Irrespective of the Label

The example we just recounted illustrates the powerful enhancement return that can result from a relatively small investment in rudimentary spiritual practices pertaining to authenticity and appropriateness in *honoring the validity of each side of an interaction*. Our objective is the *institutionalization* of Pragmatic Spirituality so that its principles become the operative base and the working lexicon interwoven with the best business practices of an organization.

On the leadership level, what we call the Dimensions of Identity, Integration, and Inspiration have been used to good effect by countless managers and leaders who have intuitively grasped their significance. The underlying hunger in the human condition to achieve greater validity and authenticity causes people to respond to leaders and management techniques that resonate with these characteristics.

Pragmatic Spirituality offers a concept and technique for communicating these time-honored attributes in a form that can be understood by people at all levels within an organization. It speaks to the members of the organization—to their personal needs as individuals and to their roles as employees. Pragmatic Spirituality creates a win-win situation; if properly done, it enhances all parties. And finally, it accesses the spiritual and intuitive resources in a nonreligious manner that should be acceptable to all belief systems or persuasions.

ATTRACTING AND KEEPING THE BEST EMPLOYEES

In addition to organizational enhancements, let us reiterate the other benefit of Pragmatic Spirituality to a company: that of attracting and retaining the right employees. As discussed earlier, organizations are metamorphosing in response to shifting world markets, resulting in the growing need for a new kind of employee—akin to a Fully Functioning Adult. What better way for an employer to attract this type of self-motivated and highly capable employee than to incorporate Pragmatic Spirituality into the fabric of the business organization?

How to Go About It

We hope that these last two chapters have piqued your interest in the potential for Pragmatic Spirituality in your organization. In the following chapter, we'll examine ways in which that can be accomplished.

Chapter 18 Highlights

Intuitive and spiritual techniques can increase an organization's acuity on all levels—as evidenced by results of using QDM. If each of the countless synapses (people-to-people business interactions) in an organization can be enhanced by just a small degree, the bottom-line impact can be enormous.

Spirituality in business must take into account the bottom line. The core concept of Pragmatic Spirituality at the organizational level is that it should enhance the effectiveness of the organization, measured by the bottom line, as well as produce other benefits of a qualitative *nature.*

Conceptually, an organization is an organism similar to an individual, influenced by Unfinished Business, identity issues, complex internal factors and external demands, and operating in a competitive marketplace. The three Dimensions of Pragmatic Spirituality may enhance authenticity and appropriateness to achieve an organizational Inner Edge—from both a quantitative and qualitative standpoint.

As an entity, each organization has a sense of self-identity. A corporation's internal values, beliefs, actions, and conscience figure heavily in how it is perceived by the outside world.

All organizations are well advised to examine their Unfinished Business. Periodically reassessing how one's company fits into the marketplace is an essential strategy. The annals of business history are full of examples of companies that floundered because of outdated belief systems and behavioral patterns, which doomed them to obsolescence or irrelevance.

The Integration aspects of the organization relate directly to how efficiently it functions and whether it survives. The prioritization of resources among many competing factors is infinitely more complex for an organization than for an individual.

Internally, each organizational unit needs to be aware of the importance of boundary issues at all levels of the organization, which also influence the organization's dealings with its many external demands.

As evidenced by the QDM examples in Chapter 17, the beneficial effects of intuition can occur in every part of an organization, enhancing not only creativity and efficiency but also satisfaction with self and work.

Ethical decisions, complex and without clear-cut guidelines, lend themselves to use of the Pragmatic Spirituality Dimensions:

- *Identity* helps to clear up Unfinished Business that might interfere in objectively dealing with the issue, and it focuses on the criteria—derived from the organization's values and principles—upon which the prioritization decisions are based.
- *Integration* is concerned with identifying each of the parties involved and sorting out the priorities of each as related to the decision at hand. Once this is accomplished, the Identity criteria can be applied and a conclusion reached.
- *Inspiration* aids in validating the process of the first two Dimensions and calls upon the resources of both the rational and intuitive minds to assist those individuals making the complex determinations.

In the new marketplace realities, survival depends on attracting and retaining self-motivated and highly capable employees. Such Fully Functioning Adult employees will be attracted to organizations operating on the basis of Pragmatic Spirituality.

There are ample precedents for many of the organizational principles and techniques we offer in this final section. Our objective is the institutionalization *of Pragmatic Spirituality, so that its principles become the operative base and the working lexicon interwoven with the best business practices of an organization.*

19

INTRODUCING PRAGMATIC SPIRITUALITY IN THE ORGANIZATION

A man of a right spirit is not a man of narrow and private views, but is greatly interested and concerned for the good of the community to which he belongs, and particularly of the city or village in which he resides, and for the true welfare of the society of which he is a member.

—Jonathan Edwards

The benefits of Pragmatic Spirituality can be introduced in an organization in one of two ways: the *bootstrap* approach or the *top-down* approach, both of which we'll explore in this chapter.

1. The *bootstrap* approach involves individual managers who decide on their own to apply Pragmatic Spirituality within their localized spheres of influence. To the extent this may be coordinated with other parts of the organization, it is done on a person-to-person basis between peer managers. Top managers may or may not be aware, but have little or no buy-in. The results may be beneficial in terms of quality of life and work efficiency, but will probably remain localized and may not survive the departure of the initiating managers.

2. In the *top-down* approach, the top managers of the organization make a commitment, both personally and for the organization, to the Pragmatic

Spirituality process, and take whatever steps are necessary to promulgate it throughout the organization. All of the organization's policies and practices are reconsidered in light of these principles. Inspiration and intuition are used to assist management decisions at all levels, including a reexamination of organizational strategy and tactics. Once established, this top-down approach should weave Pragmatic Spirituality into all facets of organizational activity, with resulting efficiencies and competitive advantages.

Let's look at each in more detail.

The Bootstrap Approach

In this scenario, one or more employees—most likely managers or supervisors—on their own initiative begin to put into practice some of the principles of Pragmatic Spirituality in the day-to-day aspects of the organization that are under their responsibility. Possibly, the bootstrapper is someone who has found the Pragmatic Spirituality process beneficial to his personal life and now wishes to bring its benefits to work, or it may be someone attracted to the intrinsic concepts of accountability, authenticity, and appropriateness.

Initially, the bootstrapper would do nothing differently; however, internally she would be assessing daily activities and procedures within the perspective of the three Dimensions: Identity, Integration, and Inspiration. Consider the following sample issues and your possible responses as a bootstrapper.

WHEN, IF EVER, DO YOU ATTRIBUTE?

As a bootstrapper applying Pragmatic Spirituality to enhance the tone and productivity in your workplace, it is totally appropriate to use terms like *accountability*, *integrity*, and even *authenticity* in communicating your ideas. If you feel that the person or people with whom you are sharing your insights would be interested in knowing more, give them a copy of *The Inner Edge*. Just be aware of the nature of words (remember our discussion in Chapter 2 about the difficulty of communicating accurately) and proceed with caution so as to not hinder your good works.

One supervisor in your department speaks to his subordinates in an overbearing manner that is demeaning to them.

You find an opportunity to have an informal conversation with the insensitive supervisor to get a feel for what's going on and how to address it. He is a nice person with some bad supervisory patterns who is largely clueless about the impact of his interpersonal style. You talk about one of your own experiences of being unaware of an interpersonal bad habit until it was brought to your attention, and then you describe how his style makes his people feel. At first he is resistant, but then he begins to wonder how he can change. You discuss some simple initial ideas and schedule a follow-up meeting. You end with a clear message that you will assist him in any way and that his behavior definitely must change.

There is a disproportionate focus on "What must be done" with virtually no attention paid to "Who we are."

In order to balance the overemphasis on Doing/Having, you schedule a short meeting with all your people about how your group fits into the overall organization. The response is good. You plan to invite the head of the sales department to come to the next meeting to talk about the new product line.

Several employees are very good at avoiding assignments and dumping their work on others.

You meet individually with the supervisors of these Teflon employees. Your message is clear: "This is unfair to their coworkers and must be corrected." You discuss specifics of dealing with the problem and get commitments from each supervisor as to a timetable. If behavior does not change, it will not be permitted to continue. You learn that one employee has been taking time off because of a terminally ill parent. You instruct the supervisor to talk with HR about special leave and to juggle work assignments to lighten this person's load for a while.

Relations are not good with part of another department that your group depends on for important data.

To determine the reason for the friction with the other group, you speak with a number of your people. Apparently it stems from the other group's perception, dating back many months, that one of your people used the other group as a scapegoat for a missed commitment—in reality not the other group's fault. You meet with the head of the other group to clear the air. She mentions some other reasons for resentments against your group, which you promise to address as soon as possible. The two of you agree to set up an informal watchdog group—two people from each group who will meet weekly to exchange progress reports and deal with gripes promptly before they escalate.

There is not an accurate accounting for personal days off, and several employees are taking advantage of the situation.
A person in payroll tells you that the root cause is that reporting is left up to the individual employee, and some are more conscientious than others. This is a problem in other departments also. After considering and rejecting various alternatives, including time sheets, someone suggests that the daily in/out sheet kept by the receptionist could be used as a basis for payroll to follow up with supervisors to determine the reason for an employee being absent. This is implemented and works well.

At the beginning of each week you meet with your boss to decide on a list of action priorities. However, during the week she adds to this list and at week's end wonders why you have not accomplished everything.
You schedule a meeting with your boss and tell her that when she adds something to your to-do list in midweek, your responsibility is to get clear direction from her as to which of the original items has been displaced in priority. She agrees in principle, but you know that you will have to make sure to hold her to this new practice until it becomes established.

With Pragmatic Spirituality's Identity, Integration, and Inspiration as a guide, you, in the bootstrapper role, can determine how best to address each area of dissonance you encounter and in what priority. The Inspiration part of the Daily PS Focus will be of particular value in determining what action might be taken. You could run your evolving plan by a trusted associate to get his reaction, after which it can be implemented in the most appropriate manner.

Factors Influencing the Effectiveness of the Bootstrap Approach

It is possible for one individual who is far down the organizational ladder to make a difference. We can all recall someone like this—a receptionist, mailroom clerk, maintenance person—who had an ability to touch people's lives. Very often, these people are demonstrating, consciously or unconsciously, the principles of authenticity and appropriateness represented in Pragmatic Spirituality.

The potential effectiveness of a bootstrapper depends on her authority to call the shots and set the ground rules within her area of responsibility in the organization. The authority of some managers is limited, either because hiring and firing and compensation decisions are out of their hands or because the boss does not delegate well. Because the application of Pragmatic Spirituality involves commonly accepted business practices, it can be done in a subtle manner without buy-in from a superior; however, as a bootstrapper it is much easier if you can make the changes under your own authority.

A key factor in the bootstrap approach is the compatibility of the organization's values with what you're trying to do. Some organizations have ingrained belief systems that are antithetical to Pragmatic Spirituality principles. These may result from Unfinished Business within the organization, or they may be a reflection of the values of people in the upper reaches of the organization.

If the underlying values or practices of an organization or its leadership run counter to Pragmatic Spirituality, there will be resistance to bootstrap measures— or any other form of authenticity and true accountability. In some cases, such negative value systems are not readily apparent—obscured or camouflaged by the personality of the leader or superficial appearances. However, when you begin to examine what *actually* happens through the clarity of a Pragmatic Spirituality perspective, you will be able to more clearly see the degree of dysfunction and deception.

Now let's examine the other way of introducing Pragmatic Spirituality into an organization—the *top-down* approach.

The Top-Down Approach

The issues of subtlety and lack of support from above don't exist with the *top-down* approach. This scenario has the top executive team fully committed to the principles of Pragmatic Spirituality, whether they choose to use that label or another. Their desire is to infuse the entire organization from the top down with the authenticity and appropriateness to achieve a true Inner Edge, to benefit the organization and its members both qualitatively and quantitatively. There are ten basic steps to achieving this goal.

1. They would begin by bringing in an outside coach who would work with the top management team on its own Pragmatic Spirituality process— both as individuals and as an organizational unit.

2. The board of directors would be involved at an early stage, both to give approval and to become aware of the process.

3. The next step would be an examination of the organization's principles, values, and belief system as compared to the "yardstick" of Pragmatic Spirituality principles. Necessary changes would be agreed upon.

4. Management at the next level down would then be invited to join the process, addressing the principles first personally and then as they relate to their organizational responsibilities.

5. As the process continues down through the organization, the application of Pragmatic Spirituality principles becomes increasingly specific to the needs and realities of each organizational segment, with management ensuring that all practices are consistent with the overriding principles.

6. Procedures and best practices are defined and memorialized, some applying to the entire organization and others to subsets. A realistic and concise code of ethics is prepared.

7. The "takeaway" for employees at all levels: the new paradigm enhances the authenticity and appropriateness of both the organization and each individual employee by holding everyone accountable for their commitments and encouraging all to grow to their full potential.

8. The new paradigm should be clearly evidenced in all of the organization's outward manifestations: customer and vendor relations, hiring and firing, government, news media, and the financial sector. Initially, there should be a modest statement of what is being done; thereafter, the fruits of the process should speak for themselves.

9. One of the clear tests will be when the need arises to terminate relations with employees—those who cannot adapt to the new paradigm or whose expertise has been made irrelevant by changes in the marketplace. Not only should these terminations be done according to Pragmatic Spirituality principles, but there should be a clear understanding by all employees about the realities of their employment status:
   — Their term with the organization is finite.
   — They will be treated fairly while employed.

— There will be a mutually fair process for their departure when it becomes necessary.

10. An ongoing monitoring and review function is established, with specific accountability to the CEO or at the board of directors level. Its responsibilities include ensuring that the organization is "walking its talk" at every level and that the code of ethics is lived and obeyed, and to serve as an ombudsman accessible from all levels of the organization to investigate and deal with possible deviations from the path.

What About Confidentiality?

At this point it is reasonable to ask, "How realistic is all of this?" More to the point, "In real life, there are 'need-to-know' and confidentiality issues—for example, details of a new product design or cutbacks planned for a certain department. How does Pragmatic Spirituality handle *that*?"

The "pragmatic" in Pragmatic Spirituality means that it must necessarily be a tool that works in real-life situations, and certainly the need for confidentiality is of critical importance in certain aspects of an organization's life. Pragmatic Spirituality does not mean setting aside common sense and business prudence— its goal remains authenticity and appropriateness. However, the difference in an organization using Pragmatic Spirituality is the manner in which confidentiality issues are decided and implemented.

In a normal organization, deciding who will and will not be privy to secrets is often done in a manner that is capricious and inconsistent from one unit to another. "Who knows what" is a strong indicator of status in an organization, so information is often withheld needlessly for "power" reasons, by both managers and subordinates. (One example of the latter is the controlling administrative assistant who makes sure the boss must come to her for contract information and schedule details.)

The three Dimensions of Pragmatic Spirituality are used to determine the way information should be limited. Identity would be the benchmark for "How open do we want to be as an organization?" and "How and on what basis do we restrict information?" Integration provides a basis for sorting out "What needs to be restricted?" "Who legitimately should have access?" and "What is the time frame for this restriction?" And Inspiration would be called upon to affirm the results of the process, with QDM assisting in particularly difficult decisions.

In short, using Pragmatic Spirituality, the handling of confidential information would be exactly the same—and possibly more effective—as in any well-run organization.

The most awkward confidentiality situation, and one where Pragmatic Spirituality can be helpful, is when the withholding of secret information could cause injury to another party. Consider the following examples:

> A department head has been told that soon after the end of the year her department will be cut by 20 percent. She has decided who must be let go. Just after Thanksgiving, one of the employees on the list to be terminated asks her to sign a "verification of employment" for a mortgage on a new house he and his wife plan to close on in December. What should the department head do?

> A relatively new employee in a specialized technical area discovers that the organization has been falsifying data in reports submitted to the government for over five years. His supervisor is openly hostile to "those EPA geeks." The company has a code of ethics that pledges environmental responsibility and encourages employees to report possible problems—but to whom? Clearly a number of people are aware of this. The employee senses that if he blows the whistle he will jeopardize his job.

Such situations represent tough moral dilemmas with no easy answers. We believe that the Pragmatic Spirituality process offers a systematic way of addressing these dilemmas and arriving at an answer you can be confident about. An organization operating on the principles of Pragmatic Spirituality would offer some flexibility to the conflicted department head in the first example, and would have a well-established process for encouraging and protecting internal feedback in the second example.

Where Pragmatic Spirituality Is Applicable

Clearly, with the top-down approach, the principles of Pragmatic Spirituality (with or without attribution to the Pragmatic Spirituality label) can be implemented throughout the organization quickly and consistently—as opposed to the limited activities of bootstrap implementation. Here are some examples of the breadth of influence of top-down implementation, addressing the tensions between "bottom-line results" and "doing things right."

SALES

Pragmatic Spirituality principles would apply to many aspects of sales and marketing, including pricing policy (fairness of discounts, uniformity of prices, calculation of rebates), advertising (veracity, choice of media, budget), incentives (appropriate basis for bonuses and discounts), equitable and legal behavior in a real-world distribution system with shady practices (competition offering money under the counter), customer complaints (handled promptly, objectively, fairly), travel and entertainment expenditures (amounts, appropriateness of entertainment, expense guideline fairness among business units), packaging and labeling (accuracy, fairness of weights), sales of obsolete or outdated product to overseas markets, and so on.

MANUFACTURING

Aspects of manufacturing affected by Pragmatic Spirituality could include choice of manufacturing locations (trade-off of many factors), treatment of workers (layoffs, increased overtime versus adding another shift), working conditions (especially nonunionized and overseas), quota setting (speed of line), worker safety and health services, quality control, grievance procedures, relationships with unions, environmental issues (effluent, waste disposal), dealing with regulatory agencies, procurement, inventory control and vendor relations, and so on.

FINANCE AND ACCOUNTING

Aspects of finance and accounting affected by Pragmatic Spirituality would include enforcement of proper accounting practices, adjustments to "make" projections, selective release of information to favored security analysts, compliance with IRS and SEC regulations, aggressiveness of tax avoidance measures, degree of cooperation and candor with outside accounting firms, rigor of internal audit function, criteria for selecting an investment banker for acquisitions, allocation of profits between offshore and domestic units, degree of preoccupation with the organization's stock price, and so on.

HUMAN RESOURCES, ADMINISTRATION, AND LEGAL

These "staff" functions in an organization often find themselves caught between a rock and a hard place when their opinion, based on a knowledge of their field, runs contrary to the desires of line management. Examples include the staff legal counsel arguing against the propriety of an activity that brings in a lot of profit, the benefits manager faced with a request by management to subtly compromise the medical plan to reduce costs, the compensation manager presented with a line manager's request for a beyond-the-guideline salary increase for a favored employee, the administrator who receives from a supervisor annual performance review forms that clearly have not been seen by the reviewed employee as company policy dictates, and so on.

Since the essence of Pragmatic Spirituality is to achieve authenticity and appropriateness in even a highly complex environment, we believe that Identity, Integration, and Inspiration have a practical application within the organizational context—especially if they have the buy-in and top-down commitment of the entire organization.

Organizations and Individuals: Intrinsic Resistance to Change

The idea of any kind of "spirituality" surviving in the harsh realities of the typical organization is something that may make many managers chuckle in disbelief—with good reason. As we have acknowledged earlier, survival is the primary goal of an organization, which would seem to preclude the relevancy of anything as esoteric and selfless as spirituality.

Bear in mind, however, that we are speaking of *Pragmatic* Spirituality. The word *pragmatic* means "active" and "practical." It is rooted in the Greek words *pragma*, meaning "business," and *prassein*, meaning "to do." These are hard-nosed, steely-eyed antecedents! By definition, Pragmatic Spirituality must be able to withstand the rigors of the real world.

As anyone who has tried to be a change agent in any type of organization knows, the ability of a group to resist new ways is extraordinary. It is in resisting change that the "little people" in the lower ranks demonstrate their passive power—along with pent-up resentments and other feelings. These produce a knee-jerk reaction, causing people to resist even those changes that have clear benefits for them.

Individuals don't like change, unless their current personal situation is extremely painful and the change will definitely bring prompt relief. Some of this resistance to change is caused by inertia, but most is wrapped around Unfinished Business issues, exacerbated by fear of the unknown and the instinct to survive. Contrast this to a Fully Functioning Adult who recognizes the need for ongoing change and has developed a proficiency in bringing about and reacting to change.

Resistance in a *group* of typical people (not Fully Functioning Adults)—such as an organization—is exponentially greater than the resistance of one single person. Resistance in a group comes not only from the aforementioned individual concerns, but also from the perception that change will alter each person's accustomed roles and interactions within the group. Status, influence, and power within a group tend to be tied to knowledge and seniority, so change brings the very real threat of making people obsolete.

IT MIGHT BE THOUGHT that organizations with a strong hierarchical structure would be most capable in achieving change due to habitual obedience of orders from the top, but often that is not the case. By their very nature, hierarchical structures become ingrained in traditional behaviors, and these entrenched patterns overpower the norms to obey.

The upper levels of management have a clearer view of the big picture of why change is necessary for the organization's well-being. For that reason, one might think that upper managers would readily support change, but that is often not the case.

Not surprisingly, the upper ranks of organizations tend to contain a high percentage of individuals whose motivational profile leans toward an intrinsic tendency to improve their influence and ability to make things happen. Thus they have a strong propensity to look out for their own interests. Unless these upper managers are convinced that a change will be advantageous for them, they may not throw all of their energies toward making it happen. (For more information on Motivational Profiles, see Appendix E.)

Overcoming the Organization's Unfinished Business

Just as an individual's Unfinished Business interferes with his ability to change, each organization has Unfinished Business that stymies progress. These include

- Value and belief systems
- Traditions
- Attitudes
- Deviations between stated policy and actual practice
- Preconceptions or prejudices of influential people

- Self-assigned importance
- Delusions of invincibility
- Looking out for self-interests at the expense of others
- Self-assigned entitlement

Identifying and dealing with Unfinished Business is an appropriate and necessary first step for introducing Pragmatic Spirituality to an organization. The following are some areas that should be examined.

THE INTRINSIC EMPLOYER-EMPLOYEE RELATIONSHIP

Each organization has a subtle but powerful value system motivating its selection of and relationship with employees. This may be alluded to in shorthand terms, such as "paternal," "supportive," "traditional," or "demanding." It most likely includes bias in favor of certain types of people, which may result in prejudice against others. Any significant change in organizational practice, such as the introduction of Pragmatic Spirituality, will require an objective reassessment of the organization's belief systems—and such a reassessment represents a threat to the privileged classes in positions of power.

MANAGEMENT STYLES AND ATTITUDES

What is the nature of the typical relationship between supervisors and subordinates? Is there a sense of mutual respect or mistrust? Is there constructive feedback that moves up the organization, or are employees expected to do their jobs and keep quiet? Are rules and policies applied in an evenhanded manner, or do supervisors play favorites? Do managers hire people who will challenge them, or do they prefer employees who "know their place"? Does the company take advantage of easily manipulated employees?

FAMILY OF ORIGIN ISSUES

As discussed in Chapter 4, organizations often become stages where both employees and managers reenact issues dating back to childhood. Whether the atmosphere is collegial or competitive, difficulties in coworker interactions usually have roots dating back to sibling situations.

BOUNDARY ISSUES

Some organizations have an intrinsic respect for boundaries: of employees, customers, vendors, the community, and so on. Other organizations feel that the good of the company justifies any kind of boundary intrusion. This may be exemplified by the assumption that employees are available during weekends and holidays, by a lack of respect for confidentiality of employees' personal data and compensation information, by a casual attitude toward ethical and legal matters, and possibly by instances of discrimination—sexual, racial, or otherwise—for which management tries to shrug off responsibility.

TOUGH VERSUS FIRM

Everyone would agree that a weak or passive manager is undesirable, but to what degree must a manager be "tough" to be effective? In the days of more primitive organizations, the floor boss was the one who could whip everyone else. That mentality of toughness bordering on harshness still has echoes in some organizations with attitudes such as, "Yes, but is she tough enough for the job?"

The Shadow in the Organization

The *Shadow* in an organization can have extreme power when it is orchestrated by a few and reinforced by many. Denial from the top down allows the organization to continue on a desired path regardless of the consequences. Recall that in Chapter 9 we discussed the necessity of dealing with the Shadow parts of your personality in order to free yourself of these limitations and open up prospects for an enhanced and expanded life.

There is an organizational parallel: so long as an organization is in denial about the dominance of its Shadow side, there is no context for authenticity or appropriateness, for the culture is impregnated with denial, emotional oppression, suppression, and delusions. However, if management is willing to step out of denial and acknowledge the Shadow on a top-down basis, the techniques of Pragmatic Spirituality offer a means with which to restore the organization.

This leads us to the next chapter, and the subject of "spirituality in business—*can it work?*"

CHAPTER 19 HIGHLIGHTS

Pragmatic Spirituality can be introduced in an organization in one of two ways: the bootstrap *approach (individual managers, on their own, act within their spheres of influence) or the* top-down *approach (beginning with commitment* by top management and the board of directors, then working down through the organization).

For the bootstrapper, the three PS Dimensions—Identity, Integration, and Inspiration—serve as a reference for noting areas of dissonance and taking appropriate action.

Bootstrap implementation becomes more problematic if individual managers are not given sufficient authority or if the underlying values and practices of the organization run counter to Pragmatic Spirituality.

The top-down approach begins with the full commitment of the top executive team and the board of directors, personally and organizationally, to the principles of Pragmatic Spirituality and to inculcating the entire organization from the top down with the authenticity and appropriateness needed to achieve a true Inner Edge.

The organization's principles, values, and belief systems are thoroughly examined and revised as needed. Procedures and best practices are defined and memorialized until each employee has been involved.

The goal of the top-down approach is enhancement of authenticity and appropriateness quickly and consistently at all levels of the organization by holding all employees accountable for keeping commitments made and encouraging all to grow to their full potential.

Matters of confidentiality are extremely important but often handled capriciously and influenced by power needs and other types of Unfinished Business. Pragmatic Spirituality can provide a highly effective means of determining how "need-to-know" issues are decided and implemented.

Pragmatic Spirituality will face resistance by the organization as a whole and by individuals within the organization. Some resistance is caused by inertia, but most is wrapped around Unfinished Business issues, exacerbated by fear of the unknown, the instinct to survive, and what is perceived as not being in one's own best interest.

Pragmatic Spirituality can overcome organizational resistance if given sufficient top-down support. It must be clear to all that it is based on enhancing both the quantitative and qualitative aspects of the company and its employees. It provides a framework for identifying and dealing with organizational Unfinished Business.

As long as an organization denies the dominance of its Shadow, the culture will be undermined by denial, emotional oppression, suppression, and delusions. Pragmatic Spirituality allows an organization to deal with its Shadow in order to create a context for authenticity and appropriateness.

SPIRITUALITY IN BUSINESS—CAN IT WORK?

Every individual has a responsibility to help guide our global family in the right direction. Good wishes are not sufficient; we must become actively engaged.

—HIS HOLINESS THE DALAI LAMA

IN THIS FINAL SECTION OF THE BOOK, we have discussed the extrapolation of the Pragmatic Spirituality principles from the micropersonal to the macroorganizational levels, reaping multiple bottom-line benefits. Bootstrap Pragmatic Spirituality by proactive individuals can create pockets of authenticity within an organization; however, these are dependent on the initiative of the bootstrapper as well as the receptivity, or at least tolerance, of superiors. Our strong conclusion is that the top-down approach is the only way to achieve Pragmatic Spirituality throughout an organization, with strong commitment from the top executive and his immediate team, and the board of directors.

Short-Term Fads Versus Top-Level Commitment

The past several decades have seen the introduction of a number of new concepts for organizational enhancement. These have led to greater sophistication in organizational development theory. Less clear is the extent of their constructive impact within organizations.

This is not for lack of trying. Many top managers have been intrigued with finding new techinques to enhance their company's ability to deal with the changing business environment. In fact, some organizations have tried to implement a succession of external change theories, leading to employee cynicism about "the fad of the month."

The problems were not necessarily that the organizational development concepts were faulty. Properly implemented, these new approaches could have achieved many benefits. Nevertheless, in spite of large expenditures on consulting fees and training materials, as well as the "lost opportunity cost" of time distracted from the work at hand, there are few ongoing success stories. The lack of return on these considerable expenditures can be attributed to many factors, but in our opinion there is one underlying core cause: the lack of commitment and involvement at the top of the organization.

The all-too-common scenario for fruitless organizational reconceptualizations might be characterized as follows:

- A CEO is intrigued by a charismatic management consultant who has a new twist on bringing enhanced productivity to organizations.

- The CEO consults with several peers, decides to proceed, sells the idea to the board of directors, and contracts with the consultant to proceed with the project.

- In his heart of hearts, the consultant knows that the key to the success of the project is the intimate involvement by the CEO; however, she is wise enough not to make that a precondition for acceptance of the assignment. (It may be that the CEO truly intended to be involved, but finds that elusive because of day-to-day demands. Or the CEO's attitude may be "Just fix it"—with no interest in being involved.)

- Implementation of the new concepts proceeds, downward or upward as the case may be, throughout the organization.

- Unless already jaded, the typical employee is reasonably open-minded, even enthusiastic, about the new ideas. He attends the one-day training seminar, then returns to work only to find a stack of urgent call-back notes.

- For a few weeks, the employee attempts to use the new concepts: they are unwieldy, and there is no support or reinforcement for their use from his boss or coworkers.

- Some time later, the employee finds the training manual buried under a pile of "in-process" paperwork on the side of the desk. Smiling ruefully, the employee drops it in the wastebasket.

Clearly, without the personal commitment and involvement of the CEO and the management team down the line, no organizational change initiative has any chance of success.

Top-Level Commitment for Pragmatic Spirituality

The need for commitment by the top executives and the board of directors includes the use of Pragmatic Spirituality in one's personal life. The CEO, those who report to her directly, and each member of the board needs to *experience* the three Dimensions—Identity, Integration, and Inspiration—on the individual level as described in Section II before the full organizational implications can be appreciated.

- **Unfinished Business:** Until you have confronted your own Unfinished Business, you are not prepared to appreciate the subtleties of organizational Unfinished Business, much less to uncover and deal with it.

- **Identity:** Gaining increased self-awareness and self-acceptance to reach a place of greater authenticity is a prerequisite for conducting the process of sorting out the elements of the organization's identity.

- **Integration:** It is only after you have objectified and prioritized the many external demands in your life that you can clearly see the equivalent issues in the organization and deal with them objectively.

- **Inspiration:** Given the left/rational brain orientation of business, each individual manager and employee needs to integrate his logical and intuitive abilities to work together at the level of Icons and metaphors in order to expand the organization's resources.

- **Self-maintenance and Self-discipline:** These are core aspects of much of the department-by-department implementation of Pragmatic Spirituality. For a manager to attempt imposing them without having experienced them personally borders on the hypocritical. Likewise, the greatest benefit

will come from each employee's sincere involvement rather than lip service. Thus, Self-maintenance and Self-discipline must come from within an
individual in a context of commitment to both personal and company
development.

- **A sense of identity based on self-understanding:** Without this, you are
  indentured to the job, prone to burnout, lacking boundaries, and likely to
  fall victim to a self-diminishing accommodation to your work and the
  demands of others. To be able to effectively implement Pragmatic Spirituality in an organization requires having done the inner work to achieve
  self-acceptance and an Inner Edge.

- Likewise, it is important that each individual in the process examine and
  recalibrate his preconceptions about *values* such as loyalty, duty, and
  accountability as a prelude to reinterpreting these concepts within the
  organizational context.

The issue can be phrased in terms of *return on investment*. There are more
significant organizational returns from Pragmatic Spirituality when the organization's members have personally committed to it. When there is little commitment, especially by top management, the returns are meager or even
counterproductive.

Will Top Management Commit?

Thus we arrive at the make-or-break question regarding successful implementation of Pragmatic Spirituality in a particular organization: "Is the CEO willing
to commit to the Pragmatic Spirituality process, both personally and as it proceeds within the organization?"

Clearly, the answer to this will vary from one CEO to the next. We see factors that argue "pro" and "con" on this issue.

The CEO Who Is Unlikely to Commit to Pragmatic Spirituality

- Has a Motivational Profile (see Appendix E) that gravitates toward power
  and influence, with a strong tendency to delegate the detailed and the
  distasteful
- Has lived in a privileged, entitled world so long that he has lost touch with
  the organization's employees

- Is a narcissistic type with a deep insecurity who finds the vulnerability involved in the Pragmatic Spirituality process very threatening
- Values media opinion and thus is not willing to jeopardize reputation on a project that might be regarded as esoteric
- Is more invested in playing a role than being an authentic leader desiring to improve the organization
- Lacks vision and awareness of the potency within management and employees to make a difference

The CEO Who Is Open to Pragmatic Spirituality

- Has a strong desire to make a positive contribution—a "payback" of lasting influence
- Sees his position as being able to leave a legacy for the company
- Recognizes the opportunity to grow, to come to terms with her own Unfinished Business and establish a role as steward for the company
- Hungers to reconcile and *integrate* his personal spiritual quest with his business activities
- Has strong empathy and a *sense of compassion* for people at all levels of the organization
- Recognizes top management perks of entitlement and privilege as illusory, preferring to work from a place of responsible and committed leadership

The CEO willing to try Pragmatic Spirituality is more likely to be either at the early stage of her career (possibly in a small company) or near the end of her career and motivated by a strong personal passion.

A Potential Change Agent — the Board of Directors

The discussion so far has assumed that the CEO is the "top dog" in the organization, as is the case in many businesses. However, in concept if not in practice, the CEO does have a boss: the board of directors. If the board is properly discharging its responsibilities, it could be the initiating agent for the introduction of Pragmatic Spirituality in an organization.

In all too many instances, the role of the board tends to be reactive or even passive. Frequently, the CEO has a strong say in the selection of new board members and controls the board's access to information. The board's contact with the organization's operation and its personnel may be filtered by the top management team.

Even without such intentional constraints, it is a challenge for board members to stay informed about the organization. To remain current with the complexity of most organizations and take action as needed involves a large investment of time and energy by board members, many of whom have busy schedules.

A look at the lists of boards of major corporations reveals a significant number of CEOs sitting on other boards. The traditional argument for this is that it gives the board the expertise of another CEO's perspective. The pernicious effects can come from the fact that CEOs may have conflicting interests that may not be obvious. For example, the board determines the compensation of its CEO and other top executives based on surveys of widespread pay scales; thus an action by a CEO sitting on the compensation committee of an outside board can indirectly enhance his own salary.

In recent years, the topic of *governance* has come into increasing prominence in the media and from a regulatory standpoint. Reports of bankruptcies and financial irregularities are quickly followed by the question, "Why was the board asleep at the switch?" Lawsuits against boards, once a rarity, are becoming more common. Some "professional" board members are reconsidering the legal liability ramifications and reducing their involvement.

Also on the positive side, there is a growing movement toward greater diversity in board composition. The involvement of women, minorities, and individuals from other disciplines brings fresh perspectives, although the offsetting downside may be a lack of business experience and acumen to ask the right questions and readily grasp the implications of a complex situation.

FOR A PUBLICLY HELD CORPORATION, the board of directors has a legally defined fiduciary responsibility to the corporation's shareholders for governance (oversight). In more closely held corporations, where most or all shares are in few or family hands, the board's role tends to be largely advisory, except in the event of disagreement among shareholders. The board's governance responsibilities become most relevant when the interests of one part of the shareholder population differ from those of another, or there is the possibility of a conflict of interest between shareholders and management.

The Opportunity for Renewal of a Board

The principles of Pragmatic Spirituality offer a board of directors an opportunity to reexamine issues of authenticity and appropriateness, both on an individual level and from the perspective of their collective responsibility to the organization. Such a reexamination and renewal could be done in a weekend retreat led by an outside facilitator. Most likely, management personnel would not be present at the initial sessions, which might focus on issues like the following:

Identity Issues
- Unfinished Business within the organization's values and practices
- Identity factors: valid and invalid
- Expectations and how they influence the board's deliberations
- Doing/Having versus Being sources of identity for the organization
- Self-acceptance for the organization
- Roles: the high expectations of the Critical Judge; the constructive Compassionate Observer
- The organization's Shadow issues

Integration Issues
- Identification of the organization's stakeholders and external demands and internal factors
- Neutralizing the excessive demands of some external demands
- Prioritizing among the external demands
- Procedures to determine situational priorities
- Ethical issues
- Boundaries

Inspiration Issues
- Establishing openness and trust in the intuitive process
- Developing proficiency in QDM techniques
- Determining the problems that need to be faced
- Creating and supporting a vision for the company
- Moving ahead: the next steps

With a renewed clarity about authenticity and appropriateness in the organization and about its own role, the board can then meet again with the CEO and other top managers to involve them in the process and seek their input. It will soon become clear just how receptive management is to going down a new path of organizational renewal.

The Bias of Short-Term Expectations

In today's publicly traded corporations, both top management and the board tend to be preoccupied with the price of the organization's stock on whatever exchange it may be traded. This has introduced a particularly pernicious bias as to what is good for the organization's long-term best interests.

A number of factors are behind this preoccupation with the short-term:

- Securities analysts who follow a company's stock base their buy/sell recommendations on how the next quarter's results stack up with past performance and projections.

- The use of stock options as management incentives strongly focuses the recipients' attention on both the stock price and the timing of their option terms.

- Compensation of top management is quite often tied to bottom-line results, which tends to shift the application of assets from longer-term to shorter-term projects.

- Statistics show that CEO compensation packages have become richer, while the average CEO tenure is decreasing. Compensation packages often include generous termination guarantees. These factors may tend to shorten a CEO's time perspective.

- In view of the rapidly accelerating rate of change of technologies and market factors, shorter-term investment of assets may in fact be more prudent than longer-term commitments in certain circumstances.

The results of the shorter-term bias are seen in the decreased amount of investment in basic research in favor of product modification or adaptation to new markets. It is evidenced in the introduction of "updated" versions of products, which for the majority of consumers have little practical advantage over their predecessors. It underlies the oft-lamented decline in customer service and near impossibility of contacting a real human being by phone when trying to resolve a problem with an organization.

The determination of appropriate time frames is one of the most difficult of management decisions: longer-term can be either statesmanlike or stupid; shorter-term can be situationally appropriate or shortsighted. We feel that Pragmatic Spirituality offers a framework for making such decisions based on Identity and Integration bolstered by the intuitive insight of Inspiration.

The QDM Vision Blocked by Top Management Myopia

The pivotal role of the top manager is amply illustrated in the experience of a respected European corporation.

CASE STUDY

The executive vice president had heard of Ron's work with intuitive decision making at another corporation. He invited Ron to give a seminar for some of his key managers. There were some reservations as to how the group would respond, since they were all very practical, hard-nosed businessmen, many with technical training.

The seminar was a great success and concluded with the participants eager for the opportunity to try QDM in a practical situation. During the seminar, several managers had alluded to their concern that the company was facing a strategic fork in the road in terms of which markets it should serve. The perception was that upper management was not addressing this issue.

A small group asked Ron if he would help them apply QDM to this matter. They asked, "Should the company focus on developing its financial and service foundation within its home base, or expand in the world market?"

The group was amazed at how well QDM worked in accessing their intuitive resources. Individuals described their Icons, and others in the group added to the interpretation. As one of the group said later, "It was one of the most intense experiences I have had. There is no question in my mind that we were operating on a higher level." One individual shared a most dynamic Icon—a world globe that expanded to a point where it exploded and fragmented. With the context of the question regarding expansion, the intuitive minds indicated that expansion could be made—but without appropriate consideration as to *limiting* expansion, the company would fragment and collapse.

The QDM process led to a unanimous decision, which the managers presented to their division head to be passed on to top management. They recommended three steps:

1. Expand carefully, monitoring each step.
2. Ensure that product development does not outpace customer service capabilities.
3. Predicate expansion on the rate of world economic trends.

Although subsequent events proved that this was exactly what the company needed to do, the eventual outcome was an extreme disappointment to the managers who had experienced this exciting QDM process.

The executive vice president excitedly shared the results of the QDM session with the president. To his disappointment, the president reacted very negatively and refused to present it to the board. The president pointed to the company's rapid growth and its success in capturing a commanding share of the market. Preoccupied with the past, and possibly blinded by arrogance and self-assurance, the president held firm to his vision for the company to continue growing at the same pace as it had in recent years.

The events of the next several years confirmed the intuition of the QDM group. The Asian recession blindsided the company's growth strategy. The president pressed on, but gradually the company lost its leadership position to another firm that had taken exactly the path recommended by the QDM group. Discouraged, the majority of the QDM group gradually left the company, further diminishing its prospects. Belatedly, the board dismissed the president, but the company remains a shadow of its previous stature.

Sadly, this case study represents another endorsement of the QDM process, as well as an example of the need for top management to be receptive to intuitive input and to act as responsive stewards to the needs of the organization.

We end this chapter by restating our strong conviction that changing paradigms are opening up opportunities for spirituality in business to make significant enhancements. However, it is only with the full commitment—individually and organizationally—of top management and the board that the bottom-line benefits of enlightened techniques like Pragmatic Spirituality can be instilled in an organization.

CHAPTER 20 HIGHLIGHTS

Organizations have tried various consultants and their organizational change theories at great expense and with few lasting results. The problem is lack of commitment by top management and the board of directors.

The top-down approach is the only lasting way of introducing Pragmatic Spirituality to an organization. This requires a willingness by top management and the board to commit to the Pragmatic Spirituality process, both personally and institutionally.

Whether the CEO is willing to become personally committed to and involved in the Pragmatic Spirituality process will differ from one CEO to another. We see factors that argue "pro" and "con" on this issue.

The CEO willing to try Pragmatic Spirituality is more likely to be either at the early stage of her career (possibly in a small company) or near the end of her career and motivated by a strong personal passion.

The board of directors could be the initiating agent for the introduction of Pragmatic Spirituality in an organization; however, many boards lack independence from the CEO or the available time to make such a commitment.

The principles of Pragmatic Spirituality offer a board of directors an opportunity to reexamine issues of authenticity and appropriateness, both on an individual level and from the perspective of their collective responsibility to the organization.

Short-term factors can create a bias that compromises an organization's long-term interests. The determination of appropriate time frames is one of the most difficult of management decisions.

Changing paradigms are opening up opportunities for spirituality in business to make significant enhancements. However, it is only with the full commitment—individually and organizationally—of top management and the board of directors that the bottom-line benefits of enlightened techniques like Pragmatic Spirituality can be instilled in an organization.

21

THE INNER EDGE AND
THE OUTER LIMITS

To see a World in a Grain of Sand
And a Heaven in a Wild Flower
Hold Infinity in the palm of your hand
And Eternity in an hour.

—WILLIAM BLAKE

WE BEGAN THIS BOOK WITH AN OBSERVATION about the "hollowness" and lack of authenticity and appropriateness that seem to permeate modern life—in spite of the technologies that have brought unprecedented comfort, convenience, and communication capabilities. The widespread response, in many forms and practices, has been an intuitive turning toward *spiritual* sources for answers and surcease.

In light of those yearnings, the strong interest in spirituality in business is understandable, reflecting a desire for greater meaning in the workplace and for achieving the potential of the organization as a force for good to resolve the challenges experienced in our communities, our country, and throughout the world.

To make use of the techniques of Pragmatic Spirituality is to actuate the profound aspects of oneself and, through practice and perseverance, move into the realm of *self-mastery*—to enable and empower oneself to function on a more optimal level and to find greater fulfillment in all aspects of life—an Inner Edge to deal with the complex world of today and tomorrow. It opens up virtually unlimited potential to change oneself and one's environment. It is, in essence, a personal renaissance—inspired, creative, deeply resonant, stretching to one's outer limits of perception—a going within to access unlimited potentials of self and, conversely, one's connection with the "outer" world. It is to reinvent, to reorganize, to reveal, and to revel in being. And it is through that increased conscious awareness and more intrinsic understanding of who we are that we can revitalize our places of work, our communities, and the world at large.

To be sure, we are not so naïve as to expect individuals and organizations to make an immediate about-face upon reading this book. At the least, we hope that this book will alter the perception that spirituality is necessarily tied to "touchy-feely," "do good for the sake of doing good," or other selfless and esoteric associations. Otherwise, the role of spirituality in business will remain transitory, superficial, and ineffectual.

The true potential for spirituality in the organization—and the organization's potential for doing good—will be realized only when the principles of spirituality are seen by hard-nosed businesspeople as having the potential to produce bottom-line results—in other words, when spirituality does not compromise their primary responsibility to the organization. That seems pretty straightforward—conventional business wisdom.

Yet we are very sure that something *more* is needed: a different kind of wisdom, one based on receptivity—an absence of skepticism and cynicism, and an openness to new ways—a *paradox*, such as the inner and the outer aspects of an Inner Edge, to address the unprecedented challenges of our tumultuous world.

We do not receive wisdom,
we have to discover it for ourselves
by a voyage that no one can take for us . . .
a voyage that no one can spare us.
—Marcel Proust

We are sure of the applicability of Pragmatic Spirituality on the individual level because we have experienced it firsthand. We also believe in its potential at the organizational level, though we are quite aware of the significant obstacles it faces. As we stated in Chapter 1, spirituality in business is an oxymoron. The organizational environment, especially that of a for-profit business, is an unlikely and unreceptive environment for any spiritual principles based on *authenticity*, *integrity*, *responsibility*, and *accountability*.

Still, remarkably, these intrinsic qualities continue to be found throughout organizations large and small in the actions of individuals at all levels and in every capacity. Acts of decency, compassion, selflessness, bravery, and integrity may occasionally come to prominence, but the great majority are known only to the few whose lives they touch. One example: the whistleblowers who risk emotional and economic well-being to bring the light of public scrutiny on unconscionable organizational practices. Truly, there are many sparks of spirituality within the complexities of organizations.

We are also aware that organizations do exist in which spirituality may be able to flourish and enhance the ability of both the organization and its members to realize their full potential. There are employees, managers, and leaders—present and future—who are not blinded by greed and power but seek an authentic balance in their lives along with an outlet for their abilities for responsible stewardship.

This book, in all its prematurity and imperfection, is written for the pioneers and pilgrims of spirituality in business. We hope it may, if only in some small way, help them find the spiritual path they seek and guide them as they travel toward their appointed goal. We bid them good fortune and the wish that the end of their journey may be graced by the age-old blessing, "Servant, well done!"

Since much of the potential of Pragmatic Spirituality is achieved through images from your intuitive resources, we offer as a final salutation a summative account of your Inner Edge journey.

THE PRAGMATIC SPIRITUALITY JOURNEY

Your desire to achieve an Inner Edge has brought you to a large wooden gate in the wall of a magnificent structure. You knock and the door is opened by a kindly guide with whom you immediately feel at ease. The guide understands what you seek and signals you to follow. You do, trusting completely that whatever the guide does will be in your best interests.

You enter a small unadorned room with two comfortable seats. Soft light seems to emanate from everywhere and nowhere. Your guide signals for you to sit; the guide takes the other chair. Closing your eyes, you let your entire body relax as you breathe deeply and steadily.

As a first step, your guide directs you to go within, deep inside yourself, down to a place you have sensed before but were not sure existed. You look about and see a door with a sign on it that states "Do not enter." You feel a sense of discomfort. Since early in your life, this place has been off-limits to you. You sense that something behind the door must be confronted before you will be free to begin your journey. *continued*

Following your guide's suggestion, you open the door and light streams in, illuminating its dusty recesses. You enter and begin exploring cluttered shelves and bookcases covered with dust and cobwebs. This is the "database" of your life: your subjective life experiences, your hopes, and your unrealized potentials. Its shadowy recesses are a jumble of facts and distortions.

The distortions are your Unfinished Business—unresolved items and outdated scripts that continue to hamper you. You can feel their negativity. At the guide's bidding, you acknowledge the existence of your Unfinished Business and its influence on you over the years. As you do this, you sense that the power of these influences is lessening.

With the guide's help, you begin to address your Unfinished Business, and as you do, the illumination in the room increases. After a while, the guide informs you that it is time for you to move on, reassuring you that dealing with your Unfinished Business will be an ongoing process throughout your lifetime— allowing you to transcend obstacles and providing new opportunities.

The guide then presents you with your Self-resolves: Self-accountability, Self-maintenance, and Self-discipline—tools for your journey.

Now that your foundations are secure and your tools are in place, the guide introduces you to the companions that will accompany you on your journey— the three Dimensions of Pragmatic Spirituality: *Identity*, *Integration*, and *Inspiration*. With a good 3D proficiency, you will be able to deal more effectively with the challenges of your journey and be guided to stay on your path.

As the final part of your preparation, the guide gives you a description of the goal you seek: the ideal of a Fully Functioning Adult. You understand that this may not be completely attainable, but it symbolizes the ideal toward which you—and all travelers on their paths—are striving.

Thus equipped, you embark on your journey.

At first it appears to be the exact path you have already traveled for so many years. But gradually you realize that this path has *two levels*: on one level are the day-to-day events that have characterized your life up till now, but there is a *new level* paralleling the old. The new level is your spiritual path, leading to the enhanced authenticity and appropriateness that constitute your Inner Edge.

You are attracted to this spiritual path, feeling a strong temptation to follow it solely. However, it is clear that you are called to *combine* the two paths, with one merging into and supporting the other. It will be challenging—and more fulfilling than following either of the two paths singly.

You move forward, well equipped to accept this challenge, on the Pragmatic Spirituality journey to achieve your Inner Edge.

YOUR PRAGMATIC SPIRITUALITY VISUALIZATIONS

THE THREE VISUALIZATIONS — Identity, Integration, and Inspiration, are presented separately here to supplement the learning process in Chapters 6, 7, and 8, respectively. In practice, the three visualizations are segued together in the 3D Visualization found on page 275. Before you begin the visualizations, be sure to set the stage.

Setting the Stage for Your Visualizations

Before doing each of the visualizations in this book, it is important that you "set the stage" in order to create a state of receptivity for internalizing the visualization. *Setting the stage* means that you create an environment that optimizes the visualization experience for yourself. It is a way of transitioning from the busy aspects of your daily routine to the special place you experience in your visualization.

- Find a comfortable setting and ensure there are boundaries against interruptions such as phone calls, beepers, doorbells, animals, visiting friends, and so on.
- A quiet room is preferable to being in a car or outdoor environment where you don't have control of the situation.
- Wear comfortable clothing; loosen any part that is restrictive.
- Take a bathroom break before you begin.

- Make sure that what you are sitting or lying on is comfortable, and that you have the time to go through the complete visualization without feeling rushed.
- You may wish to set a timer so you don't feel the need to check your watch.
- Having a pen and paper (or journal) nearby enables you to jot down things that come to mind, rather than trying to remember them.
- Begin the visualization by taking a deep breath, starting with the abdomen and inhaling into the upper chest, and then gradually breathing out. Breathe in relaxation, breathe out tension. Continue breathing comfortably.
- Relax your body, part by part, from your head down to your feet. Tell each part in turn to release any tension you may be experiencing.
- Be aware of the floor beneath your feet, the cushion under your seat, the texture of the fabric on which your hand rests.
- "Move into" an inner place, which is apart from the workings of your rational mind. As thoughts come to you, don't resist them; simply let them float away like a leaf on the surface of a stream.

Now the stage is set. You can either continue to enjoy your inner place in an undirected meditation or move into a guided visualization.

Your Identity Visualization

1. Begin by setting the stage.

2. Call on your Compassionate Observer and Critical Judge. Honor them and verify that they are working together.

3. Focus your attention on the center of your being (just below and behind your navel). Visualize this as your center of gravity (and levity).

4. Once that centeredness is clearly established, repeat the "I Accept Myself Completely" affirmation:

    Whatever my track record, whatever my imperfections,
    I accept myself completely—without reservations.

Feel the self-acceptance surround your center, as though you were holding yourself in the most loving manner.

5. Visualize a glowing sphere expanding from your center of being. This is your *identity*. See that it is a hologram made of rays from many, many sources, converging into your Identity hologram. The rays represent all the things that make you *you*, including the following:
   — Early life experiences and people
   — Behavior patterns of all kinds
   — Current relationships and affiliations
   — Your accomplishments
   Most of the rays forming your Identity hologram are bright colors—these are the valid inputs to your identity.

6. Some rays are dull and lusterless—these are Unfinished Business and behavior patterns *no longer* valid to you. Eliminate these invalid rays from your Identity hologram. Affirm your desire to remove all Unfinished Business from your life.

7. Celebrate the wonderful shining hologram of many colors that make up you! Honor all the parts of your identity. You may wish to pay special attention to a recent event or accomplishment.

8. Be aware of feeling strongly centered and grounded in your sense of self— your identity is soundly in place. You are like a well-ballasted vessel, a resilient, tall tree toughened by many winds and storms. Let this feeling permeate your sense of self and accompany you as you go through your day.

Your Integration Visualization

In the 3D Visualization, this immediately follows the Identity Visualization, which ended with the image of the hologram of many rays, each representing one of the varied inputs into your identity.

1. If you are doing this visualization separately from the Identity Visualization, begin by setting the stage.

2. Begin with the wonderful hologram of your identity, feeling a sense of self-acceptance and value.

3. Gradually become aware of the external demands that surround your identity in your day-to-day life: family of origin, spouse, children, friends, affiliations (work, religion, other organizations), activities, and so on. Honor these as realities in your life, bringing richness as well as pressures.

4. The number of external demands may feel overwhelming, but remind yourself that the choice of how to allocate your time and energy is *yours*, and that you are doing this visualization in order to make an appropriate allocation of your time and energies and to reduce the pressures on you.

5. Feel the *constricting* power of some of your external demands. See that ropes of varying thickness connect your identity to these demands. Understand that these demands have had an undue call on your energies and attention—but no longer.

6. Around you, up from the ground, a brilliant violet flame springs up and burns through the ropes. As each rope burns through (without harming you), you send forgiveness to the external demand on the other end. As the ropes of emotional encumbrance burn away, feel yourself breathing more deeply and freely, energized by this sense of freedom.

7. Without their connection to you, some of the external demands turn and exit your life. Others remain, clearly interested in continuing a relationship on a new "freed-up" basis.

8. With the undue pressures gone, you can now make a decision about how to best allocate your time and energy for today among your own needs and your external demands. Take into account the realities of the day: family situation, work situation, and your personal needs. Let your Identity Visualization help guide you as to how much you need to devote to your own Self-maintenance. The remaining time and energy is allocated among your external demands. Make the prioritization clearly, in terms of specific hours or blocks of time.

9. After your prioritization for the day is done, briefly honor all the external demands as a sign that today's prioritization choice does not reflect your overall regard for them. You will have no feeling of guilt about the "left-out" external demands, because you have made the prioritization to the best of your abilities.

10. Complete the Integration Visualization by affirming to yourself that you have done the best you can with your prioritization. If circumstances change, you will redo the Integration prioritization, but you will not second-guess the allocation you have just completed.

NOTES ON THE INTEGRATION VISUALIZATION

Especially in the early stages after you begin the Pragmatic Spirituality process, you may find that there are external demands whose ropes of attachment do *not* burn away during the Integration Visualization. This is a very useful awareness, because it highlights the very strong hold these demands—such as a parent, your boss, or an organizational affiliation—have on you. This is heavy-duty Unfinished Business, and it needs to be focused on and properly dealt with.

Remember that your prioritization of your time and energy for the day has two aspects:

- *Between* the external demands and your Self-maintenance responsibilities
- *Among* the external demands

Your prioritization should take into account your just-completed Identity Visualization, as well as the realities of your life. Some of the following factors may play into your Integration process.

- If you are physically ill or if your Identity Visualization made you aware of a need to work on your own well-being, then your Integration prioritization must provide for adequate time for yourself, with whatever trade-offs are necessary.
- If an important deadline is looming at work, your prioritization may appropriately be to devote virtually all your time and energy to completing that responsibility, vowing to "balance the books" with extra attention to other external demands and your Self-maintenance when the deadline is achieved.

• It may be that several important external demands are in conflict, such as an ailing parent and your work responsibilities. In this event, your prioritization may include such facilitating decisions as talking with your boss about modifying your workload, or setting up more resources to assist in the care of your parent.

The outcome of the prioritization and trade-off part of the Integration Visualization must satisfy two criteria:

1. Your allocation of time and energy is *realistic* (for example, you don't play the "twenty-six-hours-in-a-day delusion" with yourself).
2. You are at peace with the trade-offs, so that there will be no energy wasted on "shoulda, woulda, coulda" second-guessing. If circumstances change during the day, you will do a Quick Re-Focus and reorder your priorities. For the present, rest assured that you have made the best allocation possible and don't second-guess it.

Your Inspiration Visualization

In the 3D Visualization, this immediately follows the Integration Visualization, which ended with your Identity hologram surrounded by external demands, which you have "tamed" by appropriately prioritizing your time and energy.

1. If you are doing the Inspiration Visualization separately from the Identity and Integration Visualizations, begin by setting the stage.

2. Affirm the holographic image of your identity; notice how appropriate and grounded it feels. Acknowledge all the external demands arrayed around you, with the serenity that the Integration Visualization has properly allocated your available time and energy. You are in a safe and secure place.

3. Experience a feeling of *readiness* and *expectation.*

4. Visualize looking up from your safe and secure place. From above, emanating from a source that you trust completely, comes an intense, colored light—the light of healing—that permeates all of your being. The light affirms your Identity and Integration process and allocations.

5. Feel the light penetrating every cell of your body, bringing healing and a feeling of being loved and *completely* accepted. Feel your entire body being revitalized and healed. It is as if you are immersed in a pool of delicious liquid, completely at ease and breathing normally, entirely at peace. You are revitalized by the energy from the light.

6. Continue to "float" in that wonderfully supportive state. Whatever comes into your mind, give it free access, allow it to pass through, and let it move on. Don't try to retain or analyze; simply observe.

7. You may wish to invite the light to focus on a particular need. This might be a problem you are facing, a decision to be made, a loved one or acquaintance with special needs, or a part of your*self* in need of healing. It may be a simple question, such as "How may I best deal with this situation?" You may use a prayer, faith-based language, or symbols to articulate your needs, placing them before the divine. Or you may simply surrender to that higher power of your beliefs.

8. Relax and be open to whatever input you may receive. It may be in words, but more likely it will be in symbols and images of the right brain (Icons). Don't be impatient to translate these to your left brain; you don't want to lose the message or its nuances.

9. Even if you are not aware of a specific message having been received, trust that some part of you has received something of value that, in time, will become more apparent.

Your 3D Visualization

The 3D Visualization is a part of the Daily PS Focus. This combines the Identity, Integration, and Inspiration Visualizations into one complete visualization.

Set the Stage

A. Ensure that you are comfortable and won't be disturbed.
B. Have writing materials or a tape recorder nearby.
C. Let your body relax; move into your inner space of freely flowing thought.

Identity

1. Focus on the center of your being.
2. Repeat the "I Accept Myself Completely" affirmation.
3. Envision a hologram of many rays of light.
4. Transcend your Unfinished Business by removing any dark rays.
5. Celebrate the multicolored and shining image of your identity.

Integration

6. See yourself surrounded by your external demands (from your day-to-day reality).
7. Ropes lead to certain external demands (the most demanding).
8. Honor all your external demands. State that it is your right and responsibility to allocate your time and energies among your needs and their needs.
9. Envision a brilliant violet flame springing up around you, burning away each rope.
10. As each rope burns, send forgiveness to that external demand.
11. Free of undue demands, you prioritize your schedule for this day (among yourself and selected external demands).
12. Make it clear that your prioritization reflects today's realities, not the relative importance of each external demand.
13. Affirm that you have done the best you can with your prioritization.

Inspiration

14. Affirm the holographic image of your identity.
15. Affirm the prioritization of your time and energies.
16. Visualize a brilliant and healing light shining down from above, permeating every cell of your being.
17. Invite the healing light to focus on a specific need or challenge.
18. Take notice of the symbols or Icons that appear.

Conclusion

19. Give thanks to all three PS Dimensions as you complete this visualization.
20. Bring the positive feelings from your visualization with you into all aspects of your day.

THE RADICALLY CHANGING WORKPLACE

THE PAST SEVERAL DECADES have seen radical changes in the workplace and the underlying nature of the employer-employee relationship.

- **Organizations don't last as long.** It used to be that large corporations had an air of permanency about them. That's no longer the case. The Fortune 500 lists the largest, and presumably most stable, organizations in the United States. However, during the decade of the 1980s, 230 names disappeared from the Fortune 500 list. That's a 46 percent change! And the names continue to change through acquisitions, mergers, and other organizational metamorphoses.

- **Technologies and products don't last as long.** Consider the increasingly rapid rate of obsolescence in computers and other areas of high technology. (Someone said that if the recently genetically engineered tomato lives up to expectations, vegetables may soon have longer shelf lives than laptop computers.)

- **Skills don't last as long.** Federal Reserve chairman Alan Greenspan said in a speech, "Today, human skills are subject to obsolescence at a rate perhaps unprecedented in American history."

- **Jobs don't last as long.** The Labor Department now predicts that someone entering the job market today not only will have a dozen or more jobs, but—more significant—is likely to have two or three very different careers.

- **Organizations are structured and run in radical new ways.** Entire layers of corporations have disappeared, and the traditional hierarchical structure is giving way to the "horizontal" organization, with flexible and constantly changing work teams and outsourced services.

- **The number of "regular jobs" is shrinking.** Increasingly, businesses are relying on contingency hires and outsourcing, thus reducing the number of full-time employees.

- **The marketplaces** in which companies compete are increasingly global in nature.

- **The amount of information available** increases exponentially, and the ability to transmit it approaches being instantaneous.

Clearly, as the workplace struggles to adapt to these increasingly pervasive changes, any kind of "job security" is a thing of the past.

In fact, job security was always more wishful thinking on the part of employees than a reality in the policies and practices of employer organizations. Unionized employees have had contracts that specify, among other things, the sequence in which workers are furloughed. But the typical white-collar and office employee has believed in a sort of implicit contract between employer and employee: "Be loyal, work hard, and the company will take care of you." This contract was seldom formalized, so if a company fell on hard times it was free to take the logical steps of reducing costs, including firing employees. This happened infrequently in the slower-moving markets of the past, and a perception of normalcy was the "one-company" employee who joined the organization as his first job, worked his way up a succession of positions, and after thirty years retired with a gold watch amid echoes of a gala celebration.

As we've alluded to earlier, one of the realities of "yesterday's" workplace was that many people looked to work for part or all of their sense of being, their identity. The organization was their family, supervisors their parents, coworkers their siblings. For the good of the organization, they devoted the majority of their waking hours to their jobs, accepted corporate relocations that disadvantaged their spouse and children, and in some cases engaged in activities of questionable taste, morals, or even legality.

The more an employee believed in the implicit contract and the "company as family," the greater was the shock when employment was terminated. It meant simultaneous loss of a job, livelihood, and identity. In the latter 1980s, the implicit contract between employee and employer was broken irreversibly. *Downsizing* became an everyday term. Vast numbers of qualified employees lost their jobs. Millions of laid-off employees who had prided themselves on conscientiousness and loyalty to their companies felt betrayed and angry. Gradually the awareness grew that increased layoffs was not a temporary thing, as in the past during economic downturns, but a long-term trend.

Looking back, those turbulent and painful times did have some salutary results on the job and work scene. For one, the stigma of unemployment pretty much disappeared. Dick and his colleague, Mary Burton, saw this in the biweekly career seminar they conducted for the Harvard Business School Club of New York:

> We started the seminar in the fall of 1980. For the first several years, the number of participants was relatively low, they were all male, and most were twenty years or more into their careers. They were pretty secretive—a few would come in, sit down, and then get up and leave. There was a lot of guilt floating around. That's when we started focusing our efforts in the seminar on defusing the stigma of unemployment. As the 1980s progressed, the number of attendees increased each year. There was still a perception that unemployment was an anomaly typified by the comment: "I was amazed to find so many others here at the seminar. I thought I was the only HBS graduate out of work." Gradually the stigma diminished. In the late 1980s the number of female participants began to increase, bringing a new attitude—more interest in "self" along with "work." As we moved into the 1990s, participants were coming back to the seminar for the second or third time, saying, "Well, that wasn't the right job, so here I am back to get a tune-up for my next job search." The feeling of stigma had pretty much disappeared.

Although the radical changes in the workplace over recent years have been traumatic, they have been an unmistakable signal that the ways of the past are gone forever—which is good and bad for all employees. The good news and bad news are one and the same: it is no longer realistic to invest your identity or self-worth in a job; instead you need to independently gain an appreciation for who you are, learn the techniques for Self-maintenance, and trade the external, precarious "job security" of your past life for the solid, internally grounded sense of self-reliance.

APPENDIX C

SELF-ASSESSMENT EXERCISES FROM IN TRANSITION

As discussed in Chapter 15, "Setting Your Career Strategy" is the first phase of the Career Management Cycle. Self-awareness and market assessment are the two key components for determining your career strategy.

Exercises for Self-Awareness

There are many ways in which to achieve self-awareness, including both formal self-assessment instruments and the straightforward and realistic feedback that anyone can become more perceptive about in their normal day-to-day activities. To give you an idea of the wide scope and variety of the formal instruments, this appendix lists the self-awareness "exercises" used in the Harvard Business School Club of New York Career Seminars conducted by Dick Wedemeyer and Mary Burton for eighteen years. There are many other self-awareness instruments that can be used to equally good effect—the important thing is to *use* them!

FORKS-IN-THE-ROAD EXERCISE

Look back at the decision points in your career to date. Review decisions you've made concerning your career over the years.

- Who made the decision?
- What were the criteria for these decisions?
- Am I on *my* road or somebody else's?

BEST-CASE EULOGY EXERCISE

Write your own "eulogy" for how you would be remembered by others.

- How would I *like* to be remembered?
- If I am to be remembered thus, then from here onward I must

  _____.

LIFE MISSION STATEMENT

Write your own Life Mission Statement.

- What are my underlying life themes and desires/goals?
- How can I be faithful to these in my choice of work?

NEAR-TERM PRIORITIES EXERCISE

Rank in order of importance the "Eighteen Facets of Life" at the end of this Appendix to determine your priorities for the current phase of your life.

- Examine your completed priority list:
  —Are they valid as "current life stage" priorities?
  —*Whose* priorities are these: yours, your family's, your boss's?
  —Are these consistent with your actions, your reality?
  —Are they compatible with those close to you?
- Define your trade-offs: "Must Haves" vs. "Price Tag Factors."

VALUES & MOTIVATIONAL FACTORS

What are the values, beliefs, and other subtle factors that motivate you in your work?

- Identify these subtle but powerful forces.
- They need to be congruent with
  —Your career direction
  —Your workplace situation

MYERS-BRIGGS TYPE INDICATOR

Use the MBTI® to determine your "style" preferences (see *In Transition*, pages 64–71).

- What is your "style" vs. others' "styles"?
- What types of work/situations do you prefer?
- Enhance your flexibility and adaptability.

SKILLS

Use the Quick Job Hunt Map® to determine your "intrinsic skills" (see *In Transition*, page 78).

- Enables you to articulate your skills more credibly
- If you are making a significant career course change, this exercise will help you to define transferable skills in "industry-neutral" terms.

ORGANIZATIONAL FIT RETROSPECTIVE

Look back over your work history and define your Best-Case/Worst-Case situation regarding bosses, peers, work environment.

- Define your "Must Haves" and "Must Avoids."
- Which kinds of "political situations" trip you up?

SELF-PERCEPTION

To "see yourself as others see you," have someone describe you as an individual and coworker. Do this exercise with someone who doesn't know you well.

- Few of us are aware of how others see us.
- Get some insight as to how you "come across" when first meeting people.
- What you don't know *can* hurt you.

CONSTRAINTS	
What do you perceive is holding you back career-wise?	• Actual versus Illusory Constraints • Internal versus External Constraints • Verify them and/or transcend them!

Eighteen Facets of Life

Use these items for prioritization in the "Near-Term Priorities" exercise.

Coworkers
Contribution to society
Current income
Equity ownership
Family
Friends
Future income
Geographic location
Health
Influence and power
Intrinsic nature of work
Leisure time
Personal growth
Prestige and status
Professional growth
Security
Spouse or significant other
Workplace environment

For further details on these exercises, see *In Transition* by Mary Lindley Burton and Richard A. Wedemeyer (listed in the Recommended Reading).

ON THE JOB

Checklist for Identifying Your Boss's Expectations and Preferences

You have a new boss, either because you have just arrived or your supervisor has changed. Many of your coworkers may take a wait-and-see approach, but you understand the importance of shifting gears and fully understanding the expectations and preferences (and whims) of the new boss as soon as possible. Be proactive and get on the boss's schedule for an "orientation" meeting. And keep your eyes and ears open. Your goal is to quickly understand the person to whom you report, particularly as it may affect you and your position. Use this checklist as a guide. Not all points may be relevant to your situation, and you may wish to add others. Some of the points may be appropriately discussed during your meeting; others need to be determined indirectly.

- How would your boss like to be addressed by you?
- What is your boss's number-one priority for the next six months?
- What does your boss expect of you?
- What are your specific goals and how will they be measured?
- If at some point in the future your boss is displeased by your performance, how will you know it?
- When assigning a project, does your boss prefer to get involved with the details or just want the desired results?

- At what stage does your boss want to see feedback on an assigned project: at an early stage while options are fluid, at midproject before final determinations are made, or only in the final format?
- Is your boss OK with rough drafts or should everything you present to her be clean and presentable?
- How much does your boss want to know about a problem?
- When your boss needs to make a decision, how can you best assist him?
- Is it acceptable to ask that the boss reconsider her decision if you have relevant input?
- How often does the boss want updates from you? In what form?
- What kind of "gatekeeping" procedures (accessing the boss) should you use?
- Is the boss receptive to new ways of doing things? To what degree is he a risk taker? What is the best way for you to propose new ideas?
- What type of decisions is the boss comfortable delegating downward, and which type does she want to make?
- If you think the boss is making a mistake, what should you do?
- What are your boss's views on how E-mail should be used in the office?
- During what part of the day (or week) is the boss most open and receptive?
- What are the boss's "internal rules" about working hours, working late and weekends, personal days, sick days, and so on?
- What is the boss's attitude about intruding on employee's personal lives, calling people at home, working weekends, honoring scheduled vacations, and so on?
- How much social interaction does your boss want to have with you (and others)?
- Does the boss tend to confront situations promptly or put off dealing with them? How does that affect your dealings with him?
- How comfortable is your boss with herself? What are the implications for your interactions with her?
- Office behavior and decorum: how does your boss feel about various types of office behavior, such as confrontations and conflict, non-work–related conversation, joking and horseplay, or gossip?
- What should you do if you perceive that your work is putting you in an ethical bind?

- Is your boss on a "fast track" or is he likely to be comfortable in the position for a long time? How does that match with your career objectives?

Clearly, the answers to some of these can be only conjectural. The point is that you are focusing on the expectations and preferences of your boss, both to be able to better meet them and to recognize if any of them are a poor fit with your own expectations or objectives.

If *you* are the new boss, bear in mind that your subordinates and peers are uncertain about how they fit into the new situation and how to interact with you. You can clarify these uncertainties and start building trust and establishing an effective team by proactively clarifying your expectations—using written communication, meetings, and one-on-one conversations.

THE MOTIVATIONAL
PROFILE

DAVID C. MCCLELLAND, PH.D., was a prodigious observer of individual and collective human behavior. In his book *Human Motivation* (New York: Irvington Press, 1982), he cites three motivational categories:

1. **Craftsman:** A person high in this category is primarily motivated by competition with his own internal standards. This person feels strongly about doing things "properly" as he defines that term, rather than as other people—including the boss—define properly. A master stone carver working on intricate details tucked in crevices is the consummate Craftsman. If your supervisor says, "Your report is fine as it is," but you stay late to polish yet another draft, that's Craftsman motivation. (Note: McClelland called this category "Achievement," but that word has come to mean so many things that we have substituted the term *Craftsman.*)

2. **Affiliation:** A person high in this category is motivated primarily by concerns for the welfare of others. This person could be snowed under with work and under tight deadline pressures, but if someone said, "I've got a problem; do you have a minute?" her answer would be, "Sure, come in," and the work would be put aside.

3. **Power:** A person high in this category tends to seek out positions and other means of influence to make things happen. Although "power" may

have a negative connotation for some, here the Power motivation is *neu-tral*: it can be used for positive or negative ends.

Each individual exhibits a *combination* of the three categories, so McClel-land established a *Motivational Profile*, which indicates to what degree each cat-egory influences a person's thoughts and actions. Invariably, for each person one of the categories predominates. This concept is very useful from a self-awareness standpoint, because without this understanding, most people tend to assume that everyone is motivated the same as he or she is, which can lead to significant problems.

Opposing motivational profiles can cause problems for constructive interac-tions or relationships. For example:

- The boss (Craftsman) who criticizes a subordinate manager (Affiliation) for "wasting too much time on people."
- The salesperson (Power) who gets the promotion by cultivating the boss while the peer salespeople (Craftsman and Affiliation) are directing their attention to their customers.

More information on motivational profiles can be found in *In Transition* (see Recommended Reading, page 293).

THE INNER EDGE
CD AND SEMINARS

CD Set

In conjunction with this book, Ronald W. Jue has created a 2-CD set containing the visualizations described in *The Inner Edge* with additional guided visualizations and relaxation techniques derived from his practice and QDM seminars. The CDs, augmented by appropriate background music, set the stage for each visualization, guiding you step-by-step through the process.

The Inner Edge and Other Visualizations (two CDs)	$19.95
shipping and handling	2.85
TOTAL	$22.80

Major credit cards accepted. California residents should add 7.25% sales tax. To order, phone (888) 738-8889.

Seminars

For information on seminars, group sessions, or personal coaching on QDM and *The Inner Edge*, visit our website at www.inneredgebook.com, send an E-mail to us at inneredgebook@aol.com, or fax: (714) 447-4701. Mail correspondence can be directed to Ronald W. Jue, P.O. Box 5805, Fullerton, CA 92838.

Other Contacts

Richard A. Wedemeyer at rwedemeyer@mba1963hbs.edu

David Christel at christelentities@hotmail.com

RECOMMENDED READING

Arrien, Angeles. *The Four-Fold Way: Walking the Paths of the Warrior, Teacher, Healer, and Visionary.* San Francisco: HarperCollins Publishers, 1993. Provides a template drawn from the indigenous cultures showing how to find a spiritual locus for identity.

Borysenko, Joan. *Fire in the Soul: A New Psychology of Spiritual Optimism.* New York: Warner Books, Inc., 1993. A pragmatic book focusing on how personal growth and spiritual transformation can emerge by embracing one's life crises.

Bradshaw, John. *Bradshaw on: The Family: A Revolutionary Way of Self-Discovery.* Pompano Beach, FL: Health Communications, Inc., 1988. Useful insights on growing up and family of origin issues, including boundaries and other coping techniques.

Briskin, Alan. *The Stirring of the Soul in the Workplace.* San Francisco: Berrett-Koehler Publishers, 1996. Exploring the ways to balance a person's spiritual life with the expectations and realities of the workplace.

Burton, Mary Lindley, and Richard A. Wedemeyer. *In Transition.* New York: HarperCollins, 1991. Strategies and wisdom that still hold for today's businessperson in a world of change.

Canfield, Jack, with Mark Victor Hansen and Les Hewitt. *The Power of Focus: How to Hit Your Business, Personal and Financial Targets with Absolute Certainty.* Deerfield Beach, FL: Health Communications, Inc., 2000. How to define your own path in life and business and begin creating a plan that brings balance into your life.

Chopra, Deepak, M.D., and David Simon, M.D. *Grow Younger, Live Longer.* New York: Harmony Books, 2001. A manual for renewal of mind, body, and emotions. Includes sections on escaping the prison of conditioning, enhancing mind/body integration, and the cultivation of flexibility and creativity in consciousness.

Collins, Jim. *Good to Great.* New York: HarperCollins Publishers, Inc., 2001. A well-written and researched book providing insights into the roots of sustained corporate greatness.

Combs, Allan, and Mark Holland. *Synchronicity: Through the Eyes of Science, Myth and the Trickster.* New York: Marlowe & Company, 1996. One of the best books dealing equally well with both the scientific underpinnings of synchronicity, as well as the archetypal dimension that underlies all synchronistic occurrences.

Cooper, Robert K., and Ayman Sawaf. *Executive EQ: Emotional Intelligence in Leadership and Organizations.* New York: Grosset/Putnam, 1996. Applying the concepts of emotional intelligence to the areas of leadership and organization.

Cornell, Ann Weiser. *The Power of Focusing: A Practical Guide to Emotional Self-Healing.* New York: MJF Books, 1996. Clarifies the essential human skill of being present, focusing on ways of obtaining deep human wisdom.

DeFoore, Bill, and John Renesch (eds). *Rediscovering the Soul of Business: A Renaissance of Values.* San Francisco: New Leaders Press, 1996. Bestselling authors Thomas Moore, Gary Zukav, Charles Handy, and Matthew Fox combine their writing talents with twenty-one other contributors in this collection focusing on the spiritual renaissance in business.

Downs, Alan. *Beyond the Looking Glass: Overcoming the Seductive Culture of Corporate Narcissism.* New York: American Management Association, 1997. Addresses the shadow aspect of business that is often not seen—corporate narcissism—outlining the characteristics and methods for dealing with this phenomenon as part of Unfinished Business.

Dreaver, Jim. *The Way of Harmony.* New York: Avon Books, 1999. Based on the theme that true inner peace and freedom involve a fundamental shift in the way we perceive and experience reality, with a section devoted to spirituality in the corporate world.

Fromm, Erich. *To Have or to Be?* New York: Continuum Publishing Co., 1999. An important book explaining why the *having* mode of our existence is taking the world to the brink of psychological disaster. Also outlines a program for socioeconomic change based on spiritual values.

Gawain, Shakti. *The Path of Transformation.* Novato, CA: New World Library, 2000. Emphasizes that solutions to our personal and planetary crises reside within each of us and are within our reach.

Gerber, Michael E. *The E-Myth Revisited.* New York: HarperCollins Publishers, Inc., 1995. Recognizes and upholds that the purpose of life is not to serve one's business, but that the primary purpose of business is to serve one's life.

Goleman, Daniel. *Emotional Intelligence: Why It Can Matter More Than IQ for Character, Health, and Lifelong Achievement.* New York: Bantam Books, 1995. Offers a new vision of excellence, different ways of being smart, and defines emotional literacy.

Guiley, Rosemary Ellen. *Breakthrough Intuition: How to Achieve a Life of Abundance by Listening to the Voices Within.* New York: Berkeley Books, 2001. This is probably the best guidebook to activate and begin using your intuitive ability.

Herrmann, Ned. *The Whole Brain Business Book.* New York: McGraw-Hill, 1996. One of the earliest books on whole-brain thinking in the workplace.

His Holiness the Dalai Lama, and Howard C. Cutler, M.D. *The Art of Happiness.* New York: Riverhead Books, 1998. Focuses on the importance of inner discipline for developing a spiritual life and creating happiness.

His Holiness the Dalai Lama. *Ethics for the New Millennium.* New York: Putnam Publishing, 1999. His Holiness re-examines our Western assumption regarding the basic characteristics of man and focuses on the goodness of man's essential nature.

Houston, Jean. *Jump Time: Shaping Your Future in a World of Radical Change.* New York: Jeremy P. Tarcher/Putnam, 2000. Challenges the reader in recognizing that our individual destiny is inextricably linked to the world's unfolding.

Jaworski, Joseph. *Synchronicity: The Inner Path of Leadership.* San Francisco: Berrett-Koehler Publishers, 1996. An inspirational story of a business leader's journey toward understanding the deeper issues of leadership and discovering that one's way of Being is greatly impacted by leadership.

Judge, William Q. *The Leader's Shadow: Exploring and Developing Executive Character.* Thousand Oaks, CA: Sage Publications, Inc., 1999. An examination of the inner dynamics of executives in top leadership positions. Adds dimension to *The Inner Edge* chapter on Unfinished Business with a focus on leadership characteristics.

Kabat-Zinn, Jon. *Wherever You Go, There You Are.* New York: Hyperion, 1994. The heart of Buddhist meditation made clear, concise, and readily accessible to the Western mind.

Krishnamurti, Jiddu. *To Be Human.* Boston: Shambhala Publications, Inc., 2000. A splendid introduction to this spiritual figure's integration of psychology, philosophy, and spirituality for walking the path of personal truth.

Levoy, Gregg. *Callings: Finding and Following an Authentic Life.* New York: Three Rivers Press, 1997. An examination and guide for discovering your calling in life and to create the passageways that lead you to greater authenticity and personal power.

Maslow, Abraham H. *Maslow on Management.* New York: John Wiley & Sons, Inc., 1998. A seminal work on human behavior in the workplace. Extols the virtues of collaborative and synergistic management.

McGraw, Philip C. *Self Matters: Creating Your Life from the Inside Out.* New York: Simon & Schuster Source, 2001. Explores the way we define ourselves and our aesthetic being.

Miller, Alice. *The Truth Will Set You Free.* New York: Basic Books, 2001. Avoids psychological jargon and gets to the heart of Unfinished Business, providing insights on early childhood development and how we might liberate ourselves from parental conditioning.

Mountain Dreamer, Oriah. *The Invitation.* San Francisco: HarperCollins Publishers, 1999. A guidebook reflecting on how to live more deeply, honestly, and passionately.

Myss, Caroline. *Sacred Contracts: Awakening Your Divine Potential.* New York: Harmony Books, 2001. Synthesizes psychology and spiritual insight for creating a path of greater self-awareness.

Pearson, Carol S., and Sharon Seivert. *Magic at Work: A Guide to Releasing Your Highest Creative Powers*. New York: Bantam Doubleday Dell Publishing Group, Inc., 1995. Shows how the magic of human imagination can help us thrive in challenging times.

Pehrson, John B., and Susan E. Mehrtens. *Intuitive Imagery: A Resource at Work*. Boston: Butterworth-Heinemann, 1997. One of the first books offering valuable insights into how the intuitive mind can assist corporations in navigating through business matters and into the new millennium.

Purce, Jill. *The Mystic Spiral: Journey of the Soul*. New York: Thames & Hudson, Inc., 1980. A wondrous book illustrating in pictures how the cosmic symbol of the spiral represents the hero's journey to the still center of one's being.

Rabbin, Robert. *Invisible Leadership: Igniting the Soul at Work*. Charlottesville, VA: Hampton Roads Publishing, 2002. Highlights the importance of a clear mind, an open heart, and present-centered attention as basic ingredients for Transcendent Leadership.

Ray, Michael, and Rochelle Myers. *Creativity in Business*. New York: Bantam Doubleday Dell Publishing Group, Inc., 1986. Shows how our creative resources can be lived out in each moment and brought to bear within business organizations.

Ray, Michael, and Alan Rinzler (eds.). *The New Paradigm in Business*. New York: Jeramy P. Tarcher/Putnam Books, 1993. Numerous contributors provide unique perspectives concerning the effect of global changes on old, limiting, and ineffective business paradigms.

Renesch, John E. *Getting to the Better Future: A Matter of Conscious Choosing*. San Francisco: New Business Books, 2000. A vision of historic transformation for all humankind and a global future full of possibilities. Highlighted in this book is the potential for the business community to lead the rest of world in an incredible transition for all humanity.

Renesch, John, and Bill DeFoore (eds.). *The New Bottom Line: Bringing Heart and Soul to Business*. San Francisco: New Leaders Press, 1988. Prompted by the debate concerning spiritual values in business, this collection contains the writings of the chief debaters: Tom Peters, Anita Roddick, Ken Blanchard, Angeles Arrien, and Thomas Moore, among others.

Sanders, T. Irene. *Strategic Thinking and the New Science: Planning in the Midst of Chaos, Complexity, and Change.* New York: Simon & Schuster Inc., 1998. Highlights the importance of looking at the world as a whole system, rather than as a collection of deterministic principles, and the importance of integrating intuition with intellect.

Schaef, Anne Wilson. *Living in Process: Basic Truths for Living the Path of the Soul.* New York: The Ballantine Publishing Group, 1998. Teaches an action philosophy that will reconnect you with your deep, long-forgotten spirituality.

Talbot, Michael. *The Holographic Universe.* New York: HarperCollins, 1991. A seminal book outlining a new conceptual model for how our brain and body work in tandem with the intuitive mind.

Vaughan, Frances. *Shadows of the Sacred.* Wheaton, IL: The Theosophical Publishing House. Addresses the shadow side of idealized spirituality and asks us to come back to the practical task of nurturing spirituality as a source of healing and wholeness.

Warner, Jim. *Aspirations of Greatness: Mapping the Midlife Leader's Reconnection to Self and Soul.* New York: John Wiley & Sons, Inc., 2002. Confronts the disillusionments of people in midlife who appear to "have it all" yet yearn for purpose and provides a blueprint for positive change.

Wheatley, Margaret J. *Leadership and the New Science.* San Francisco: Berrett-Koehler Publishers, Inc., 1992. The new sciences of quantum physics, chaos theory, and new biology shift our perspectives on reality and our assumptions on how we do business.

Whyte, David. *Crossing the Unknown Sea: Work as a Pilgrimage of Identity.* New York: Riverhead Books, 2000. The workplace is focused on as a great opportunity for self-discovery and growth, and a place where we can cultivate a greater sense of presence.

Wolf, Fred Alan. *Taking the Quantum Leap: The New Physics for Non-Scientists.* New York: Harper & Row Publishers, 1989. A humanized view of how quantum mechanics, God, and human thought and will are related.

Wolman, Richard N. *Thinking with Your Soul: Spiritual Intelligence and Why It Matters.* New York: Harmony Books, 2001. A thoughtful inquiry into the spiritual dimensions of life and its place in the twenty-first century.

Zohar, Danah. *The Quantum Self: Human Nature and Consciousness Defined by the New Physics.* New York: William Morrow and Co., Inc., 1990. With considerable clarity, the author shows how the insights of modern physics can illuminate relationships with ourselves, with others, and with the world at large.

Zohar, Danah, and Dr. Ian Marshall. *SQ: Connecting with Your Spiritual Intelligence.* New York: Bloomsbury Publisher, 2000. Collective evidence has established a third type of intelligence: SQ. This handbook shows how to access SQ to develop personal potential and meaning.

QUOTE SOURCES

Alda, Alan. Quoted in *Do It! Let's Get Off Our Buts*, Peter McWilliams, Los Angeles: Prelude Press, 1994, page 28.

Blake, William. Quoted in *Bartlett's Familiar Quotations*, John Bartlett and Justin Kaplan, eds., Boston: Little, Brown and Company, 1992, page 359.

The Dalai Lama, His Holiness. *The Path to Tranquility*. New York: Viking Arkana, 1999, page 221.

Edwards, Jonathan. Quoted in *The Forbes Scrapbook of Thoughts on the Business of Life*, Forbes Magazine ed., Chicago: Triumph Books, 1992, page 259.

Emerson, Ralph Waldo. Quoted in *Bartlett's Familiar Quotations*, John Bartlett and Justin Kaplan, eds., Boston: Little, Brown and Company, 1992, page 431.

Gawain, Shakti. Quoted in *The Book of Positive Quotations*, John Cool ed., New York: Gramercy Books, 1999, page 113.

Goldberg, Herb. Quoted in *The Book of Positive Quotations*, John Cool ed., New York: Gramercy Books, 1999, page 320.

Hardy, Dorcas. Quoted in *The New Beacon Book of Quotations by Women*, Rosalie Maggio ed., Boston: Beacon Press, 1996, page 582.

Hillel. Quoted in *Bartlett's Familiar Quotations*, John Bartlett and Justin Kaplan, eds., Boston: Little, Brown and Company, 1992, page 102.

Jung, Carl. Quoted in *Simpson's Contemporary Quotations*, James B. Simpson ed., Boston: Houghton Mifflin Company, 1988, page 133.

Lao-tzu. Quoted in *The Word Lover's Book of Unfamiliar Quotations*, Wesley D. Camp ed., Paramus, NJ: Prentice Hall Press, 1990, page 443.

Lawrence, D. H. Quoted in *The Book of Positive Quotations*, John Cool ed., New York: Gramercy Books, 1999, page 323.

Ortega y Gasset, Jose. Quoted in *Encarta Book of Quotations*, Bill Swainson ed., New York: St. Martin's Press, 2000, page 709.

Proust, Marcel. Quoted in *The Word Lover's Book of Unfamiliar Quotations*, Wesley D. Camp ed., Paramus, NJ: Prentice Hall Press, 1990, page 442.

Quinn, Doris Kerns. *Christian Science Monitor* (June 2, 1976).

Repplier, Agnes. Quoted in *The New Beacon Book of Quotations by Women*, Rosalie Maggio ed., Boston: Beacon Press, 1996, page 195.

Ross, Steven J. Quoted in *Simpson's Contemporary Quotations*, James B. Simpson ed., New York: HarperCollins Publishers, 1997, page 200.

Shafranske, E. P. "Factors associated with the perception of spirituality in psychotherapy." *Journal of Transpersonal Psychology* 16 (1984): 231–241.

Shaw, George Bernard. Quoted in *The Concise Columbia Dictionary of Quotations*, Robert Andrews ed., New York: Columbia University Press, 1989, page 37.

Szasz, Thomas. Quoted in *Simpson's Contemporary Quotations*, James B. Simpson ed., New York: HarperCollins Publishers, 1997, page 392.

Watson, Thomas J. Quoted in *The Forbes Scrapbook of Thoughts on the Business of Life*, Forbes Magazine ed., Chicago: Triumph Books, 1992, page 202.

INDEX

Accountability
    deadlines and follow-up, 174–75
    interpersonal, 173–74
    intrapersonal, 172–73
    as "litmus test", 177–78
    one-way, 171
    in peer-to-peer interactions, 175
    as scorekeeper, 172, 178
    Self-, 47–48
    service and, 229, 230
    summary of chapter on, 178–79
    in supervisor-subordinate
        interactions, 175–76
    Teflon employees, 176–77, 179,
        237
    two-way, 171–72
Accounting practices, 243
Adaptability
    defined, 149, 158
    examples of, 149–50
    feedback and, 109–10
    importance of, 150
    loyalty, responsibility, and, 161–69
    office politics and, 156–58
    as purpose of PS, 18
    Quantum Decision Making and,
        151
    rapport and task, 153–54

    resistance to, 110–11, 159
    summary of chapter on, 158–59
    of today's employee, 121, 149
    Unfinished Business and, 150–51,
        154–56
    vulnerability and, 151–53
Advisers, on-the-job, 124–25
Affirmations
    Affirmation of My Potential, 21,
        25–26, 102
    "I Accept Myself Completely"
        Affirmation, 64–65, 124,
        270–71, 276
    Self-Maintenance Affirmation, 50
Alda, Alan, 3
Ambidextrous mind (QDM), 136
Ammonites, xvii
Anger
    characteristics of, 112–13
    management techniques, 113–15
    as secondary emotion, 113
Appropriateness of actions
    in Fully Functioning Adult, 18
    in organizations, 219, 228–30
    as PS goal, 10, 99
Authenticity
    defined, 10
    in managers, 153

in organizations, 219, 228–30
  as PS goal, 18, 99
Authors, about the, 315–16

Being versus Doing/Having
  in the organizaton, 223
  at personal level, 62–63
  in the workplace, 124
Benefits of PS
  in the organizaton, 24–25, 207, 217,
    220, 231
  at personal level, 22–24
  in the workplace, 22–24
Blake, William, 263
Blind allegiance, 163
Board of directors
  as change agent, 255–56
  PS at personal level for, 253–54
  renewal through PS, 257–58
Bootstrap approach to PS in an
    organization
  description of, 235, 236–39
  versus top-down approach, 247–48
Boss checklist, 190, 285–87
Boss-subordinate interactions
  accountability contracts, 173–74,
    175–76
  deadlines and follow-up, 174–75
  hiring employees, 137–38, 215–16
  Teflon employee confrontation,
    176–77, 179, 237
  termination of employee, 152–53
Bosses
  attitudes of, 246
  compassionate, 153
  difficult, 215
  insensitive, 237
  myopia of, 259–60
  tough versus firm, 247
  toxic, 109, 155–56

Boundaries
  defined, 78
  establishing, 79–81
  healthy, 78, 79
  inadequate, 78–79
  isolating, 78, 79
  organizational, 226, 246–47
  workplace, 109, 128–29
Boundary-setting
  external demands and, 77–78
  as Self-discipline, 53
  as Self-maintenance, 51
Bradshaw, John, 78
Brain functions, right/left, 87–88
Burton, Mary, 279, 281, 284, 303
Business. *See also* Pragmatic
    Spirituality in the workplace;
    Pragmatic Spirituality on
    organizational level
  changing world of, 14–15
  compartmentalization in, 15
  spirituality and, 5–6, 13–14, 251–61
  workplace changes, 119–21, 277–79

Career management, Career
    Management Cycle
  career strategy, 183–86
  CEO of your career, 191–92
  in the job phase, 183, 189–91
  networking, 188–89
  obstacles to, 192–93
  PS as foundation of, 181
  self-assessment exercises, 281–84
  self-marketing, 187–89
  summary of chapter on, 193–94
  three principles of, 182
CEO
  board of directors and, 255–56
  compensation packages, 258
  PS at personal level for, 253–54

PS, commitment to, from, 254–55, 261

short-term fads and, 251–53

CEO of your career, 191–92

Change
 in business world, 14–15
 resistance to, 65–66, 244–45
 in workplace, 119–21, 277–79

Change agents in organization, 131, 133, 244

Checklist, boss, 190, 285–87

Childhood injunctions, 40–42

Christel, David, xiii, 292

Co-dependent personality, 61

Commitments
 external, 50–51
 Self-discipline and, 48, 50–53
 to yourself, 51–53

Compartmentalization, 15

Compassionate managers, 153

Compassionate Observer
 defined, 16
 at personal level, 63, 66–68
 in the workplace, 124–25

Confidentiality issues in organization, 241–42, 248

Consultants, dealing with, 211

Continuum of self-interest, 54

Contracts, accountability, 173–74

Cottle, Donald R., 207

Critical Judge, 66–68, 124–25

Cultural differences, QDM
 overcoming, 211–12

Customer service training, 228–30

Daily PS Focus
 description of, 20–22, 102
 on the job, 125, 191
 responsibility and, 167–68
 summary of, 100

3D Visualization, 21, 22, 100, 102, 125, 275–76
 as top priority, 101

Dalai Lama, xi, 12, 251, 304

Deadlines, 174–75

Decision Making, Quantum (QDM)
 defined, 136–37
 examples of, 137–39
 intuitive feedback, 145
 intuitive proficiency, 136
 at organizational level, 207–18, 226–27
 specific questions for, 135–36, 137, 141–42
 summary of, 146–47
 three levels of perception in, 139–41
 three-part process, 141–44, 147

Decision making in the organization
 benefits of QDM, 207, 217
 essential aspects of QDM, 213, 218
 examples of, 208–12, 213–17
 strategic issues, 226–27
 top management myopia and, 259–60

Definition of spirituality, 9–10

Dependent personality, 61

Derived identity, 61

Dimensions of Pragmatic Spirituality (PS)
 Identity, 18, 19–20, 57–71
 Inspiration, 18, 19, 20, 85–98
 Integration, 18, 19, 20, 73–83
 PS journey and, 265

Distractions, internal, 12–13

Doing/Having versus Being
 at personal level, 62–63
 in the organization, 223
 in the workplace, 124

Dysfunctional workplaces
  attraction to, 155–56
  limits of PS in, 130–31, 133

Early injunctions, 40–42
Edwards, Jonathan, 235
Emerson, Ralph Waldo, 197
Employees, Employee
  adaptable, 149–59
  attracting and keeping, 231
  boss checklist for, 190, 285–87
  employer's relationship with,
    203–4, 246, 277–79
  exploitation of, 162–63
  firing, 152–53
  hiring, 137–38, 215–16
  as an individual, 202–3
  job security of, 14, 120, 201–2,
    277–79
  today's versus yesterday's, 120–21
  training, 228–30
  as a worker, 201–2
Ethical decisions, 227–28, 232
Exercise (physical)
  for enhancing identity, 69
  as Self-maintenance, 51, 53
Exploitation of employees, 162–63
External demands
  boundaries and, 77–81
  examples of, 73–74
  neutralizing, 74–77
  prioritizing, 74

Fads, short-term versus top-down
  commitment, 251–53
Family-assigned identity, 58
Female, being, 105–6
Finance and accounting, 243
Firing employees, 152–53
Flexibility (adaptability)

  examples of, 149–50
  feedback and, 109–10
  importance of, 150
  office politics and, 156–58
  as purpose of PS, 18
  Quantum Decision Making and,
    151
  rapport and task, 153–54
  resistance to, 110–11, 159
  summary of highlights on, 158–59
  of today's employee, 121, 149
  Unfinished Business and, 150–51,
    154–56
  vulnerability and, 151–53
Four Rs, the
  defined, 37, 46
  examples of using, 43–45
  Recognition (first R), 37–38
  Research (third R), 37, 38–42
  Responsibility (second R), 37, 38
  Retrofitting (fourth R), 37, 42–43
Fully Functioning Adult
  flexibility of, 109–11
  as idealized concept, 18, 266
  negative emotions in, 112–15
  real-life examples of, 101, 102–9
  the Shadow and, 45, 46, 111–12
  summary of chpater on, 115

Gawain, Shakti, 85
God, limited human perception of,
  87
Goldberg, Herb, 85
Gossip, 157
Greenspan, Alan, 271

Hardy, Dorcas, 161
Health issues, 107–8
Henson, Jim, 303
Hillel, 73

Hiring employees, 137–38, 215–16
Human resources, 243–44

"I Accept Myself Completely"
    Affirmation, 64–65, 124, 270–71
Icons, intuitive
    defined, 91, 92
    guidelines for processing, 92–97,
        143–44
    for hiring employees, 137–38
    for intervention with difficult
        manager, 215
    in Quantum Decision Making, 20,
        139–41, 142, 143–44
    for recruitment problems, 210–11
    for redesign of product line,
        208–10
    for transcending disparate cultures,
        211–12
Identity, Identity Dimension of PS
    board of directors and, 257
    Compassionate Observer and, 63,
        66–68
    defined, 19–20
    Doing/Having versus Being, 62–63,
        124, 223
    ethical decisions and, 227
    external demands and, 76
    external factors and, 57–58
    how identity evolves, 59
    in an organization, 222
    job as identity, 120–22
    reestablishing locus of, 63
    Self-acceptance and, 63, 64–65
    sources of, 58–60
    summary of chapter on, 70–71
    undeveloped, 60–62
    in the workplace, 122–24
Identity Visualization, Your, 63,
    69–70, 270–71, 276

In Transition, 181–82, 188, 191, 290,
    303
In Transition self-assessment
    exercises, 281–84
Inadequate boundaries, 78
Independent Contractor Model,
    166–67, 169
Injunctions, childhood, 40–42
Inner Edge, The
    book, 7, 236
    CD set, 291
    seminars, 291
Inner Edge
    benefits, 4
    description of, 3–8
    journey, 265–67
    Pragmatic Spirituality for, 7–8,
        17–26
    spirituality in life and business,
        9–16
Inner factors. *See also* Unfinished
    Business
    defined, 3–4, 19, 20
    ethical decisions and, 228
    intuition, 91–97
    at organizational level, 226, 257
    at personal level, 85–98
    right/left brain theory, 87–88
    source of, 86–87
    summary of chapter on, 97–98
    ways to access, 4
    in the workplace, 129–30
Inspiration Visualization, Your,
    89–90, 271–74, 276
Institutionalization of PS, 230
Integration Dimension of PS
    balance and, 82–83
    board of directors and, 257
    boundary-setting, 77–81
    defined, 19, 20, 73

ethical decisions and, 228
external demands and, 73–77
obligation to higher cause and,
    81–82
in an organization, 224–25
Self-maintenance and Self-discipline
    in, 77
summary of chapter on, 83
in the workplace, 126–29
Integration Visualization, Your, 80,
    81, 271–74, 276
Interpersonal accountability, 173–74
Intrapersonal accountability, 172–73
Introducing PS in the organization
    bootstrap approach for, 235,
        236–39
    confidentiality issues, 241–42
    resistance to change and, 244–45
    summary of highlights on, 247–49
    top-down approach for, 235–36,
        239–41
    top-down implementation
        examples, 242–44
    Unfinished Business and, 245–47
Intuition. *See also* Icons, intuitive.
    accessing, 92
    examples of, 91
    patience and, 97
    two modes of, 91–92
Intuition in the organization
    benefits of, 207, 217
    essential aspects of, 213, 218
    examples of, 208–12, 213–17
    summary on, 217–18
Intuitive Icons
    defined, 91, 92
    guidelines for processing, 92–97,
        143–44
    for hiring employees, 137–38
    for intervention with difficult
        manager, 215

in Quantum Decision Making, 20,
    139–41, 142, 143–44
for recruitment problems, 210–11
for redesign of product line,
    208–10
for transcending disparate cultures,
    211–12
Intuitive proficiency, 136
Isolating boundaries, 78

Job, PS on the
    accountability, 171–79
    adaptability, 18, 149–59
    application of, 119–33
    benefits of, 22–24
    Career Management Cycle, 181–94
    limits of, 130–31, 133
    loyalty and responsibility, 158,
        161–69
    Quantum Decision Making
        (QDM), 129–30, 132, 135–47
Job security, 14, 120, 201–2, 277–79
Journaling, 26, 145, 147
Jue, Dr. Ronald W., 12, 25, 88, 91,
    130, 136, 138, 161, 207, 208, 209,
    210, 211, 259, 291, 304–05
Jung, Carl, 17, 45

Kelly, Walt, 192
Koren, Alan, xv

Lao-Tzu, 57
Lawrence, D.H., 135
Left brain functions, 87, 88
Logo, corporate, 138–39
Loyalty and responsibility
    as core life values, 162
    as double-edged sword, 81–82
    in evolving organization, 165–66
    exploitation related to, 162–63

as impediments to adaptability,
161–62
Independent Contractor Model,
166–67, 169
negative implications of, 164–65
reciprocation of loyalty, 108
redefinitions of, 166–68
summary of chapter on, 168–69
in traditional organization, 163–64

Male, being, 104–5
Man in the Gray Flannel Suit, The,
127
Manager-subordinate interactions
accountability contracts, 173–74,
175–76
deadlines and follow-up, 174–75
hiring employees, 137–38, 215–16
Teflon employee confrontation,
176–77, 179, 237
termination of employee, 152–53
Managers
attitudes of, 246
compassionate, 153
difficult, 215
insensitive, 237
top management myopia, 259–60
tough versus firm, 247
toxic, 109, 155–56
Manufacturing, 243
Market assessment, 185–86
McClelland, Dr. David C., 289–90
Metaphor, realm of, 140
Misconceptions, workplace, 131–32
Motivational Profile, 289–90

Nautilus, as metaphor, xvii
Negative emotions
anger management, 113–15
characteristics of anger, 112–13
Networking, 188–89

Objectivity, 185
Obligation to higher causes, 81–82
Office politics
defined, 156–57
judgmental attitudes and, 157–58
Organization, PS in the
benefits of, 24–25
commitment to, 251–61
ethics, 277–78
evolving versus traditional
organization, 197–205
introducing, 235–49
potential for, 219–33
Quantum Decision Making
(QDM), 207–18
Ortega y Gasset, José, 99
Overview of Pragmatic Spirituality
(PS)
benefits, 16, 22–25
core elements, 17, 18
daily application, 20–22
description of PS, 7–8, 10, 15–16
objective of PS, xvi, 18
three Dimensions of PS, 18,
19–20
three levels of PS, 22–25
underlying premise, 18–19

Personal level, PS at
benefits of, 22–24
Fully Functioning Adult (FFA), 18,
99–115
Identity Dimension, 19–20,
57–71
Inspiration Dimension, 20,
85–98
Integration Dimension, 20, 73–83
three Self-resolves, 47–55
Unfinished Business, 18–19,
29–46
Peter Pan syndrome, 60

Physical activity
  for enhancing identity, 69
  as Self-maintenance, 51, 53
Pragmatic Spirituality (PS)
  benefits of, 16, 22–25
  core elements of, 17, 18
  daily application of, 20–22
  defined, 7–8, 10, 15–16
  journey, 265–67
  objective of, xvi, 18
  three Dimensions of, 18, 19–20
  at three levels, 22–25
  underlying premise of, 18–19
Pragmatic Spirituality Dimensions
  Identity, 18, 19–20, 57–71
  Inspiration, 18, 19, 20, 85–98
  Integration, 18, 19, 20, 73–83
  PS journey and, 266
Pragmatic Spirituality (PS) on
    personal level
  benefits of, 22–24
  Fully Functioning Adult (FFA), 18,
    99–115
  Identity Dimension, 19–20, 57–71
  Inspiration Dimension, 20, 85–98
  Integration Dimension, 20, 73–83
  three Self-resolves, 47–55
  Unfinished Business, 18–19, 29–46
Pragmatic spirituality (PS) in the
    workplace
  accountability, 171–79
  adaptability, 18, 149–59
  application of, 119–33
  benefits of, 22–24
  Career Management Cycle, 181–94
  loyalty and responsibility, 158,
    161–69
  Quantum Decision Making
    (QDM), 129–30, 132, 135–47

Pragmatic spirituality (PS) in an
    organization
  benefits of, 24–25
  commitment to, 251–61
  evolving versus traditional
    organization, 197–205
  introducing, 235–49
  potential for, 219–33, 263–67
  Quantum Decision Making
    (QDM), 207–18
  receptivity to, 263–67
Pragmatic Spirituality visualization
    techniques
  Identity Visualization, 69, 270–71
  Inspiration Visualization, 89–90,
    274–75
  Integration Visualization, 80, 81,
    271–74
  setting the stage for, 269–70
  3D Visualization, 21, 22, 100, 102,
    125, 275–76
  What Were Your Early
    Injunctions?, 40–42
Prioritization. *See also* Integration
    Dimension
  at organizational level, 224–25
  at personal level, 74
  in the workplace, 126–27
Proactive versus reactive thinking, 13,
    16
Product line, redesign of, 208–10
Progress, tracking, 26
Proust, Marcel, 264

Quantum Decision Making (QDM)
  defined, 136–37
  examples of, 137–39
  intuitive feedback, 145
  intuitive proficiency, 136

specific questions for, 135–36, 137, 141–42
summary of, 146–47
three levels of perception in, 139–41
three-part process, 141–44, 147
Quantum Decision Making in the organization
benefits of, 207, 217
essential aspects of, 213, 218
examples of, 208–12, 213–17
strategic issues and, 226–27
summary of chapter on, 217–18
top management myopia and, 259–60
Quick Re-Focus
description of, 21, 22, 100, 103
on the job, 125
purpose of, 101
Quinn, Doris Kerns, 29

Rapport and task principle, 153–54
Reading, Recommended, 293–99
Recognition, 37–38
Recruitment problems, 210–11, 215–16
Religion versus spirituality, 10, 86
Repplier, Agnes, 171
Research (one of Four Rs), 37, 38–42
Responsibility and loyalty
as core life values, 162
as double-edged sword, 81–82
in evolving organization, 165–66
exploitation related to, 162–63
as impediments to adaptability, 161–62
Independent Contractor Model, 166–67, 169
negative implications of, 164–65

redefinitions of, 166–68
summary of chapter on, 168–69
in traditional organization, 163–64
Responsibility for behavior, 37, 38
Restatement of Self-resolves, 21. *See also* Self-resolves
Retrofitting (one of Four Rs), 37, 42–43
Right/left brain concept, 87–88
Ross, Steven J., 119

Sales and marketing, 243
Self-absorbed people, 54
Self-acceptance
description of, 63, 64–65
"I Accept Myself Completely" affirmation, 64–65, 124, 270–71
workplace issues and, 122–24
Self-accountability, 47–48
Self-assessment exercises, 281–84
Self-assigned identity, 60
Self-awareness, 184–85, 281–84
Self-discipline
commitments and, 50–53
defined, 48
Integration Dimension and, 77
as often omitted tool, 49
Self-maintenance and, 48–49, 51
signs of lack of, 53
in workplace, 127–28
Self-esteem
adaptability and, 155
customer service and, 229
in enablers, 157
Self-interest continuum, 54
Selfishness, 77
Self-maintenance
affirmation, 50

defined, 48
Integration Dimension and, 77
as often omitted tool, 49
Self-discipline and, 48–49, 51
signs of lack of, 53
ways to take care of yourself, 51
in workplace, 127–28
Self-marketing, 187–89
Self-mastery, 263
Self-resolves
    as often omitted tools, 49–50
    Restatement in Daily PS Focus, 21
    Self-accountability, 47–48
    Self-discipline, 48–49, 50–53
    self-interest continuum, 54
    Self-maintenance, 48–49, 50
    summary of chapter on, 54–55
Shadow, the
    defined, 45, 46
    as guide, 111–12
    in the organization, 247, 249
Shaw, George Bernard, 149
Short-term expectations, 258–59
Short-term fads versus top-level
    commitment, 251–53
Situationalists, 158, 159
Socially assigned identity, 58–60
Spiritual awareness, 86
Spiritual issues, 4–5
Spiritual practices. *See also*
    Visualization techniques
    Daily PS Focus, 20–22, 100, 101,
        102
    Pragmatic Spirituality (PS) and,
        7–8
    search for effective, 6
Spirituality. *See also* Overview of
    Pragmatic Spirituality
    in business, 5–6, 13–14, 251–61
    compartmentalization and, 15

defined, 9–10
greater effectiveness through,
    11–13
growing interest in, 11
judgment distorted by, 221–22
perception of God, limited human,
    87
religion versus, 10
Supervisor-subordinate interactions
    accountability contracts, 173–74,
        175–76
    deadlines and follow-up, 174–75
    hiring employees, 137–38, 215–16
    Teflon employee confrontation,
        176–77, 179, 237
    termination of employee, 152–53
Supervisors
    attitudes of, 246
    compassionate, 153
    difficult, 215
    insensitive, 237
    tough versus firm, 247
    toxic, 109, 155–56
Szasz, Thomas, 47

Teflon employees, 176–77, 179, 237
Termination of employee, 152–53
3D Visualization
    in Daily PS Focus, 21, 22, 100,
        102
    detailed description of, 275–76
    on the job, 125
Three Self-resolves, The
    as often omitted tools, 49–50
    Restatement in Daily PS Focus, 21
    Self-accountability, 47–48
    Self-discipline, 48–49, 50–53
    self-interest continuum and, 54
    Self-maintenance, 48–49, 50, 53
    summary of chapter on, 54–55

Top-down approach to PS in
    organization
  bootstrap approach versus, 235,
    236–39
  description of, 235–36, 239–41
  summary of, 247–49
Top-down implementation examples,
  242–44
Top-level commitment needed
  board of directors, 253, 255–58
  CEOs, 254–55
  executives, 253–54
  short-term fads versus, 251–53
Toxic workplaces
  attraction to, 155–56
  limits of PS in, 130–31, 133
Traditional organization
  changes in, 14, 119–20, 198,
    277–79
  evolving organization versus,
    198–205
  job security in, 14, 120, 201–2,
    277–79
  loyalty in, 163–64
  yesterday's versus today's employee,
    120–21
Transcendence, defined, 11–12

Undeveloped identity, 60–62
Unfinished Business
  adaptability and, 150–51, 154–56
  career problems and, 192–93
  defined, 18–19, 29
  distortions as, 266
  Four Rs for dealing with, 37–45
  inner scripts, 30–35
  office politics and, 157–58
  in an organization, 222–23, 245–47
  reenactments, 35–36
  resistance to change and, 65–66

  roots of, 33
  Self-accountability and, 47–48
  self-sabotage and, 29–30
  the Shadow, 45, 111–12, 247, 249
  summary of highlights on, 46
  workplace-specific, 131–32

Visualization techniques
  Identity Visualization, 69, 270–71
  Inspiration Visualization, 89–90,
    274–75
  Integration Visualization, 80, 81,
    271–74
  setting stage for, 269–70
  3D Visualization, 21, 22, 100, 102,
    125, 275–76
  What Were Your Early
    Injunctions?, 40–42
Vulnerability, 152–53

Watson, Thomas J., 219
Wedemeyer, Richard A., 281, 284,
  292, 303–04
Whistleblowers, 264–65
Wisdom, 136, 264
Work and the Identity Dimension
  Doing/Having versus Being, 124
  job as identity, 120, 121, 122
  self-acceptance, 122–24
  summary of, 132
Work and the Inspiration Dimension
  intuitive resources, 129–30, 132
  Quantum Decision Making
    (QDM), 129–30, 132, 135–47
Work and the Integration Dimension
  boundaries, 109, 128–29
  prioritization, 126–27
  Self-maintenance and Self-
    discipline, 127–28
  summary of chapter on, 132

Workplace
  misconceptions, 131–32
  radical changes in, 14, 119–21,
    277–79
Workplace, PS in the. *See also*
    Pragmatic Spirituality in the
    organization
  accountability, 171–79
  adaptability, 18, 149–59

application of, 119–33
benefits of, 22–24
Career Management Cycle, 181–94
limits of, 130–31, 133
loyalty and responsibility, 158,
    161–69
Quantum Decision Making
    (QDM), 129–30, 132, 135–47

ABOUT THE AUTHORS

RICHARD WEDEMEYER, after growing up in suburban Philadelphia preoccupied with school, church choir, Boy Scouts, and the pressures of an upwardly mobile family, received a B.A. in chemical engineering in 1958 from the University of Rochester. This was followed by three years on a U.S. Navy destroyer in the Pacific; he ended up as engineering officer and received a Secretary of the Navy Commendation. After considering going into the ministry, he instead earned an M.B.A. from Harvard Business School in 1963, then spent the next nine years with the Rohm and Haas Company in a variety of positions: research and development, field technical rep, sales manager training a new sales force for the Australian subsidiary, and deputy general manager for the Spanish subsidiary, overseeing the start-up of a new manufacturing plant.

Dick returned to the United States and held several management positions with smaller companies, culminating in a painful but necessary career crisis and time of introspection. His resulting midcareer course change, from technical marketing management to operational head of Jim Henson's Muppets for fourteen years, formed the basis for his fascination with the topic of career management. This resulted in his widely acclaimed book, *In Transition* (Harper Business, 1991). Coauthored with Mary Burton, it is based on their experiences conducting the ongoing Career Seminar for the Harvard Business School Club of New York over an eighteen-year period.

A pivotal event in Dick's life journey was the sudden death of his wife of fifteen years, Shirlee, soon after he joined the Muppets, leaving him a single parent to Laura, twelve, and Trevor, ten. This, along with his career transition, initiated a process of discovery on a variety of paths, leading eventually to his meeting Ron and writing this book.

Dick is making a transition from full-time work to less-structured activities, including several board responsibilities, counseling and consulting, reading, reconnecting with friends, and working in his shop. He lives in Greenwich, Connecticut, with his wife Jane. They met eighteen years ago playing music at a friend's party, and music and travel continue to be their favorite forms of recreation, along with time spent with their children and grandchildren around the country.

RONALD JUE is a third-generation Chinese-American, born in San Francisco and raised in the Bay area. Upon completing his undergraduate work in the biological sciences at California State University, San Jose, he found momentary relief from Western Newtonian-Cartesian thinking by selecting elective courses in Eastern philosophy. His newfound love of Eastern philosophy took him on an eighteen-month journey around the world, where he spent a great deal of time in India, Burma, Thailand, and Japan. There he met many teachers who validated his inner life, and his study of Vipassana and Zen meditation techniques helped him to understand the workings of the inner world.

Returning to California, he taught secondary school science, but his love of Eastern philosophy was still burning strongly. In 1970, he received a Fulbright Teaching Fellowship to Indonesia. There, his interest in Eastern thought grew with the study of the spiritual traditions of the Indonesian culture. This period of study proved pivotal as Ron found through his studies that altered states of awareness could be used to affirm faith in a higher power and to reestablish ties to humankind's spiritual heritage in order to create harmony within a society.

After a year in Indonesia and his return to California, Ron set off in yet another direction by studying clinical psychology, which served as a context for bringing together his interests in cultural anthropology, religious studies, and science. His interests then led him to serve as president of the Association for Transpersonal Psychology from 1985 to 1991, and to working with His Holiness the Dalai Lama. With the Dalai Lama, he worked with the World Business Academy in San Francisco and the World President's Organization, Washington, D.C., in creating dialogues on the topic of spirituality in business. His interest in integrating spiritual values with business led him to assisting in the development of the PBS television series, "Healthy People/Healthy Business"; teaching for the TEC Organization in San Diego; and working as a mentor, coach, and trainer for CEOs interested in personal and organizational transformation.

Ron is currently the president of Quantum International, based in Newport Beach, California, an educational and training corporation for businesses. To learn more about Quantum International, visit his website at www .intuitive-qdm.com.

Ron doesn't see retirement on the horizon. He enjoys traveling with his wife of thirty-five years and two daughters who share his interests in travel, art, music, and the path of spirit.